Courting Desire

The Politics of Marriage and Gender: Global Issues in Local Contexts

Series editor: Péter Berta

The Politics of Marriage and Gender: Global Issues in Local Context series from Rutgers University Press fills a gap in research by examining the politics of marriage and related practices, ideologies, and interpretations, and addresses the key question of how the politics of marriage has affected social, cultural, and political processes, relations, and boundaries. The series looks at the complex relationships between the politics of marriage and gender, ethnic, national, religious, racial, and class identities, and analyzes how these relationships contribute to the development and management of social and political differences, inequalities, and conflicts.

Honor and the Political Economy of Marriage: Violence against Women in the Kurdistan Region of Iraq by Joanne Payton
Courting Desire: Litigating for Love in North India by Rama Srinivasan

Courting Desire

Litigating for Love in North India

RAMA SRINIVASAN

RUTGERS UNIVERSITY PRESS

NEW BRUNSWICK, CAMDEN, AND NEWARK, NEW JERSEY, AND LONDON

Library of Congress Cataloging-in-Publication Data

Names: Srinivasan, Rama, 1982- author.
Title: Courting desire : litigating for love in North India / Rama Srinivasan.
Description: New Brunswick : Rutgers University Press, [2020] |
Series: The politics of marriage and gender: global issues in local contexts |
Includes bibliographical references and index.
Identifiers: LCCN 2019010435 | ISBN 9781978803541 (hardback : alk. paper)|
ISBN 9781978803534 (pbk. : alk. paper)
Subjects: LCSH: Marriage—India, North. | Marriage law—India, North. |
Courtship—India, North. | Couples—India, North.
Classification: LCC HQ670 .S647 2020 | DDC 306.810954/1—dc23
LC record available at https://lccn.loc.gov/2019010435

A British Cataloging-in-Publication record for this book is
available from the British Library.

♾ The paper used in this publication meets the requirements of the American
National Standard for Information Sciences—Permanence of Paper for
Printed Library Materials, ANSI Z39.48-1992.

www.rutgersuniversitypress.org

Manufactured in the United States of America

To women in Haryana who make choices and fight for them . . .

CONTENTS

Conclusion: Closures, New Beginnings,
and Happily Ever After? 161

FOREWORD

The politics of marriage (and divorce) is an often-used strategic tool in various social, cultural, economic, and political identity projects as well as in symbolic conflicts between ethnic, national, or religious communities. Despite having multiple strategic applicabilities, pervasiveness in everyday life, and huge significance in performing and managing identities, the politics of marriage is surprisingly underrepresented both in the international book publishing market and the social sciences.

The Politics of Marriage and Gender: Global Issues in Local Contexts is a series from Rutgers University Press examining the politics of marriage as a phenomenon embedded into and intensely interacting with much broader social, cultural, economic, and political processes and practices such as globalization; transnationalization; international migration; human trafficking; vertical social mobility; the creation of symbolic boundaries between ethnic populations, nations, religious denominations, or classes; family formation; or struggles for women's and children's rights. The series primarily aims to analyze practices, ideologies, and interpretations related to the politics of marriage, and to outline the dynamics and diversity of relatedness—interplay and interdependence, for instance—between the politics of marriage and the broader processes and practices mentioned above. In other words, most books in the series devote special attention to how the politics of marriage and these processes and practices mutually shape and explain each other.

The series concentrates on, among other things, the complex relationships between the politics of marriage and gender, ethnic, national, religious, racial, and class identities globally, and examines how these relationships contribute to the development and management of social, cultural, and political differences, inequalities, and conflicts.

The series seeks to publish single-authored books and edited volumes that develop a gap-filling and thought-provoking critical perspective, that are well-balanced between a high degree of theoretical sophistication and empirical richness, and that cross or rethink disciplinary, methodological, or theoretical boundaries. The thematic scope of the series is intentionally left broad to encourage creative submissions that fit within the perspectives outlined above.

Among the potential topics closely connected with the problem sensitivity of the series are "honor"-based violence; arranged (forced, child, etc.) marriage; transnational marriage markets, migration, and brokerage; intersections of marriage and religion/class/race; the politics of agency and power within marriage; reconfiguration of the family: same-sex marriage/union; the politics of love, intimacy, and desire; marriage and multicultural families; the (religious, legal, etc.) politics of divorce; the causes, forms, and consequences of polygamy in contemporary societies; sport marriage; refusing marriage; and so forth.

Rama Srinivasan's *Courting Desire* is an ethnographically rich analysis of "court marriages" in North India. While investigating cases of elopements and "love marriages" that are mediated through legal interventions, Srinivasan explains how the politics of consent and choice is embedded into courtroom spaces and processes and highlights how these legal interventions transform marital patterns and preferences by shaping local interpretations of an ideal marriage and choice of a marriage partner. Her book is a fascinating story of a normalization contest, or, in other words, of a symbolic conflict between the value regimes of family-arranged matches and "love marriages." It also offers readers a nuanced insight into how the dominant patterns of citizens' engagement with the state and its laws are changing in contemporary North India.

Péter Berta
University College London
School of Slavonic and East European Studies

PREFACE

I have ruminated a good deal on the question of ethical responsibilities, which extends far beyond protecting interlocutors and their identities. In my mind, I have wrestled endlessly with both the critique that anthropologists do not adequately describe their own positionality in the field and the counter-critique that they have priortized themselves over the ethnographic voices. My transcriptions of interviews and life history narratives have made me realize that I have been truly fortunate to be presented with such diverse and unique stories that for the most part can be retold independent of the researcher's story.

I cannot accurately comment on whether my profile evoked responses that other researchers may not have encountered, but I do know that the openness with which some of my interlocutors, both women and men, shared information regarding their intimate lives, including "taboo topics" such as sex, has not been available to many South Asianist ethnographers with whom I have interacted. Several factors may have contributed to this: my race, gender, age (almost no one believed that I was over thirty), affliation with an American university (locally considered more progressive than Indian communities), and finally, the fact that the groups I interacted with in the rural areas were not exposed to the kind of research I conducted, in terms of both its themes and its duration.

One issue that constantly troubled me was the interlocutors' curiosity about my own personal life, which was certainly justified, considering the nature of my questions. Initially, I revealed details of my personal life only to a few people who were my primary hosts. This was partly because I did not possess the vocabulary to explain a biracial relationship to many people. But more importantly, I was already marked—despite my best efforts, I could never pass as a local— and I knew that the information would spread quickly given its novelty. Interlocutors were not bound to secrecy the way I was, and why should they be?

It was only toward the end of my fieldwork that I divulged details to some of the interlocutors with whom I was close. Like some of the couples quoted in this book, I was able to cloak the news in the respectability conferred on the institution of marriage, even though I was only intending to get married at that point. It would be fair to ask why I needed this cloak of respectability, given my radical feminist politics. Concerns about personal safety and the durability of the research project dominated my decisions, given the documented evidence of disrepute attached not only to interfaith and intercaste relationships but also to biracial relationships when the woman is Indian/South Asian. The literature on this and my own experiences would fill many pages, but that is a conversation for another project.

The second ethical question I confronted was during the writing process. It is difficult to say with certainty whether some of my analysis stems from personal experiences or my personal life trajectory has, in some ways, been molded by lessons from ethnographic encounters. It seems relevant to mention my own situation during the months I spent at the Punjab and Haryana High Court in Chandigarh city and how these experiences are also part of my memories from the field. In February 2015 I started collecting the paperwork required for my partner to file an application for "establishment of civil union" with the registrar in his hometown in Germany. As I continued to track eloping couples at the court who sought validation for their relationships from the judges, I waited for the German state, through its embassy in New Delhi, to investigate my background, purportedly to decide whether it could approve our union.

This long process included some light moments, such as when my bemused parents were asked by a private investigator whether it was a "love marriage" or an "arranged marriage." It also involved two distressing interviews at the embassy—one was particularly brutal in its cold bureaucratic framing—where I was asked to divulge many facts, dates, and details regarding the relationship, including whether my parents had approved the match. By the time I received a visa to "establish a civil union" in Germany, I had experienced some of the challenges eloping couples at the court routinely face, including a naked scrutiny of one's personal life and the precarity of the subject position state spaces produce. Though I have relative privilege in India, I experienced a racial inferiority complex that comes from holding Indian citizenship and documents issued by the Indian state, in the latter the German state professedly has no faith. I also realized that like the eloping couples I was tracking, I sought approval from the state *despite* its exacting terms because of my aspirations for the future. This would become one of the key analytical tropes in my research.

*   *   *

In my first year of graduate school at Brown University, a visiting professor speaking at an ethnographic methods seminar, Gabriela Vargas Cetina, described what she saw as a trend toward performance observation. As she spoke, she turned to me and added in jest, "So you have to study the process of elopements by also trying it out yourself." I did not know then that this question would arise in the future and under peculiar circumstances. Given the uncertainty and lack of transparency we faced with the German state agencies, many well-wishers advised me and my partner to get married in Denmark, a preferred location for Germans who sought a quick and easy wedding. I would undoubtedly have learned something valuable from the elopement experience with the Danish state as a key player, but we decided not go down that path. The legal provisions were such that the marriage would not have ensured togetherness—German bureaucracy would have simply changed the term *fiancée* to *spouse* and continued with the same procedure.

I finally received my German visa in November 2015, eight months after the application process began. By this point I had developed an affective relationship with bureaucratic paperwork. Legal processes were viewed through the lens of a sentimental affinity I had earlier seen among many eloping couples. The eloping couples in my research study had the perseverance to complete an extraordinary journey, and moreover, through what they saw as the *right* (legal) way to do things. My own journey is textured by these ethnographic lessons. They not only helped me check my privilege every time I felt frustrated with global and racial inequalities but also kept reminding me that researchers follow similar moral prescripts to craft our own futures, especially those that are slightly unusual. For me, the relationship with the state was not defined by a "cruel optimism," and the eloping couples in my study are responsible for this lesson.

Aicha vorm Wald,
Germany,
January 2019

Courting Desire

Introduction

Living and Loving in North India

W_e live in an age where words do not mean what they are supposed to mean—a postmodern condition, perhaps. Using the word *love* is loaded with great risks, in academic settings and elsewhere. Romantic love is allegedly a Western liberal construct that does not adequately describe ideas and emotions from the Global South. Love in North India has spiritual and aesthetic connotations that are ostensibly corrupted by sexuality and lust in practice. If love does not quite mean what it is supposed to mean, what would litigating for love involve?

When the Supreme Court of India decriminalized homosexuality in September 2018, "LoveisLove" trended on all media platforms from India. In the context of the judgment, the uncritical usage of the word was deemed acceptable. The long struggle to decriminalize homosexuality, which originally began with the need to support marginalized communities affected by AIDS and other sexual health issues, was transformed into a rallying cry for love without an asterisk. Perhaps love has now been salvaged from its heteronormative roots in the Western liberal universe. A more compelling explanation is that the idea of love in this context is celebrated in a diverse, inclusionary form that finally completes its meaning. Context is a familiar friend and foe for an anthropologist. It allows for criticisms against using a Western lens to perceive gender and sexuality questions in the Global South but also for resisting cultural, often essentializing, explanations for gender discrimination and inequality. Telling the story of love and marriage in North India is riddled with these risks. In addition to using words essential for communicating the trends I discuss—words that will be immediately flagged—I have also set out to describe sexual and marital relations in a region known for its quantifiably poor performance on gender and other social inequalities.

The endeavor here is to trace the existence of choice and consent in intimate relationships through a study of elopements and "love marriages." My interlocutors almost always connected with the term *love marriage*, immediately grasping that my enquiries pertained to what are locally understood as courtships that led to elopements and marriages based on choice. Ethnographic honesty demands that because I enquired after love marriage, using English words in Hindi sentences, I reproduce the interactions accurately. I learned to think of the term with several virtual asterisks, or even scare quotes. My hope is that over the following pages, the readers, too, will imagine some scare quotes, or if it is easier, simply assume the term to be accurate for the purposes of this book.

According validity to a contextual fiction is an idea sourced from the other half of this project, which deals with the legal validity of marriages based on choice and consent. As a legal anthropologist I have drawn on the concept of legal fiction—assumed accurate for the purposes of a case though it may be only partially true or even completely false. Love marriage falls somewhere on that spectrum of truth. The idea of love is assumed to be accurate for the purpose of legal cases. For other case studies, based on intensive ethnographic research and life history narratives, I attempt to trace what love means in the context of the word's usage. There was, for example, a strong preference for the term *care* among my interlocutors who spoke about their loves and lovers. This care, as I will explain in chapter 3, emerges from a larger history of severely skewed gender hierarchies and a socially sanctioned neglect of and indifference to women's lives and well-being.

Works on the anthropology of emotions have highlighted how emotions are politically and socially conditioned (Lutz 1988; Abu-Lughod 1999). Love marriage in North India is a phenomenon with political resonance, one that affirms marriage as a relationship of choice when family-arranged marriages are still, overwhelmingly, the norm. The trend of seeking legal validation for marriages through litigation processes attests to the fact that eloping couples see their decisions as based on citizenry and rights, even if they do not often assert these verbally in a legal or social space. Those who prefer choice in intimate relationships and exercise that choice end up making a political statement, regardless of how apolitical they may otherwise be.

The opposition to elopements and love marriages, by contrast, is more openly political. In North India, this movement began with a revitalization and politicization of *khap panchayats*, caste conclaves often associated with the locally dominant caste of Jats. From issuing fatwa-like decisions on the separation of couples who violate caste norms, encouraging public boycotts of couples and families (predominately the grooms' families, who are seen as co-conspirators), felicitating the murderers of couples in "honor killings," khap panchayat leaders have both politicized themselves and instrumentalized these campaigns to establish individuals' political careers.[1]

Although honor killings continue, the politicized campaigns on courtships and love marriages are on the wane in Haryana, but in neighboring Uttar Pradesh they have been given a new life by the ruling Bharatiya Janata Party (BJP). Currently, two separate campaigns are underway, one attacking interreligious married or affianced couples and the other harassing presumably courting couples. The former, popularly known as the "Love Jihad," is a multipronged campaign with national outreach that involves interventions in administrative and judicial spaces. The Love Jihad rhetoric, which demonstrates the ruling party's larger political and ideological leanings, alleges that Muslim men "lure" Hindu women into marriage in order to effect their religious conversion. The campaign is a core component of a nationwide Hindu supremacist agenda that warns against purported dangers from minority communities.

The second campaign, run by so-called anti-Romeo squads, is a more localized campaign closely associated with regional strongman, Uttar Pradesh chief minister, and bellicose monk Yogi Adityanath. Anti-Romeo squads formally seek to protect women and their dignity from unwanted attention from male suitors, commonly called Romeos in North India, after the famous Shakespearean lover. In practice, the squads have been known to curtail or prevent any form of contact or conversation between the genders as they consider courtships to be alien to Indian culture.

Both the anti-Romeo squads and the Love Jihad campaign are extensions of the politics practiced by khap panchayats in the early 2000s in that they seek to delegitimize women's desire for and consent in friendships, courtships, and marriage. In asserting that women are lured or brainwashed into falling in love and forging intimate relationships, all these campaigns show a lack of understanding of sexual consent. This is not especially surprising for North Indian states such as Uttar Pradesh, Haryana, and Rajasthan, which record high instances of sexual assaults.[2] But another troubling factor, which is often debated and disputed, is that a significant number of these registered offenses are by unofficial agreement seen as consensual relationships "gone wrong." That is, in some cases of elopements and courtships, sexual assault charges are levied retrospectively, sometimes at the insistence of parents. Lawyers, activists, and police officers have unofficially spoken to me about this aspect of sexual assault cases, but there are no official statistics on it. Distinguishing cases of sexual assault from courtships is riddled with difficulties, because rapes and sexual assaults are routinely disputed in courtrooms by defense lawyers as consensual encounters. Pratiksha Baxi has extensively studied this phenomenon as part of her study on rape trials (2014), whereas my focus is to trace the existence of consent in tales of love and litigation.

Narratives of love and consensual relationships exist and persevere in an atmosphere characterized by violence, especially gender-based violence. That violence, I would argue, is normalized in the regions where I conducted research. The ethnographic context in Haryana, where I lived and observed local communities, immersing myself in its often gender-segregated environs, was one saturated by discourses that normalized violence. Clear and present danger of sexual assaults was something women invariably spoke about in gender-segregated settings. In cross-gender settings, what was left unspoken hung, stagnant, in the air we breathed.

A Lifeworld of Violence

On February 17, 2016, Haryana's state government announced that the Jat community would be accorded Special Backward Caste status and 20 percent reservations in government employment, in response to their long-standing demand for Other Backward Caste (OBC) status and 27 percent reservations. Given that the previous federal government's decision to grant Jats OBC status had been held constitutionally unviable by the Supreme Court of India, the government of Haryana had been forced to come up with a compromise to appease this numerically and politically strong community.[3] Their offer was rejected, and protests turned violent in large parts of Haryana. Jat agitators claiming a socially backward status indulged in a blatant display of brute power, destroying public and private property with impunity as many Jat police officers abandoned their posts.[4] Some of the blame for the carnage was attributed to the "provocative" comments of Rajkumar Saini, a member of parliament from the ruling party in power at both the federal and state levels. In criticizing the conduct of Jats Saini had quipped, "A Jat is your friend when you have a stick in hand. Agar dhandha haat mein nahi hai toh gardan pakadenge" (If you don't have a stick then they will be at your throat). In their rampage, Jat agitators targeted not just Saini and his community to "make them pay" for his comments, which is usually the case with communal violence in many parts of India; instead, they disproportionately destroyed businesses of another community, the Punjabi traders. This was violence for its own sake, violence that was its own reward.

Jats have not forgiven the ruling party for choosing a non-Jat chief minister, a member of the Punjabi trading community who is seen as a political lightweight. Jats have dominated regional politics since the state was created in 1966, and in the last two decades their supremacy has remained unchallenged irrespective of the party in power. "CM [chief minister] is always ours," is a refrain I have often heard in a community that has, through its dominance and aggression, alienated both upper and lower castes. In popular culture, violence and aggression is often synonymous with the Jat community, but not in any way particular to it. Violence is both political and normalized in contemporary North India, as Saini's ostensibly provocative remark demonstrated.

The question of choice-based marriages and the role of marriage in social transformation is structured around this pervasive violence, manifested most clearly in the phenomenon of honor killings of intercaste or consanguine couples. Caste conflicts such as the 2016 events described above also make this violence visible, but gender-based crimes highlight the pervasiveness of this violence on an everyday basis. Women's lives are negotiated around this aggressive display of masculine power in public life, and many women acknowledge being sexually harrassed on a daily basis, most often during their commutes to educational institutions or workplaces. At times, women learn to deploy violence to protect themselves against sexual harassment, but as a news report about the two Sonipat sisters showed, patriarchy (embodied by both women and men) does not take kindly to such usurpation of "masculine traits.".[5] In this context, care emerges as a salient but subtle critique of the society and a political statement against gender inequality and violence against women.

As part of my ethnographic research, I also soaked in this atmosphere of pervasive violence. As Veena Das has said of pain caused by sexual violence, an ethnographer cannot hope to locate pain in language without considering the relationship between pain, language, and body (1997, 88). Building on Wittgenstein, she argues that "the pain of the other not only asks for a home in language but also seeks a home in the body" (88). Tracing this pain was a complicated and confusing experience for my embodied identity as a feminist and Indian cisgender woman. In interviews where warm and affectionate women told me they supported instances of "honor killings" that had taken place in their village, or as I sat in a courtroom listening to a police officer calmly lecture that eloping couples should be murdered (more on this in chapter 5), violence in the region emerged as endemic, molding those inhabiting the space (including me, the researcher) in subtle and not-so-subtle ways.

Violence is, to draw on Edmund Husserl's conceptualization, the *lebenswelt*, or lifeworld, in this region. Husserl perceived a given world as a natural attitude, limited to our experience of it (1970). Similarly, the pervasive normalization of violence, especially sexual violence, can numb even ethnographers, at times, because conceptualization depends on one's experience of the world. Husserl would tell us that one cannot experience the world in its entirety, but only in its intersubjective dimensions; that is, with those with whom we coexist in spatial and temporal intimacy. There were moments in my fieldwork when cultural immersion was so near complete that sexual harassment had become a "normal," everyday part of my own life. Although I had previously experienced harassment growing up in Delhi, back then I had reference points that reinforced the idea that one must not allow harassment to become normalized. Immersion in the cultural landscape of rural North India allowed me to experience and understand masculine aggression and the normalization of sexual harassment and crimes without such reference points. This violence is a phenomenon with history and a material culture that supports its perpetuation. Whereas for Husserl, lebenswelt is historically conditioned and pretheoretical everyday life, as Throop and Desjarlias have summarized, in my account Haryana and its pervasive violence are presented as "a dynamic, shifting, and intersubjectively constituted existential reality" (Desjarlais and Throop 2011, 91).

Interviews on the question of marriage delved on hope and happiness for the future, but the violence in society and the wariness it produced was always a lurking presence in the background. Testimonies of women who recounted verbal, physical, and sexual assaults at home and beyond described a pain akin to that discussed in anthropological texts on "social suffering" (Kleinman and Kleinman 1995; Das 1997; Biehl 2013b). Honor killings are just one example of this violence, though they have come to dominate the mainstream media's image of Haryana. While news of honor killings is met with shock elsewhere in India and the rest of the world, in the prevailing political and social climate violence is woven into the discourse and instances of lawlessness are taken for granted, even by law enforcers at the local level.

In the aftermath of the 2016 violence, two questions emerged in mainstream Indian discourse: Why do Jats, who are clearly privileged, want reservations (anyway), and why are they so angry? This book locates some possible answers in the individual aspirations and intimate lives of young (twenty- to thirty-five-year-old "millennial") Haryanvis from different communities. The 2016 events were a manifestation of both the pervasiveness of violence in the society and the frustrated aspirations of millennials. Aggressive masculinity as a strong affective force ensures the exclusion of women from political and public life.[6] Violence has increasingly become the only tool with which men from dominant communities, frustrated in their aspirations, can attempt to keep women and people from lower castes from claiming their space in public life.

My research suggests that the anger among men from dominant communities such as the Jats, Bishnois, and Rajputs stems from the fact that their privileged position in an agrarian society is on the wane, and younger men are now expected to compete for their place in a nonagrarian future. Unlike women, whose bleak present is giving way to a future of potential opportunities where few or none had previously existed, men, and Jat men in particular, are looking at a future of diminished importance. Land ownership, which accounted for their privileged position as well as their political domination, is declining, and men from dominant castes must compete for alternative resources and opportunities with women and people from other communities. Jat men in North India, more than men from other dominant communities, feel entitled to resources and opportunities as well as their position of political domination, and these two factors feed off each other.

This ethnographic moment shapes larger contestations on marital choices and decisions. At the same time, it highlights how marriage has always been about the political economy. Exchange of women, Gayle Rubin argues, is a shorthand to refer to social relationships of kinship structures where rights are unequally bestowed. Kinship systems exchange "sexual access, genealogical statuses, lineage names and ancestors, rights, and people—men, women, and children—in concrete systems of social relationships. These relationships always include certain rights for men, others for women" (Rubin 1990, 46). Transformations in political economy make mutations in kinship systems not only possible but even inevitable. My ethnography is concerned with how social relationships transform choices in marital partners but also how rights are negotiated and/or redistributed in periods of social crisis. Gender-based violence, including honor killings, is emblematic of both extant inequalities and renewed contestations.

Despite Haryana's notoriety as the land "synonymous with the honor killings,"[7] parts of which are considered "no place for women,"[8] there is little scholarly work on the recent history of the state. In the next section I briefly trace the history of this state to contextualize the male sense of entitlement and anger at the potential loss of privilege. In chapter 5, I will build on this summary.

Toward a Gendered History of Haryana

Prem Chowdhry has produced several acclaimed books on the history of the region (1994, 2007, 2011), tracing the colonial roots of some of the trends we see today in Punjab and Haryana, especially the exploitation of women's productive and reproductive roles. She has also analyzed elopements recorded in the annals from colonial India, where the disruption in the exchange of women represented a threat to masculine control over women's productive labor in agriculture and reproductive labor as suppliers of personnel for the British army (2004, 2007). Similarly, the alienation of women's labor in postcolonial agrarian societies has been researched by feminist scholars such as Bina Agarwal (1994) and Smita Jassal (2012).

For Haryana, which was carved out of Punjab on linguistic lines in 1966, land ownership and the alienation of women's labor have profound implications, as large parts of the state were co-opted in the federal government's Green Revolution project. The state-sponsored scheme, which aimed to achieve higher yields through irrigation and chemical fertilization, changed the landscapes of both riverine regions and the arid lands close to Rajasthan and Delhi. The transformation of the arid landscape to lush green represents a social transformation: some peasant communities in North India became extremely prosperous within a short period and began influencing local hierarchies and political equations. While Jats and Bishnois benefited from the increase in agrarian yields and could consolidate political power in the state, land-owning Yadavs in southeast Haryana remained subregional players until recently because the Green Revolution project did not extend to the districts in that region. In western Uttar Pradesh, Jats remain one of the few beneficiaries of the Green Revolution in a state whose political establishment was otherwise dominated by Yadav communities. With the expansion of the National Capital Region into Haryanvi districts such as Gurugram and Rewari, the Ahirwal/Yadav community members have prospered from land sales but remain disgruntled at the political clout of Jat leaders who had mediated these real estate deals.[9]

In addition to changing the fortunes of select communities, the Green Revolution also changed the relationship of the people to the state, which had successfully become a benevolent provider. Moreover, the scientific advancements in agriculture and the corresponding rise in individual fortunes were likened to a miracle. One might say, following Fernando Coronil, that the powers of the state were imbued with magical properties. Writing about Venezuela, Coronil holds that illusionary powers of the state are condensed through a combination of its resources—the people and the land (1997). Whereas in Venezuela this was achieved by the discovery of oil fields, in the North Indian states of Punjab, Haryana, and western Uttar Pradesh it was through agriculture. This was particularly important, as I will explain in chapter 4, for the arid regions on the Rajasthan-Haryana border where I conducted parts of my fieldwork. The nation-state had performed a conjuring trick that had beholden Haryanvi subjects for much of the twentieth century, and the illusion is likely to continue into the postagrarian future through the clamor for government jobs. The widespread aspiration for public sector jobs may appear disproportionate to external observers, given the state's inability to cater for the sheer number of aspirants, but it is also a testimony to the special regard the people of the region have for the Indian state and the hopes and expectations they invest in its institutions.

Similarly, the trend of litigating for love is in some ways a testimony to the people's faith in the magical powers of the state. Though elopements and marriages based on choice (especially without parental approval) are generally regarded with contempt and accorded scant validity, when eloping couples visit the courts the social perception transforms. The couples themselves often come to see themselves as married through the courts' intervention. In this book, I locate the existence of an emerging conceptual category called *court marriage*, which appears to encompass ideas of both normative, "respectable" unions reserved for marriages based on kinship rules, and nonnormative, choice-based unions popularly known as *love marriages*. The existence of this new category is a testimony to the creative potential of the law and legal spaces.

Those who remain ambivalent or critical of the trend of elopements lend credibility to the concept by deploying it in speech acts. Such marriages are produced through interactions between citizens and state spaces, where the former learn to project their individual aspirations onto the state and its laws. But what is construed as legal is not restricted to the letter of the law alone. The intermediate space between the letter of the law and the spirit is, I believe, a liminal one—a temporary ritualistic space that can create marriages as if through magic.

The term *court marriage* is hardly referenced in scholarly literature from India. The only mention I have come across is in Perveez Mody's *The Intimate State*. As part of her research, Mody tracked cases of "court-marriage," which she has described as civil marriage or registration of Hindu weddings (2008, 103), at an administrative court in Delhi (the sub-divisional magistrate's court). In the context of intercommunity marriages, she quotes interlocuters in Delhi alluding to these court-marriages as both "steel-proof," in that the couples will not be separated from their dissenting families, and a union of dubious social legitimacy (109–111). In Mody's fieldwork "the court" refers to a magisterial office or the executive branch of the state, whereas in my study it pertains to the judiciary.

Combining the analysis of judicial proceedings with themes from classical kinship studies from South Asia (Ortner 1978; Raheja 1988), which perceive marriage as a rite of passage conducted in ritualistic terms, I delineate the specific settings within which such marital unions are forged and receive validity, both legal and social. In the following sections, I discuss the scholarship on state, law, and legal orders that my book builds on.

Feminist Scholarship on Indian State, Law, and Legal Orders

My ethnographic data resonates with several long-standing feminist debates, especially those from a postcolonial context, on themes such as law versus customs, individual and community rights, and the interaction between jurisprudence and legal practice. South Asian feminist scholarship on jurisprudence, in particular, has emphasized how cases involving women's rights are often inaccurately framed as a confrontation between traditionalist societies and a modern state. Feminist scholars in both the West and the Global South have pointed out how the modern state is thoroughly enmeshed in the private lives of its citizens, especially through its control over the institution of marriage (Pateman 1988; Okin 1989; Agnes 1999; Vanita 2011).

Feminist scholarship on law in India, especially works by Nivedita Menon (2004), Ratna Kapur (2013), and Flavia Agnes (1999), has critiqued the binary that pits laws against customs, highlighting that laws governing family and inheritance extend the rule of the patriarch. The laws instituted by the state, feminist scholars have argued, carry the perceptions of the dominant caste patriarchy and, in fact, further its goals as the designs of governance. As Menon points out in *Seeing Like a Feminist*, the state has become the space where the Brahmanical/upper caste and the Victorian patriarchy have found compatibility (2012, 24). Pratiksha Baxi, who followed court proceedings more closely, describes how adjudications on love marriages tend to view women as abject bodies (2006, 74) with conflicting claims of custody (62). In cases of elopements that are framed as abductions, Baxi locates a nexus between kinship and the state that, for her, symbolizes a privatization of public law (62). Baxi and Chowdhry address this in their work on abduction cases where an eloping bride is conceptualized in the court as a kidnapped subject and the judge is required to settle the question of her custody (Baxi 2006, 2014; Chowdhry 2004, 2007).

Veena Das signals a shift in the analysis of the Indian state's patriarchy, perceiving it as something of an adjudicator or arbitrator who lays down terms of a contractual relationship between women and their male guardians (2007). The official discourses surrounding the birth of the nation represented, according to her, a "state of disorder" because partition of the Indian subcontinent had "dismantled the orderly exchange of women" and "correct matrimonial dialogue between men" (Das 2007, 21). Through the figure of an abducted woman, the new state constituted "a particular relation between social contract and sexual contract—the former being a contract between men to institute the political and the latter the agreement to place women within the home under the authority of the husband/father figure" (21). But rather than see the social contract that privileges patriarchal authority as "natural or originary," Das suggests that it is a "predication of fatherly authority based on consent" (34). It was initiated by the Indian state, which, moved by the scale of violence it witnessed during the partition, assumed that state action was expected by the subjects.

The rule of law, according to Das, is premised on an assumption of consent given in a state of disorder, where women ostensibly "agree" to be placed under the guardianship of men and men agree to self-discipline. Though patriarchal control was consolidated in the process, following Das I also see the state as a possible site for questioning and weakening its control—where consent for the contract could be rescinded, especially in times of "normality." In viewing fatherly authority over women, ostensibly for their own protection, as a state-mandated contract rather than part of a nonnegotiable patriarchal ideology, Das appears to underline a theory where the state is not merely an extension of the family and kinship.

When the rule of the patriarch is seen as a social contract enforced by the state, the state's mediation in cases where the patriarchy is challenged is not only an opportunity but even a necessity since the patriarch can approach the state to seek redress and restoration of legal guardianship. One could even argue that in order to be perceived as individuals with rights (and not as wards), women, too, must enter state spaces at some point in their lives. Das and Deborah Poole address this very question in their edited volume *Anthropology at the Margins of the State* (2004), arguing that the state can be located not only in institutional spaces but also in the community and even in individuals.

As they write in the introduction, the ethnographies collected in the volume demonstrate that, at times, the state itself may not be invested in its legibility in that "it is continually both experienced and undone through the *illegibility* of its own practices, documents and words" (10; emphasis in original). And people who are traditionally understood as outside of and/or opposed to the state come across as vital actors in this undoing. As Jyoti Puri argues, recognizing states themselves as subjective allows us to focus on how preoccupations with managing sexual practices and forms of sexual labor are discursively producing the state itself (2016). Governing sexuality, she writes, helps sustain the illusion that states are a normal feature of social life, "intrinsically distinct from society, and indispensable to maintaining social order" (2). In other words, the legal order that is presumably reshaping other normative orders is itself produced through the expectation that it should regulate sexual practices.

Livia Holden's ethnography on divorce proceedings in courts in Central India illustrates how state spaces are molded through such expectation. The lawyers, who are Holden's informants, not only show an astute understanding of the customs that allow women from lower castes to divorce and marry several men, but they also help the women validate their relationships in courts (2016). To end their marriages, these women often used a "notary public," who functions as an extension of the state where people try to fit their refashioned personal lives within legal frameworks. As Holden summarizes: "The notary public, in spite of a cold paternalistic attitude, appears wisely to manipulate a vast range of legal and metalegal categories and thereby creates for his clients the sufficient platform for a legal recognition of their customs. Whereas we would have expected a narrow interpretation of the law, we have instead a clever bridge in relation to the official setting" (144). Holden seems to suggest that when the legal text cannot serve the needs of some, citizens often believe that the state is still obliged to, and those whose job it is to interpret the text might manipulate legal procedures to provide closure when the official law falls short. Building on her argument, I propose that legal processes gain their credibility not only through the letter of law but also through the acknowledgment they receive among community members.. Legal consciousness shapes nonstate normative orders, determining the relationship between competing and complementary regulatory frameworks.

If feminist scholarship has played an important role in disrupting the binaries of law versus custom and kinship versus state, this body of literature still largely focuses on the ideological impulses of a patriarchal state, whose power is perceived as coercive and omnipresent. Without losing sight of the

FIGURE 1 Night view of the Punjab and Haryana High Court.
Photo: Janaki Srinivasan.

state's patriarchal dispositions, this ethnography goes beyond ideological mechanizations to focus on the interplay between distinct but overlapping normative orders. To borrow from Sally Merry, this approach aims at examining the ways in which "social groups conceive of ordering, of social relationships, and of ways of determining truth and justice" (1988, 889).

For the legal order to have any legitimacy, it needs the acknowledgement, grudging or affirmative, from the community itself. As I will highlight using examples of protection petitions in chapter 5, courts create an opportunity to forge a marital union seemingly sanctioned by the state. This process represents a juridification of love marriages, a phenomenon wherein local conflicts are adjudicated as part of a universal and ostensibly impersonal framework for rights. The next section discusses the literature on juridification that has closely informed the chapters on my courtroom ethnography from the Punjab and Haryana High Court (figure 1).

Juridification of Love Marriages

The negotiations couples undertake fall under what Upendra Baxi would term "politics for human rights" rather than "politics of rights"; the focus is on "practices and forms of transformative politics for dignity and justice for all humans everywhere" (2012, 276). Baxi redirects the emphasis away from advocacy efforts undertaken within the human rights framework and toward everyday, individualized negotiations, a scholarly move that is particularly relevant for legal anthropologists. Building on his work, Julia Eckert and colleagues argue in the introduction to *Law against the State* that we should trace the gradual process of change in normative orders, which has not been imposed from above—that is, not through the initiative of state institutions. They propose that we instead study the "effects of people's legal choices, trials and errors in eclectic situated processes of juridification" (Eckert et al. 2012, 3).

In my research, I focus on a localized phenomenon that holds the potential to inform and mold global discourses on human rights as well as state institutions. The protection petition is a writ petition filed for safeguarding one's fundamental right to life and liberty where the state (specifically, federal states such as Haryana and Punjab) is the main respondent and family and kin groups, who are named as people threatening to harm or separate the couples, are secondary respondents. But the protection petitions do not just signify the application of state law against the state, as juridification processes in human rights litigation do. I argue that they also mobilize the state and its bodies to participate in potential conflicts within social and community orders.

Couples in my study rarely asserted their rights explicitly within community or state spaces, but the protection petition gives them the opportunity to phrase their demands with docility; that is, without directly challenging political and social hierarchies. Leaving the task of articulating the existence of marital or citizen rights to judges signals a depoliticization that is typical of juridification processes, as Eckert and colleagues have noted (2012). If courts adjudicate on a case-by-case basis, couples make individualized, depoliticized claims, asserting only their own aspirations and the life choices they have made.

Couples prefer this ordered process to the messy negotiations they must undertake with their parents, who might be disapproving if not outrightly hostile. Advocate Tanu Bedi (real name), who has also served as a legal officer for the court on this issue, insisted in a conversation with me that only a miniscule percentage of the couples who got the court order actually approached police officials at district levels for protection. She had come across couples, she said, who had not even spoken to their families about their intentions to elope and were completely clueless about whether the wedding would be opposed, let alone whether they should fear physical harm. Her extensive experience has led her to view many such petitions as a waste of precious judicial time. But in this book I aim to show that the protection petition is not just about protecting life but about creating the life it was meant to protect—a life where the subject has the liberty to choose their partner. Various interlocutors in this ethnographic study underline the productive potential of law (I acknowledge the Foucauldian turn here) through their life experiences and inherited ideas on citizenship.

As Eckert has discussed in "Rumours of Rights," a chapter in *Law against the State*, subjects are also well aware of their vulnerability when it comes to legal processes. Law, she argues, is the site of both hopes and fears, where rumors of rights come with the uncertainty that is inherent to how rumors usually work (Eckert et al. 2012). But where Eckert's informants in Mumbai slums are acutely aware of the ability of law to "make people illegal" (2012, 150), my own observations from the courtrooms in Chandigarh reveal a process that may end in subjects *becoming legal*. Marriage, in this context, is a rite of passage that also ends up reinforcing adulthood and rights.

Jurisprudence professor Anil Thakur at the Chandigarh-based Panjab University stated in a private conversation with me that there is a strong tendency among the people in the region to "bring facts to the knowledge of the state."[10] Sometimes petitioners did not appeal for resolutions but rather sought to "inform the courts" of facts pertaining to their lives—possibly to ensure that they were still leading legitimate lives. This represents a willingness to embrace the subjectivity of the state in order to live legally tenable lives. As João Biehl has noted while surveying the trend among Brazilians to sue the state for their medical expenses, the effort is not just about "extending life." He finds it significant that his informants use the expression *entrar na justiça*, "to enter the judiciary" or, literally, "to enter justice" (2013a, 421), when referring to their lawsuits. They assert that they no longer want to live outside the zone of justice and also tacitly accept that the space of the court is, in fact, the space of justice. According to Biehl, realizing their citizenship through this interpretation allows citizens to remake both the spaces and themselves (422). I propose, in turn, that eloping couples feel the need to enter the zone of justice, a seemingly neutral state institution, where they can be assured that they are leading legally tenable lives despite having made a contentious marriage. The number of these actions also suggests that marriage itself as an institution may be transforming via this interaction with the state and its bureaucracy.

In some ways, marriage is a bureaucratic instrument in modern liberal states. Ruth Vanita traces the evolution of the institution as a bureaucratic effort in European countries that eventually gave the state absolute control. In "modern western states" this absolute control transformed an institution that was previously based on mutual consent (and that alone) into a bureaucratic one (2011). Vanita cautions against the bureaucratization of marriage in India, which she locates in the attempt to make registration compulsory, arguing that this will make the nation less democratic and reduce the diversity of its sexual practices. Vanita's argument pursues a familiar trope in feminist scholarship that distrusts state interventions on issues pertaining to gender and sexuality. An increased role for state institutions in intimate relationships will, as Vanita has argued, undoubtedly lead to more classification and routinization of sexual unions in terms legible to the state, but in my research, I have found the bureaucratic state to be a productive site in this regard.

Consequently, I argue, in variance from Vanita's thesis, that in some cases bureaucratic control could actually increase the chances of entering relationships based on consent. I admit that my research deals primarily with heterosexuality, while Vanita's article is a broader exposition on the topic of marriage equality. But the idea of mutual consent in relationships, regardless of sexuality, is usually presumed. Like the idea of social consent in democracies, presumption of mutual consent needs to be problematized. This ethnographic study and my intellectual trajectory as a feminist scholar lead me to argue that consent requires continuous articulation and cataloguing.

Legal Interventions on Consent

In March 2013, the government of India passed the Criminal Law (Amendment) Act, which finally supplanted Victorian conceptualizations of rape and sexual assaults. The backdrop for the proactive legislation on sexual offences was the December 2012 *Nirbhaya* rape case and the protests that ensued accross the globe. The new law, which expanded the definition of rape beyond the Victorian law's terms that limited it to genital penetration, also destabilized a well-established judicial procedure that Pratiksha Baxi termed a medicalization of consent in rape trials that eventually harms the complainant (Baxi 2014, 61). Two high-profile cases against well-known public personalities have since utilized the law's specific provisions, with one of them—that of scholar and artist Mahmood Farooqui—reaching a conviction at a special court in Delhi in 2016. In September 2017, the Delhi High Court reversed this judgment with a statement that goes against the current transnational trends in conceptualizing consent as "no means no" by disregarding the complainant's utterance as a "feeble no."[11] Also, in distinguishing the complainant through her presumably elite social status, the judgment held that the terms under which a refusal of sexual consent is recognized must by necessity be different than when the complainant comes from a more "conservative" background. The judgment, which was subsequently upheld by the Supreme Court, has been widely criticized for classifying sexual crimes according to the complainant's social location as well as for differentiating between forms of refusal. This case in particular poses some vital questions for scholarly research: How can we reinvent the Indian judiciary's role in adjudicating and affirming sexual consent in intimate relationships and encounters beyond legislating new laws? Can the definition of sexual consent be universal (and should it be)? I address these questions individually.

In a web article for the feminist journal *Signs*, legal scholar Janet Halley (2015) had some cautionary words for American feminists who campaign for institutionalization of affirmative consent. In particular, she is wary of the "possibility of a vast new criminalization," associating the trend with the sex-negative tendencies of those she calls "dominance feminists." In Halley's analysis, moves toward affirmative consent represent two distinct features: Liberalism with a capital *L* and liberalism with a lowercase *l*. Whereas capital-*L* Liberalism represents attempts to "promote individual freedom to decide the course of one's own sexual engagements" as part of a broader orientation toward individual liberty, lowercase-*l* liberalism, Halley argues, represents a socially conservative ideal, realized through an engagement with the state and through the cooperation of male paternalistic elites. She questions the politics of feminists who put the weight of the state and of punishment behind the norm of affirmative consent, and proposes that we instead put the norm "into legal proceedings in the real world" (2015).

In this book I explore how sexual consent evolves both in the real world, of which I consider the legal world to be an integral part, and through the weight of the Indian state when the focus is not on cases of rape or sexual assault but on cases where sexual consent is exercised and validated through the moral authority of the state. In my research on elopement cases, I locate the idea of sexual consent in a broader framework of socioeconomic transformations and changes in marital patterns in North India. Legal validation of intimate relationships based on choice and consent assumes critical importance in this ethnographic context, with even those who remain critical of love marriages recognizing them after the state has ostensibly weighed in on the case.

In the processes I examine, affirmative consent dialogue is achieved not by the activism of dominance or governance feminists but rather by the actions of women and men who seek certain rights from the state in their individual capacities as adult citizens. Sexual consent in intimate relationships here represents an effort to tap into the promises of capital-*L* Liberalism, especially individual liberty, and reroute its moral value back to the real world. It is indeed concerned with the state's moral authority and power but specifically its power to adjudicate on and validate certain universal rights.

Consent *sans* Context?

As the Farooqui judgment highlighted, part of the difficulty of writing on sexual consent lies in recognizing that sexual relationships are located within relations of power that are context-specific but are not always encompassed by them. Much of feminist and anthropological writing since the 1990s has focused on understanding sexual and gender relations as culturally relative, following Marilyn Strathern's intervention (1991), and as shaped by postcolonial structures and institutions, following interventions from subaltern studies. One must necessarily revisit cultural relativism and the dangers of accepting "radical alterity" among different groups, as some anthropological works have done (e.g., Wardlow 2006), when they are deployed in legal cases as means to contextualize and consequently absolve perpetrators of sexual crimes.[12] Farooqui's acquittal also signals the importance of some universal values, including but not limited to human rights, which have been displaced in efforts to decolonize women's voices, as postcolonial feminism has done, or to highlight the intersectional nature of women's experiences, especially of violence. If postcolonial feminism has, as Sumit Sarkar has alleged, fragmented women's experiences (1999, 312), intersectional feminism has, Nivedita Menon argues, far exceeded its conceptualization by Kimberlé Crenshaw as a legal instrument, posing the danger of consolidating intersecting identity categories as homogenous and undifferentiated in the name of resisting the universal (2015, 8).

The trouble with addressing the gravity of the Farooqui judgment, beyond its egregious statements on the "feeble no," is that in the vital work feminists have undertaken to resist white, Western feminist scholarship—contextualizing women's experience of violence and injustice—we have also displaced stable and recognizable definitions. Consent, sexual or otherwise, and the rule of law that upholds it today stand on shaky ground as conservative Liberalism with a capital L, whose imposition from above we are called on to resist.

The importance of balancing context with universal rights as well as the law with the "real world" will be highlighted in this book through multiple comparisons of Haryanvi cases with a case from the southern state of Kerala. In the case of Hadiya, formerly a Hindu woman in her mid-twenties who first converted to Islam and later married a Muslim man, her exercise of consent was disputed at the Kerala High Court and the Supreme Court. The high court annulled her marriage and forced her to return to her parents' house, and the Supreme Court even ordered an investigation into possible terror links in the case before paving the way for her eventual reunification with her husband.[13]

Kerala, the original site for the Love Jihad campaign, had found judicial backing for the political campaign that eventually spread from the state to North India. Ironically, Kerala has some of the best gender development indices, while in Haryana, which scores poorly in this regard,[14] weddings based on choice are today no longer as politically controversial and the high court does not usually adjudicate on the validity of marriages. Hence, context depends on a variety of social and political factors that may, at times, produce paradoxical results. My research data and the contrasts it draws against the cases of Farooqui and Hadiya demonstrate the importance of legal processes, not only for conceptualizing affirmative consent but also for highlighting how context-specific exercise of consent can inform transnational conversations on the issue. To summarize, legal intervention on sexual consent can be both context-dependent and context-defining, and often operate in conjunction with "real world" conditions. In the next section, I propose an alternative theorization of consent that remains cognizant of the ethnographic context but also of Liberalism and liberalism.

Consenting Adults in Societies of Consent

The idea of consent itself, apart from its association with sexuality and marriage, has been richly explored in the field of political philosophy. In liberal democracies, the state, its agents, and its citizens view themselves as parts of societies of consent bound by a social contract. This social contract is not necessarily an informed one. It evolves from the ideas of Rousseau and Hobbes, who understood it is as a set of obligations on part of the citizens as well as the governments. As Stanley Cavell and Judith Butler have pointed out, the credibility of the government and its policies derive from the popular will in societies of consent. Butler writes in her book on political assembly that a lack of trust among "the people," however exclusionary this term might be, undercuts the government's ability to function with any claim to credibility (2015). Yet, although it is the support of the people that allows the government to function, Cavell is doubtful of the extent to which consent can be withdrawn if the government deviates irreversibly from our vision. Psychological exile, Cavell tells us, is not an exile (1990, 107). The role played by the courts (and specifically, writ petitions) become especially important when governments no longer respect popular will and the people cannot withdraw their consent to the governing state. Eloping couples, in their act of suing the state governments, hold the state accountable to the contract, when even elected leaders often side with community, abstractly defined, to restrict civil liberties of adult citizens.

Although some individual lawsuits end in failure, on a larger scale, the sustained filing of petitions, received on a daily basis, precludes the state from losing sight of its obligation. The miscarriage of the law is in this way individualized—an accident, as Socrates viewed the verdict in his case (Arendt 1972, 58). In my observation, judges strove to largely appear as neutral agents committed to upholding laws unlike some political leaders who regularly questioned them. Instead, the judges channeled their biases into comments that do not appear in any legal documents. These comments are uttered in the courtroom only for the benefit of those present, including all the couples who have been assigned to their courts on a given day. It is easy to discount the role played by the writ petitions filed by eloping couples in contemporary India, where instances of violence and injustice (even on the court premises) occur with impunity.[15] Yet, such petitions require analysis on various levels—marriage, family, kinship, law, and state. In this current phase (2016–2019) of seeming "lawless-ness" in India, what do laws mean to people and the agents of the state?

As Hannah Arendt argues in *Crises of the Republic*, phases of lawlessness or rises in petty crimes are indicators of weak governments, and the perpetrators of violence are best understood as opportunists. These periods suggest a situation ripe for revolution, though it may never materialize (1972, 69–72). Lawlessness, especially in the case of opportunistic Hindu supremacist activists in India, can also result in a renewed commitment by "the people" (especially those with less social or political capital) to the Constitution of India, which is a powerful sym-bol, and to the courts, which are one of the key sites where redress is possible.

Courts facilitate conversations in moments of heightened emotions and mandate that state and state agents listen to "the people." The trend of filing of writ petitions has grown during periods of shrinking liberties and greater num-bers of political injustices. The people's faith in the judiciary continues, despite some serious doubts raised about the impartiality of courts.[16] Writ petitions are today fulfilling the function of enforcing the social contract and demanding that the state remain lawful and just. Though the trend of filing protection peti-tions predates the BJP regime, the governments's role in this large and diffused set of writ petitions that today constitutes a mode of resistance cannot be dis-counted. Protection petitions generate conversations on civil liberties and on consent, which are essential for societies ostensibly founded on the latter. These petitions, along with other types of writ petitions on civil liberties, serve to constantly remind the state of its obligations under the contract. Love mar-riages and protection petitions may consitute a "waste of judicial time," even for some human rights advocates I have spoken to, but they serve a vital func-tion in extending civil liberties, especially at a time when the political dis-course promotes their curtailment. Even in their seemingly apolitical and nonagential form, elopements rattle judges because couples appear to be sug-gesting that they have fulfilled their obligations to the state and it is now the state's turn to fulfill its obligations to them.

In this book, I have built on and extended feminist scholarship on the state and law, but I propose here a reconceptualization of the state where sexual sub-jectivity is not only a source of marginality and vulnerability but also an aspira-tional goal. That is, the positionality of a subject can and does afford a limited space for creatively interpreting state laws and legal procedures and crafting desired life situations.

Plan for the Book

In the first chapter, I focus on the nation-state and its legal designs for mar-riage, through a discussion of parliamentary debates on the Special Marriage Bill, which introduced choice and consent as crucial aspects of the institution of marriage. Chapter 2 explores the tropes of romantic love, bureaucratic governance, and sentimental justice in popular culture and cinema and how these interact with local and global aspirations from the field. Chapter 3 traces intergenerational transformations in ideas about love, sexuality, and marriage, with a specific focus on how care in intimate relationships seeks to subvert gender-based inequalities. Next, I track aspirations for career and mobility in an increasingly postagrarian society through ethnographic observations and quantitative data on education indicators among women and men.

Chapters 5 and 6 are based on ethnographic observations and interviews in and around courtrooms, where the focus is on protection protections and sexual consent in cases that are popularly identified as court marriages. Chapter 7 is a theoretical exposition on alternative ideas for future, where belonging to the state and laws emerge as dominant frameworks for contextualizing the aspirations of eloping couples.

Ethnographic Context and Methods

In order to provide a holistic account of marital patterns and contextualize the terms love and court marriages, I conducted ethnographic fieldwork in both rural Haryana and in Chandigarh city, the capital Haryana shares with the state of Punjab. In rural Haryana, research was primarily carried out in three districts close to the Rajasthan border: Fatehabad, Hisar, and Sirsa. These districts are popularly known as the *baagri* belt, after the dialect of Hindi spoken in the region. Interviews and participant observation in the baagri region were conducted from August to December 2014, and during shorter visits in March 2015, June 2015, and January 2018. I resided on the campus of a women's college and thus interacted with many young women between the ages of eighteen and twenty-five. Ethnographic research was also conducted within communities and kin groups, especially during events such as weddings.

Interlocutors included young women and men, often students, who either anticipated being married in the near future or had been married recently. Other groups included in the study were parents of young Haryanvis (more often mothers than fathers); university and college professors, local reporters, and writers and poets; and current and past elected representatives, including *sarpanchs* (village heads) and one former member of parliament. In Chandigarh city, I interviewed young Haryanvi students and professors at Panjab University, government employees and bureaucrats, and professionals in the private sector. Follow-up interviews were conducted in 2018.

Research in courtrooms that handled cases of eloping couples was conducted from May to August 2012 and January to August 2015 (but not in June, when courts are on a vacation break). Interviews with litigants were completed in lawyers' chambers in the court complex. I also had extended conversations with lawyers, both women and men, in the bar rooms and in their offices on and outside the court complex in 2012, 2015, and 2018. Real names have been used only in the cases of a few professors and human rights advocates who shared their views as experts. All other interlocutors, including lawyers who worked on protection petitions and other state actors including judges, were assigned pseudonyms.

As a project on nonnormative heterosexual marriage, this study includes voices of both women and men, and it is important to describe the nature of my interactions with both. In addition to interviews with key informants such as lawyers, I interacted with approximately forty to forty-five men in rural Haryana and Chandigarh city (more in the latter site); these were often rather formal, structured interactions. The number of women interlocutors in the research data is slightly higher (around fifty-five to sixty), and I interviewed more women in rural areas than in the city. But my interactions with women in both sites were usually much more extensive, with several opportunities for follow-up interviews and life-history narratives where intimate details were shared. Jest and frivolity as well as tragic confessions were often part of group or one-to-one conversations with women, but not often encountered in my interactions with men. Nevertheless, my interviews with men, especially young men, gave me a unique opportunity to analyze some prevailing trends in masculinity, though perhaps with less authority than I can with regard to femininity. As a feminist project on marital patterns and gendered norms and aspirations, this book examines narratives of both women and men, but through different entry points.

PART ONE

Localizing Marriage

1

Civil Marriage in Postindependence India

Birth of a Utopic Idea

In scholarly work, the institution of marriage represents a quintessential conflict between state law and community customs, where the former is often presumed to impinge on the latter. Notwithstanding feminist contributions to the literature, the state and laws continue to be perceived even in academic and intellectual circles as modern, liberal artifacts that threaten or reform traditions, depending on one's perspective. Clifford Geertz had critiqued these binaries as an anthropological mischief that had reduced custom from thought to habit and law from thought to practice (1983, 208). Geertz treated law and customs—that is, rule following in general—as forms of local knowledge, arguing that a legal mind feeds on muddle as much as it does on order (217). Laws and customs are both ideational, borne of a disorderly dialogue as much as a well-planned design. In this chapter I focus on the nation-state, its legal designs for the institution of marriage, and the political dialogue that resulted in the Special Marriage Act of 1954.

Under the colonial regime, state agents had already undertaken massive codification drives to collate customs and draft personal laws, a process well documented in feminist historiographic works (Poonacha 1996; Uberoi 1993; Chowdhry 1994). This included carrying forward both the bureaucratic impulses of the state, which was needed to record customary practices in order to better govern the colony or "manage the population," and take forward the modernizing zeal to "reform" the society. The drive to record customary practices is evocative of James C. Scott's work on how the modern state reconceptualizes its subjects in its efforts to make the latter legible (1998).

According to Chowdhry, when it first took charge, the colonial government found the marriage patterns in the Punjab and Haryana ill-defined and questionable. She notes that any attempts at enforcing marriage registration were "rejected on the grounds that it was practically impossible to define what constituted marriage" (2007, 30). British administrators, who had undertaken the massive codification drive to "understand" local kinship networks, framed marriage as an "economic necessity" (29). This framing was tactically constructed to facilitate better management of the high agricultural revenue produced by the region as well as the large numbers of personnel (predominantly from the Jat community) needed for the colonial armies. The colonial government's aim was maintainence of the status quo rather than change or "reform." They recognized certain relationships as "marriages" so that the families were kept intact and could be tapped as productive and reproductive resources of the region. In their endeavor they were assisted by senior men in the community who acted as informants on customary rules. Though the British codifiers may have been skeptical of some of the norms and customs cited by these community spokespersons, they chose to go along with what they were told (29).

Codified customs were sourced from the community before they became tools in the hands of the government, but Chowdhry reveals that male elders in Punjab and Haryana used these codification drives as opportunities to mold state law to their advantage, making the rule of the patriarch more stringent in the process (90). In North India, codification also defined and regulated what constitutes marriage through a dialogical process. Marriage laws in postindependence India similarly evoke both this dialogue and the patriarchal bias. The Hindu Marriage Act, 1955 and the Special Marriage Act, 1954 carried forward the state's efforts to make the population legible by making registration practices obligatory or appealing in different parts of the country, and by molding the institution in bureaucratic terms—something I will examine more closely in the next chapter.

Despite its vulnerability in the face of caste patriarchy, the Indian judiciary has maintained a tenuous balance as the proverbial benevolent patriarch. Judicial intervention on questions of marriage and family is imbued with concerns about the financial and physical protection of women, and it largely maintains that women's guardians (kinsmen or husbands) must ensure their well-being, at least in the corporeal if not the psychological sense of the term. Jurisprudence on marital troubles in India espouses values of a liberal modernity marked by equal rights, friendship, and companionship, but in practice it settles for pragmatism and compromise.

In her study of family courts that adjudicate on marital disputes and domestic violence, Srimati Basu finds that the law functions both at a utopic level where gender equity is an end goal and as a strategy where resolution is prioritized over persistent discord (2015). The intractable legal problem of marriage demonstrates that as an institution it is, by definition, "persistently associated with conflict, deprivation and exclusion" (3). To smooth over this ideological dilemma, the judiciary enforces a "coercive harmony" that does not necessarily resolve conflicts over power or property but nevertheless addresses them messily (4). The trouble with marriage, as several feminist scholars before Basu have also highlighted, is that the state is unable to live up to its utopic promise of an equality-based ideal family situation. This is not only because legal processes are long and inefficient in achieving their goals—and social beings are also not completely molded by legal frameworks. According to Basu, the law operates as a strategy or force although we perceive it through the powers vested in state institutions and agents.

My research suggests that law is a process as well as an ongoing dialogue. My ethnographic data does not support the conclusion that there is resolution—there are, however, openings and closures. Closures are not to be confused with end goals. I agree with Basu that law does not resolve the "trouble with marriage," but law can take the conversation forward or end one that has stagnated or deadened. I will discuss this idea of closures and openings more thoroughly in chapter 7, but in this chapter I focus on the conversational aspect of law. In the following discussion of the archival research I conducted at the parliament library in New Delhi, I delineate the terms in which marriage was defined and regulated in liberal, utopic frameworks in the early years of postindependence India.

This historical perspective assumes importance in the context of my ethnographic research that deliberates extensively on what constitutes a valid marriage. According to the letter of the law, validity for marriages can be sourced from either the civil marriage law or personal laws based on religion. The Hindu Marriage Act, 1955 and the Anand Marriage (Amendment) Act, 2012 (for the Sikh community) were passed by the Indian parliament, whereas minority communities such as Muslims and Christians are regulated by personal laws instituted under the colonial government.[1]

The Special Marriage Act of 1954 allows for intra- and intercommunity marriages as well as the registration of a marriage previously solemnized under a personal law. Unfortunately, in the public mind the law is often associated with interfaith marriages only, and its benefits for intrafaith couples are underemphasized. Several lawyers I spoke to were ignorant of the fact that the Special Marriage Act was applicable to any heterosexual couple.

While there is a rich scholarly literature on personal laws and legal practice associated with them (Agnes 1995; Vatuk 2008; Sinha 2012), civil marriage finds attention only in Perveez Mody's *The Intimate State* (2008), in which she analyzes the Special Marriage Act of 1872. The later Special Marriage Act of 1954 was a fresh legislation, not an amendment on the colonial law pertaining to the Brahmo Samaj, a rationalist community in East India that sought the registration of weddings conducted without rituals. Although both laws pertain to marriages that can be solemnized without religious ceremonies, the institution itself is defined in divergent ways. The Special Marriage Act of 1954 drew on multiple sources, both religious and secular, but both laws represented a liberal modern thrust—one was rooted in a civilizing mission undertaken by a colonizing government and the other was an early assertion of an aspirational democracy and a young nation-state (that is, India). The rest of this chapter will analyze aspects of the parliamentary debates on Special Marriage Bill to highlight the conversational aspect of law, preceded by a brief discussion on conceptualizing secular marriages, as this question guided the debates in subtle ways.

The Idea of Secular

Civil marriage laws in India draw on some religious conceptualizations, troubling the popular notion that civil marriage is secular whereas personal laws are not, by definition and design. But what does "secular" mean in the context of marriage, or more ambitiously, what does civil marriage bring to a secularizing society? These questions are contentious when the nation-state appears to be dropping the idea of secularism and calls for a Hindu nation are getting increasingly clamorous.

A stock question I asked many of my interviewees is whether they believed marriage to be religious, social, or legal. In the communities I studied marriage is determined not by religious rituals but, overwhelmingly, by social validation. And this view is not limited to North India, where I conducted my research; customary forms of marriage across South Asian communities are traditionally defined and validated by the social witnessing of rituals (Ortner 1978; Raheja 1988; Fruzzetti 1993). According to the Hindu Marriage Act, whether a couple seeks to marry in a registry office or to register a marriage previously solemnized through rituals, witnesses are key to ensuring the validity of a marriage.

In many ways, the importance of religion lies in the position it enjoys in state law. I focus here on Hindu marriages and the Hindu Marriage Act because Haryana is overwhelmingly Hindu (with a few isolated pockets of Meo Muslim communities). The Hindu Marriage Act recognizes religious weddings, as well as customary forms of marriage, even when the bride has not attained the age of consent (eighteen). That is, the weddings of girls over the age of fifteen years are considered valid, even though her parents and spouse may be held criminally culpable for arranging a wedding of a minor. Marital rape, incidentally, is currently recognized only in case of marriages involving legal minors. Because it provides for marriage registration, the Hindu Marriage Act is responsible for the increasing popularity of religious and Arya Samaj weddings, which require *saptapati* (seven steps around the fire), over certain customary rites among different caste and indigenous groups.[2] The aspiration or even necessity to secure state certification of marriage reflects the importance of the state in everyday lives. The need to be legible to the state has resulted in an increasing homogenization among Hindu communities, which, I argue, also reflects a secular impulse that coexists with meanings that to a certain extent depend on religion. That is, the motivations for having a religious wedding are largely secular, even if the origins of the law are not.

The Hindu Marriage Act, consequently, has resulted in a gradual, if mostly invisible, secularization of the community, where the standardization of wedding rites has come to represent the power the state vests in them through its control over validation processes.[3] This secularism is not atheistic but the original intention was to bring religious laws under a state-regulated framework where the state could intervene to ensure greater individual freedoms with regard to marriage and family rights, which religion and customary provisions had circumscribed. Though the law recognizes customary practices of weddings, the customary and caste rules on marriage alliances, exclusions, and specific incest taboos are not enforceable on individuals who defy kinship norms. Caste conclaves, for example, have sought to forbid consanguine marriages and invalidate unions that violate incest taboos, known locally as intra-*gotra* marriages, but these efforts have been overruled repeatedly by the national government and the courts.[4]

Hindutva politics threatens to erode secularization and greater individual freedoms in the community by making the state subservient to its own designs. It is the Hindu supremacists' ultimate revenge against the advances made by the majority community in securing individual freedoms through legislation. In a curious turn of events, the Indian state today presents greater opportunities for Muslim women to petition for the reform of marriage practices such as *triple talaq* and polygamy—not to promote greater freedoms for Muslim women but to target what Hindu men often see as the privileges enjoyed by Muslim men.[5]

Hindutva politics has also advanced this movement through its Love Jihad campaign, aggressively targeting intercommunity marriages under the Special Marriage Act. On July 20, 2018, the Punjab and Haryana High Court struck down key provisions of the Haryana government's "Court Marriage Check List" for marriages conducted under the law. The Haryana government had sought to send notices to the parents of couples who had petitioned to marry under this law, a move that was struck down by the high court as a violation of the (now) fundamental right to privacy (and also beyond the purview of the Special Marriage Act). Additionally, in relaxing the domicile requirements for proof of address and ensuring privacy by dissuading the public display of applicants' names, Justice Rajiv Narain Raina made a statement that challenges recent trends in national and regional politics pertaining to marriage and religion. According to his court order, "The State is not concerned with the marriage itself but with the procedure it adopts which must reflect the mind-set of the changed times in a secular nation promoting inter-religion marriages instead of the officialdom raising eyebrows and laying snares and landmines beneath the sacrosanct feet of the Special Marriage Act, 1954 enacted in free India to cover cases not covered by any other legislation on marriages as per choice of parties for a court marriage."[6]

Justice Raina defiantly claimed that India is a secular nation where the state's role should appear in sync with the broader social trends, at a time when leaders of the ruling party are seeking to institute a Hindu nation-state and curtail individual rights. By holding executive action to be excessive and tantamount to moral policing when procedures are implemented or designed with the intention of preventing rather than facilitating marriages under this law, Justice Raina further stressed that the state's role is one of a facilitator rather than a regulator.

Here, the judiciary is seeking not only to bring marriage under the purview of the state but also to clearly delineate and limit the powers of state agents on the question of marriage. Secularism re-emerges here as a moral force that can maintain state's power over the concerns of the society and religious representatives and secure individual freedoms. As a legal process and dialogue, the high court judgment strives to uphold both the utopic ideals that the judiciary is ideologically inclined toward and the original promise of the Special Marriage Act, which Justice Raina holds sacrosanct. Being secular can be a revered goal, just as civil marriage can draw on religion without being subsumed by it.

Debating Secularity, Sexuality, and Severance: Conversations on the Special Marriage Bill

The Special Marriage Act, 1954, opened up the possibility of individuals marrying out of personal choice (and for the first time, across religious lines), before foreclosing it by instituting requirements many prospective couples found daunting. The most crippling provision is the one-month application period, during which family members can register their disapproval of the proposed wedding. Threats of honor killings and other less drastic measures to prevent such weddings make the long waiting period unviable in parts of North India and elsewhere. Additionally, the publicly displayed list of couples registered to get married under the act can prompt threats that may not have otherwise existed. Justice Raina's judgment struck down this provision through a Supreme Court judgment on the right to privacy. Legal experts have often focused on such procedural hurdles, and some lawyer-activists are determined to make the law viable for eloping couples, but my research focuses on understanding the discursive frameworks behind the law's institution.

In order to gauge the logical limits to which this law can potentially take us, I analyzed the philosophical orientations that governed its introduction and the historical context in which it was written. While I acknowledge that the legal text can be, and often is, interpreted outside its specific context, I view this law as part of the Indian nation's grand narrative—the original set of promises the nation-state made to its citizens. It is within this context of a grand narrative that I place the voices that emerge from the records of parliamentary debates on the draft bill. In the debates, parliamentarians in postindependence India seemed to have believed they were engaged in building the young nation by detailing rules by which citizens were to marry and produce a liberated populace (Council of States Debates 1953, September 16, 2535–2538). Some lawmakers, both men and women, also backed the bill out of concern for Indian women's status in the family and society. They believed that it would improve women's lives in significant ways. Those who objected to the bill cited concerns that ranged from how marriage was defined under the law to the perceived threats its divorce provisions could pose to perceived sexual morality in society.[7] Yet another group professed a lack of interest in what they called a "women's interest bill," which according to them diverted precious time away from other, "more important" matters with respect to nation building. Yet, their expressed disinclination did not necessarily prevent them from engaging in the debate. Many provisions of the bill were taken apart and intellectually stimulating arguments ensued as the draft law went through more than four years of debate in both houses of the parliament and deliberations in a Joint Parliamentary Committee.

The Special Marriage Act reflected the aspirations of the leaders and what they believed the public sought from the new nation-state. Although the postpartition concerns about kinship and the exchange of women that Das discussed in *Life and Words* (2007) were not part of the debates in any major way, certain parallels between the parliamentary debates and Das's arguments on sexuality and social contract can be drawn. First, the debates dwelled on whether marriage was a sacrament or a contract and how the lawmakers expected the marriage law to be perceived. Second, the bill was seen as a key component of nation building as it conceptualized how the citizens who (could) procreate should enter a union. The elected representatives also discussed in great detail the purported injury to male authority figures caused by the exercise of choice and individual will in marriage. Where the debates deviated substantially from Das's premise was in their explicit attempts to perceive married citizens outside of family and kinship bonds. The bill's most bitterly debated provision was its severance clause, according to which couples were expected to forgo family ties when they got married under the law. I discuss these aspects individually in the following sections.

A State Blessing: Sacred or Contractual?

The question of defining the institution prompted a rich discussion on whether marriage in India constituted a contractual agreement or a sacrament. Several parliamentarians argued that marriage was considered a contract in Islam but not in the (Brahmanical) Hindu religion. Rajagopal Naidu of the Upper House or Rajya Sabha, then known as the Council of States, claimed that the Hindu marriage is sacramental but also contractual by way of being "a gift of the bride," as were *Gandharva* weddings (which are choice based and have no witnesses) and marriages among the Brahmo Samaj community in Bengal (Council of States Debates 1952, August 7, 3329).[8] The law minister in the early 1950s, C. C. Biswas, claimed that the new law extended to all citizens the option of legal registration, which was previously available only to the Brahmo Samaj under the Special Marriage Act of 1872. Since the new legislation did not call for interfaith couples to renounce their faiths in order to marry, it could be argued that marriage could still be treated as a sacrament by theistic couples.

Biswas and the government envisaged an alternative to divine blessing, a contract that would satisfy couples that they had been married through due processes rather than through rituals. This legal alternative was seen as liberating citizens from the mandated social witnessing of marriage ceremonies, with the state itself serving as witness. Shrimati Jayashri observed: "From a rational point of view, I should say marriage is a voluntary association of two individuals attached to it. It is the duty of the state to protect its rights and enforce its obligations. Marriage, therefore, must be a civil contract as far as the State is concerned" (House of the People Debates, 1954, May 21, 8021).

The powers these early lawmakers sought to entrust to the state and its procedures were akin to the powers of the magical state discussed in the introduction. According to Coronil, the deification of the Venezuelan state, which condensed the multiple powers dispersed throughout the nation (1997, 4), imbued the state with magical powers and dazzled the citizens with illusions. The state representatives, Coronil wrote, "appeared on the state's stage as powerful magicians who pull social reality, from public institutions to cosmologies, out of the hat" (2). Early lawmakers in India seem to have grappled with this idea of the state taking over sacred powers. While the law's magical properties were never completely realized, legislators not only revisited the definition of marriage itself (as a sacrament or a contract) but also significantly revised it during the debates. Justice Raina's impassioned order that called for the law's sacrosanct aspects to be respected is evocative of the state's illusionary powers.

Marriage and the Problem of "Ungovernable Sexualities"

Notwithstanding this expansive discussion on the definition of marriage, it invariably got entangled with ideas of procreation and sexual morality in the debates, in ways that are not completely unconnected to the discussion of sacraments and contracts. Hindu legislators, in particular, were wary of the contractual aspects of civil marriage, where divorce emerged as a threat to their own definitions of the institution. Another prickly topic was the requisite age for brides and grooms. Increasing the age of sexual consent and restricting child marriage had been important considerations and a site for activism in colonial and postindependence India, but when it came to the question of choice-based marriages the arguments proceeded on divergent tracks. Although the Indian representatives in colonial legislatures had repeatedly opposed British laws that sought to raise the minimum age for sexual consent, as historian Himani Bannerji has pointed out (1998), some parliamentarians in postindependence India attempted to increase the marriageable age under the Special Marriage Bill. Several arguments were offered in support of this move, including Kishen Chand's claim that women between eighteen and twenty-one are emotional and "high-strung" (Rajya Sabha Debates 1954, September 22, 3046) and Tajamul Husain's contention that older parents would be better capable of reproducing strong and brave Indians "who can defend the country in times of need" (Council of States Debates, 1954, May 5, 5209).

Since the age of sexual consent for women was fifteen in 1954, when these arguments were made, early marriage was still valid under several laws. Increasing the requisite age for civil marriage appeared to serve the purpose of reducing the likelihood of a choice-based marriage since parents could arrange for weddings before women were eligible to exercise their right under the proposed law.[9] But Chand's and Husain's arguments still deserve a closer engagement. Given that the civil union law was envisaged with utopic ideals for the nation-state—for the state to "condense its powers"—for these lawmakers, regulating the reproductive potential of its citizens represented an opportunity to create a populace previously characterized by its colonial masters as a weaker race. Perhaps, in the view of some lawmakers, not everyone was capable or even worthy of participating in this nationalist project.

Pragmatism prevailed, however, as the amendments for increasing the minimum age to as high as twenty-one for women and twenty-five for men were rejected on the grounds that this would completely defeat the purpose of giving Indian citizens the option to marry of their own accord. Both the proponents and the critics shared an aspiration for what we today would call a biopolitical project of managing populations and managing bodies (Foucault 1990), where state power can be seen as productive rather than just oppressive.

At the heart of these discussions lay a Victorian anxiety about sexuality—in that it could not even be named directly by some. As Biswas put it, almost ominously, "Suppose two young persons have made up their minds to marry and you place all these obstacles in their way. Certain very undesirable consequences may follow" (Council of States Debates, 1954, April 29, 4565). Even as he performed his role as the enlightened leader, Biswas seems to have been unable to contain or express his fears about ungovernable sexualities. He could not shrug off the image of the child stigmatized with an "unrepentant, reprobate sinfulness" (Nandy 1983, 15), a morally degenerate entity who needed to be rescued, according to the British colonizers. The proposed age increases speak to this anxiety, in which, Foucault claimed, the sexuality of the child was both denied and feared (1990, 27–30).

The postcolonial state continued to wrestle with the colonial mission of rescuing the sinful child, and of making men and women out of subjects who had been deemed children for a long time. In determining who was still a child and who was capable and levelheaded enough to indulge in sexual activities, marry, and procreate, the parliamentarians were wary but ultimately summoned the collective will to release the proverbial child from the stigmatizing sin of sexual proclivities. The legislation process, then, was also in part an effort at psychologically registering and phenomenologically experiencing a hardwon independence through reiterations of the collective self's adulthood. Some promoters of the bill accepted that a legal adult of eighteen years was "intelligent enough" (Council of States Debates, 1954, April 29, 4565) to make a decision on marriage. Biswas, however, stressed that the lawmakers should help young couples to marry, as far as possible, "without any great violence to our cherished sentiments or to ordinary considerations of prudence and propriety" (4565).

Lawmaker Seeta Paramanand, who spoke at length on women's status in India, also worried about wrong choices and spousal abandonment, where parental consent (especially in cases of intercaste or intercommunity marriages) as well as sexual respectability were seen as providing women with security (Rajya Sabha Debates 1954, September 22, 3040; Council of States Debates, 1954, May 5, 5205). The state's role was to both provide these "respectable" options and ensure the protection of women's interests within such relationships. It may not be coincidental that these anxieties arose at a time when the "orderly exchange of women" had been disrupted, as Das (2007) discussed. Choice-based marriages, too, were expected to take place in an orderly manner.

Over the course of my fieldwork, I observed that male and female judges of protection cases approach the question of women's security, financial and logistical, in their own individual ways. This resonates with discourses that emerge from the parliamentary debates. A feminist reading makes us wary of the morality discourse, which included S. Mahanty's allegation that the women in the parliament "have lowered marriage to the morass of sex" under the pretext of equality of rights and status (Council of States Debates 1954, April 29, 4616). But sexual respectability concerns continue to be pertinent today. In my ethnographic experiences as well as in the experience of lawyers I interviewed, women who elope expect to get married immediately in spite of procedural hurdles such as being a legal minor (under eighteen years of age). In rural Haryana as well as on the high court premises, those who had engaged in premarital sex confessed to me that they felt an obligation to marry their partners despite having doubts about their relationships. Parmanand's argument resonates with such testimonies where respectability confers security in the relationship in the eyes of both state and nonstate actors.

On the topic of sexual respectability, two radical reformers of independent India diverged considerably. Anticaste leader and constitutionalist B. R. Ambedkar, who conceived intercaste marriage as one of the modes by which caste patriarchy could be weakened, believed in the importance of sexual respectability (Ambedkar and Rege 2013). In contrast, the South Indian anticaste, self-respect movement founder "Periyar" E. V. Ramaswamy claimed that chastity and norms of respectability constrained women, and therefore they should refuse marriage in order to liberate themselves (Geetha 1998). While Ambedkar was keenly attuned to the pain that accrued to Dalit women who were denied sexual respectability, Periyar saw chastity as a virtue that constrained both upper-caste women, who were required to maintain it, and lower-caste women, who learned to aspire to it because it was routinely denied.

Periyar, incidentally, did not support the Indian state, because freedom from colonialism had not resulted in a liberation from caste and gender oppression. Ambedkar, for his part, had pinned his hopes for liberation from caste patriarchy onto the Indian nation-state. By the time the Special Marriage Bill was debated, however, Ambedkar had resigned from the Congress Party and his position as law minister because the Hindu Code Bill had been derailed by conservative lawmakers (Sinha 2012). He made brief appearances in the parliamentary debates I studied, arguing that the Special Marriage Act of 1872 could be extended to other communities and therefore there was no need for the new law. He certainly did not share either the aspirations for the proposed law or the anxieties it generated in some parliamentarians.

Severing the Umbilical Cord?

One of the bill's most heatedly contested provisions was the clause of severance from the family. A citizen who opted for a marriage under this law was expected to sign a legal deed of separation from her family at the time of the wedding, though the opportunity to "legally reunite" at a later date would always exist (Council of States Debates 1954, April 29, 4571–4572). Biswas stubbornly upheld this clause, because, for him, it was important that the citizen fully understood the enormous significance of the decision to choose her spouse (1954, May 5, 5181–5190). S.S.N. Tankha also supported the clause, calling it a deterrent. Only those who are ready to bear the consequences of family alienation, he claimed, should make such a decision (Council of States Debates 1954, May 5, 5155–5157). This legal deed of severance was conceived as a critical rite of passage. The lawmakers, it appears, insisted on bestowing certain rights only on those who were ready to accept individual responsibility for their actions.

This presumed individualizing tendency of choice-based marriages was cited by my informants at court complexes and elsewhere as one of its perceived ills—that it splits families and disrupts kin relations. The separation and return, if it is possible, is enacted through movement from community to state spaces rather than through a legal deed. Eloping couples who visited the high court often returned to the community, to live either with the groom's family or in a separate establishment close to home. In kinship literature from South Asia, marriage is understood as a rite of passage where rituals provide a space for transition (Ortner 1978; Fruzzetti 1993). For the state, it is the bureaucratic procedures that facilitate this out-of-the-ordinary event in which couples come to be seen as married. According to Mody, elopement made couples "not-community," while the court acted as a normalizing agent to facilitate their return to the community (2008).

A marriage of choice can also achieve the vital break an individual yearns for. Three women lawyers in Chandigarh explicitly stated in interviews with me that women who are very oppressed or constrained at their natal homes are often the ones who elope. The discursive framework on choice-based marriages, as represented in the debates, even appears to mandate such a break. When kin and community do not offer a safe space, men and women can achieve a decisive break through choice-based marriages. This is especially significant because the marriage institution helps to perpetuate kin networks and the political and economic system they favor, making it a viable site for disruption.

The Rule of Law and the Role of the State

The parliamentary debate records for the year of the law's passage included the sole intervention made by a noted politician of that time, Vijayalakshmi Pandit.[10] She allayed her fellow lawmakers' fears that the proposed law, and especially its divorce provisions, would encourage a proliferation of sexual desire. She predicted that the law would not immediately have many takers but that the next generation, emancipated by the state's efforts to educate and "liberate" its populace, would demand the right to choose their partners. She conceived of choice marriage as a calculated, rational decision rather than the emotional one some of her colleagues pictured (Lok Sabha Debates 1954, September 1, 812–816). In Pandit's conception, the law, too, was meant to be a carefully orchestrated design. She argued that a freedom willfully granted is better than a freedom that is "taken" (815).

There are two key aspects to Pandit's intervention here: the first is concerned with how marriage was perceived in the new nation and the second deals with the state's role in marriage and maintaining social order. Like other women representatives, she believed that choice in marriage and state protection for married women would improve lives. Where she deviated from her colleagues was in asking her fellow lawmakers not to fear the law, because it aimed to cater to a select audience. She also warned that denying this group the right to choose their partners would have consequences. She was concerned not with sexual mores but rather with the challenges the newly politicized subjects might pose for the state. Her statement did not necessarily seek safeguards against a possible rebellion. Instead, she was proposing, I argue, that the state should stay ahead of the public—that is, be a little more progressive than its subjects—so that friction could be avoided.

My short analysis of the historical debates suggests that the aspirations of a liberal governmentality, a benevolent but wary patriarchy, and a new disciplinary regime had converged in the creation of the marriage law. Lawmakers across gender and community lines accepted that the state had a prescribed role as a protector and benefactor of women, even if they had doubts regarding the law itself.

The Special Marriage Act proved to be largely ineffective in facilitating the marriage of legal adults whose parents opposed the match.[11] Still, the discourses surrounding its scripting provide a viable framework for understanding some of the state's mechanizations on choice-based marriages conducted today. In their effort to provide legal cover for "irregular relationships" (Council of States, 1954, May 5, 5180), the lawmakers ensured that two closely linked ideas gained credence: contested marriages most likely needed state approval; and the state is the site where marriages that do not find credibility in society will ultimately get mediated. Here, the state provided openings as well as potential closures for strained family ties.

In summary, by spelling out the potential terms of marital intimacy and endearment in a politicolegal space, the lawmakers provided the crucial juridical backing for the exercise of choice in sexual partnership in independent India. They laid down their reasonable vision for citizens who would be in the position to exercise their newly acquired freedom in an ordered world. For these lawmakers, the liberal ideas were a necessary component of a modern nation and companionate marriages were an essential accompaniment.

Whereas this section has dealt with the aspirations associated with the authorship of the civil marriage law, the next section analyses the sociocultural milieu in North India and the contestations in the region on the question of elopements and love marriages. The idea of court interventions reveals an understanding of civil marriage that is both connected to and independent of the Special Marriage Act in discursive terms.

Haryana's Lost Opportunity

Marriage in both classical anthropological tradition as well as in legal terms is a ritualized act that requires witnesses. As mentioned earlier, a Gandharva wedding, where the nuptials are solemnized without witnesses, is not recognized under the Hindu Marriage Act. The law finds its potency in laying out the terms for registration of weddings, which is a governmental record of a wedding previously conducted according to religious and/or customary rules. Although Haryana state does have a Compulsory Marriage Registration Act, at present it does not serve its intended purpose. The practice of registration is not widespread in this region, and in particular the law is of no assistance to eloping couples who would like the state to acknowledge a wedding where the community has not. Among other provisions, the law requires affidavits (notarized testimonials) from both sets of parents and other relatives, making the terms of registration similar to a socially approved wedding ritualistically witnessed by the community/kin groups. By adding such requirements, the Haryana government ensured that registration is in many ways superfluous. A wedding already sanctioned and witnessed in the community is not seen as requiring registration and validation from the state. According to the law, unregistered weddings may invite penalties, but these are not currently being enforced. Registration of weddings is more widespread in urban regions and parts of South and East India, which have seen significant social movements in support of women's education and empowerment. The processes of obtaining employment, banking, property, and identity documents such as passports also make registration of marriage prudent. But the Haryana government has created procedural hurdles for the implementation of both the Hindu Marriage and Special Marriage Acts, ensuing that a civil wedding or a proof of marriage through registration eludes eloping couples who require the documentation for their survival and togetherness.

The eloping couples in my research study preferred religious establishments where the priest who presided over the ceremony could provide a certificate. Chandigarh city's Arya Samaj offices, Hindu temples, and Sikh *gurudwaras*, where some sections of the Hindu population from this region are customarily obliged to wed, are relevant for this reason. Couples often lamented that religious sites in rural areas closer to home did not provide the certificate "needed to file a petition in courts." In these situations, the religious wedding is only a nominal ceremony conducted in order to approach the courts, with the high court in Chandigarh being the most favored. The court does not explicitly validate the claim of marriage, but couples and communities construe what it does as a sanction, a theme I discuss further in subsequent chapters. Yet, in forcing couples to jump through these hoops to obtain confirmation of their love marriages that still leaves room for ambiguity, the state and its institutions have clearly sought to play regulator instead of facilitator, a development Justice Raina takes exception with in his judgment. But Justice Raina had also missed an opportunity to stress that the Special Marriage Act pertains not only to interfaith but also to intrafaith couples. The latter group crowds the Chandigarh-based high court on every business day, and couples could benefit enormously from the law if its procedures were simplified, their privacy was protected, and the domicile requirements were relaxed. As such, the connections between the guiding principles of the Special Marriage Act and the high court proceedings are abstract but ubiquitous.

The authors of the Special Marriage Act signaled an impulse to normatively order Indian society, but they also imbued the law with their aspirations for the nation-state, defined in both personal and political terms. It is a law that many citizens may not be familiar with, but some of its provisions are widely known and acknowledged as specifying rights the Indian state upholds. The right to marry a person of one's choice is seen as something the state allows but it is acceptable to community members only after state mediation. The trend of filing protection petitions has accelerated after the 2006 Supreme Court judgment *Lata Singh v. the State of Uttar Pradesh*, which mandated the state governments to safeguard couples against crimes such as honor killings. These cases reflect how the need for state approval can create an entire legal apparatus devoted to facilitating marriages that ideally should have been served by the Special Marriage Act.

Court proceedings dealing with protection petitions evoke salient themes extensively addressed in the debates, including a tendency among some judges to approach the question of women's protection as being about more than just physical safety. One male judge, for example, routinely asks grooms to create a fixed-deposit bank account for their new brides. Commenting on this practice, one young Haryanvi lawyer claimed that unlike his peers, he did not see the requirement as an irregular legal procedure. The need to protect women's interests, he claimed, governs judicial rationale in cases ranging from divorce to dowry harassment and domestic violence. Procedurally, the protection petition comes across as an incongruous option for those who choose their spouses, but I argue that in epistemological terms, it covers one of the motivating factors behind the law's passage.

Court proceedings also visually demonstrate the potential of choice-based marriages to sever family ties. Elopement cases often result in high drama, with parents of the bride appearing in court to contest the wedding. When dealing with cases where the legal claims of couples and their parents are hopelessly at odds, some judges choose to order that the court record statements made by all parties involved and announce the date for the next hearing. Many of these cases reach a resolution (either a durable marriage or in the bride's return to her natal family) as the event of the wedding recedes in memory. In one case that I will discuss at length in chapter 5, the bride and her parents disagreed over her legal age, with the parents claiming that she was still a legal minor. The parents explicitly stated that putting off the case for another date would not serve any purpose—if they left the courtroom without their daughter, the case was as good as lost. I interpreted their insistence on closure as a recognition of the fact that when courts "allow" couples to live together for even a brief period, they bestow conditional legitimacy on the relationship and the break from the family is regarded as complete.

The ritual of a high court visit is the performance of a scripted text that transforms the performers in irrevocable ways. For the couples, seeking state mediation is what Victor Turner calls an act of repeating scripted texts in a liminal space that both reconstructs the text and the performer of the text (1986). This text could also be seen as a contract the couples write in association with the courts. For the couples who return to an ostensibly normalized life, the trip to the court provided an opportunity to realize and reconstruct their selfhood, even if temporarily, where emancipation is achieved not before marriage, as Pandit had predicted, but rather *after* the wedding and court visit.

2

Of Rebellious Lovers and
Conformist Citizens

The legendary stories of North India and Pakistan, part of a rich repertoire of ritualistic songs and folktales, portray rebellious lovers as social outcasts who are banished and eventually killed (Hansen 1992; Chowdhry 2007). In these tales, rebellious love that challenges social norms and disrupts kinship order is often treated as an irresolvable crisis; the couple's return to the community is unimaginable and their survival even as outcasts continues to threaten social order. In other words, only their deaths can restore social balance. In many instances, folktales celebrated rebellious love but also stressed that what we today call "honor killings" are inevitable in order for the society to persist after the rupture caused by this love and desire.

When compared to these love legends, the contemporary cases of elopements, as represented in my ethnographic data, present a two-part problem of contextualizing empirical evidence within the contemporary cultural landscape and then redefining the positionality of lovers who survive despite violating social norms. This chapter tracks popular culture artifacts, including the larger-than-life spectacle of Bollywood films that draw on the folktales but are not limited by them, and then proposes a framework for understanding contemporary elopements and choice-based marriages.

Apart from the cinematic representations, these tales of transgressive love are also featured in songs sung at prewedding women's gatherings across North India and Pakistan as cautionary tales. Although the tragic stories were meant to deter young lovers, they also were designed to fuel the imagination and desires that can be realized in the realm of fantasy (Chowdhry 2007, 235–236). Daljit Ami researches the motifs and socioeconomic references that capture both the timelessness and the historicity of these tales. According to him, love legends such as *Mirza Sahiban* adapt to transformations in the state, in historical discourses, and in the material conditions of cinema itself in India, Pakistan, and diasporic communities in Canada; they can absorb historical traumas, aspirations, and tensions (2016, 1). Love legends provide templates on which contemporary narratives of desire and love are constantly rewritten, and Ami attributes this to the enduring themes of mobility, masculinity, individualism, and the surveillance state (3–4). In fact, the surveillance state and its biopolitical regime resurface with different ideological motivations in different temporal and spatial settings to play a major role in this drama.

As Strathern (1991) has theorized, partible aspects of self facilitate the creation of hybrids and networks and define persons through shared notions of belonging. This can pertain to one's immediate society as well as, I would argue, the state. In a 2004 piece, Strathern builds on this theorization and argues that the role played by the legal technique in fabricating persons and things rehearses issues that have long troubled anthropologists studying marriage arrangements (202). The stories of star-crossed lovers can be conceptualized as hybrids of all the times and spaces they have previously inhabited, at once reminiscent of and divergent from the societies they have formerly dwelled in and the states that have governed them. Adaptations found in South Asia and North America fabricate persons and objects from the immediate material world but rehearse familiar issues and conflicts.

Contemporary popular culture provides us with important clues about these hybrids of fabricated lives, including, at times, the intimate and sentimental relationship people forge with the space of the state. While the last chapter dealt with the ideological dispensation of the postcolonial state, here I survey the cultural representation of the state and the role it inscribes for the state—marked as a mystifying bureaucratic maze—on the question of love marriage.

The objective of eloping couples represented in my research data is not to quit a rigid, exploitative society and live in the wilderness but to return and dwell within its restrictive boundaries. The survival of the marriage and of the married couple itself depends on securing social sanction of their wedding through court intervention and thus resolving (to some extent) the social crisis. The state, as a routine and everyday presence in the community (see Das and Poole 2004), offers abstract solutions and bureaucratic paperwork (see Holden 2016) that are entered into social circulation to form new hybrids. This chapter is concerned with both the transforming nature of love legends and the popular perception of this routine, mundane form of the bureaucratic state, which does not present utopic or ideological pretensions.

Rebellion to Conformity: Love in Popular Culture Tropes

The tale of forbidden love was spectacularly mounted with contemporary motifs in the iconic film *Qayamat Se Qayamat Tak* (From doom till doom; dir. Khan 1988), where young lovers (nineteen to twenty-two years of age) from warring

Rajput clans elope and live in seclusion before finally being murdered by their families. *QSQT*, as it is popularly known, does not draw its inspiration directly from popular folktales but captures the tales' essence of the social rupture created by forbidden relationships, which can be mended only by the lovers' deaths. The movie, as the title suggests, begins with the catastrophe of an illicit relationship that is "set right" by murder and ends with another catastrophe—brutal double murders of a pair of star-crossed lovers whose relationship has no explicit social sanction (see figure 3 for more context). The eloping couple attempt to forge a licit relationship by solemnizing their wedding themselves (this can be viewed as a Gandharva wedding) literally as social outcasts in wilderness, but within the narrative arc of the film, togetherness and cohabitation are portrayed as transitory and ambiguous. The text, in other words, captures the instability of a situation created by a relationship that is neither licit nor illicit, anticipating the doom prophesied in the title.

According to Chowdhry, who draws on Sohini Ghosh's works, pre-1990s films valorized such rebel lovers who resisted family opposition: "Family pride and honour had to suffer defeat in the face of love" (2007, 7). Since the 1990s, she continues, most films have been urban romances that fell in line with patriarchal authority: "Approval of parents, even against heavy odds, is considered masculine" (8). Preserving Indian culture and values in matters of marriage emerged as a way of retaining the indigenous moral and cultural superiority from other cultures and societies, particularly Western society (8). Hence, film scholars such as Jyotika Virdi claim that we have witnessed the resurfacing of patriarchal authority and enforcement of community's purity (2003, 181) that was more explicit in films such as *QSQT*. As if to capture this generational divide, *Humpty Sharma ki Dulhania* (The Bride of Humpty Sharma; dir. Khaitan 2014) pairs young lovers working hard to secure patriarchal approval from parents who had themselves defied social norms and made what turned out to be a successful intercaste marriage.

It seems that the tales of love and gore were being replaced by stories where lovers survive and return to the community (or never actually quit the community), albeit after assuaging the sentiments of an injured patriarchy. Rebellious young lovers from timeless folktales had suddenly become conformists, eager to please elders and prove themselves worthy of their desires. Within the universe of these films, the contest between couples who seek choice in intimate relationships and patriarchs who are unable to relinquish authority played out in kinship spaces. Post-1990s films did tame the lovers and reinforce patriarchal authority but they also brought back the lovers from their mandatory exiles and violent deaths, an aspect Chowdhry touches on without according it much importance.

Such contests are, as yet, difficult to pursue in rural settings, where communities are far more interconnected in a chain of clan and supra-clan networks.

According to my interlocutors, deviations have resulted in summons to caste conclaves, which frequently become a setting for the community to intimidate and crush individuality or rebellion at its inception. In general, I observed repeatedly that surveillance in rural regions is intricate and rebuke/backlash could be swift if community elders were inclined to intervene. In Bollywood films, negotiations in the urban milieu or between urban characters temporarily in rural settings give rural Indians an opportunity to vicariously experience resolutions to love stories, a spectacle rarely witnessed in their immediate lives.

Early conformist films such as *Maine Pyar Kiya* (I fell in love; dir. Barjatya 1988) and *Dilwale Dulhaniya Le Jayenge* (The Big-hearted will take the bride away; dir. Chopra 1995) portrayed urban characters, and in the case of three of the four protagonists, even global citizens temporarily living in rural settings. The love stories do not defy community norms (in both films the lovers have similar caste backgrounds) but instead seek to defy the rule of the patriarch on the question of marriage. Violence from patriarchs and kin groups is borne with grace and their final approval is gratefully acknowledged.

Violence in the so-called romantic films gradually disappeared and by the first decade of the twenty-first century, popular culture began to refer to honor killings, directly and not within the melancholic framework that *QSQT* deployed. Tragic losses of life due to transgressive love no longer hold romantic appeal. Haryanvis, who were overidentified with the trend of honor killings, were often essentialized or caricatured, as in films such as *Khap* (dir. Sinha 2011). They were, until very recently, the "rednecks" of India, unable to reconcile with the globalizing society and often juxtaposed against a starkly distinct urban society. *Matru ki Bijli ka Mandola* (Matru's Bijli's Mandola; dir. Bhardwaj 2013), an absurdist drama which revolves around a wealthy Jat landowner and industrialist, is well populated with redneck caricatures, and the term "honor killings" is casually mentioned in connection to choice in marriage in a throwaway line to please the mainstream audience's indentification of the phenomenon with Haryana.

Honor killings as a phenomenon was better represented more recently in the noir/risqué thriller *NH10* (dir. Singh 2015), where the antagonists are fleshed-out characters identifiable within their own context. The crime in the movie was inspired by the famous Manoj-Babli double murder in the Kaithal district of Haryana but the plot revolves around the struggles of its urban protagonists from Gurugram (a suburb of Delhi that has one of India's highest GDPs) who accidently witness the crime.[1] The divide between the first world the urban characters inhabit and the third world of their rural antagonists is portrayed as dystopic. Both *Matru ki Bijli ka Mandola* and *NH10* have very little to offer by way of romance; the tragic loss of lives is a cruel joke in one and a dystopic event in the other. Neither film attempts to recapture the appeal of folktales from the region.

The retelling of folktales in contemporary settings has become more performative, even taking a surreal and abstract form in *Mirzya* (dir. Mehra 2016), which is based on the Punjabi folktale *Mirza Sahiban*. The predictable murders of the lovers are presented with aesthetic detachment, with very little blood to repulse the viewers apart from also requiring less emotional investment on part of the audience. In *Aaje Nachle* (Come, let's dance; dir. Mehta 2007), after delivering a performance of another love legend from Punjab, *Heer Ranjha*, Imran, a Muslim character, confesses to his colleague and lover Anokhi, a Hindu woman, that he would not like to perform it again because he doesn't want to witness the woman he loves "die" at the end of every show. Set in contemporary Uttar Pradesh, which has recently seen campaigns such as the Love Jihad (against Hindu-Muslim relationships) and the anti-Romeo squads, their interreligious love story is portrayed as less controversial than their mentor's earlier elopement with an American photographer. Highlighting the intergenerational transformation in the reel world, the mentor's elopement had been triggered by excessive surveillance and curtailment of the lovers' individual freedoms, whereas Imran and Anokhi remain unfettered. The mentor's rebellion and flight to obscurity is treated as an echo from another time and place, like the story of Heer Ranjha had been to the film's young performers.

The crux of conformist-era love is that the popular culture, and indeed the political society it caters to, do not find rebellious love or its temporary success over patriarchal authority appealing in its traditional form. Forbidden loves were not plot drivers but rather incidental to larger sociopolitical struggles and negotiations. The dilemma involves placing romantic love in its specific socio-economic context, where the timelessness of folktales may inform the narrative but its moral message struggles to find resonance. Rebellion that ends in tragedy is no longer persuasive.

It is important to acknowledge not only the shaky ground on which the conformist-love genre is judged as regressive but also the fact that transgressive love came out of its romanticized social banishment, refusing to die a gory death to create insidious, cautionary tales for the next generation of potential lovers. The folktales and songs make the idea of transgressive love irresistible while also ensuring, according to Chowdhry's accounts, that women largely live out these fantasies within performative spaces (2007, 235–236). As the next section highlights, aspirations are today rehearsed in divergent performative spaces.

Performing Gender: Global and Local Lives

Spending sleepless nights in the company of women who sang about love and lust as part of prewedding rituals in Haryana, I found curiously few younger women and adolescents at these gathering. They were, at times, embarrassed by the bawdy lyrics and dance forms or confessed that they found them difficult to learn and participate in. My own keen interest in recording and archiving this disappearing art form did not blind me to the fact that these songs were no longer young people's most important resources for understanding sexuality and desire. These ethnographically rich experiences provided a valuable glimpse into a stark and visible generational shift, a theme I will expand on in chapter 3. But it is important to stress here that transgressive love of the young and restless in rural India does not belong to popular culture artifacts any more than it does within cinematic tropes. Younger women and men from this region did not find their lives represented in either popular urban films or the ritualistic songs, but they did find their aspirations represented in the former in ways the latter could not quite satisfy.

Young men were enamored of testosterone-fueled Punjabi-Hindi Bollywood songs and misogynistic rap music inspired by British Indian pop icon Yo Yo Honey Singh. Singh and the genre of music he has spawned offer rural men of North India a toxic mix of global worldview and parochial masculinity, serving as accessible points of entry into aspirations and questions of identity that cannot be captured by traditional cultural artifacts. As far as young women from the baagri region are concerned, they listen and dance to Punjabi-Hindi music because they are attracted to the access it provides to the global world of opportunities. It was more difficult to track their quest for identity symbols, given the lack of role models in the public sphere. I finally found a curious and almost hidden fascination for popular Rajasthani folk music artistes. My interlocutors shared with Rajasthani women artistes their dialect as well as a worldview that was localized even as it looked outward. Traditional, gender-exclusive singing events turned women inward (Chowdhry calls them "inner voices") toward hidden interiors of the intimate family space. The quest for younger women was to find a vocabulary to express aspirations that were global but needed to be realized within the familiar community and region.

In summary, the demise of the rebellious love trope as well as the increasing detachment from traditional art that celebrates love and lust may invoke nostalgia in researchers like me but also signals an exploration of a desire that will not be relegated to the margins but will be directed to the very center of an increasingly connected and networked world, as the Eiffel Tower replica in figure 2 also reveals. In this world, love and longing is part of a broader set of aspirations that may require both conformity and resistance; where challenging social norms can sometimes result in a greater bargaining power in the society.

Contemporary Expressions of Desire

The eloping couples I interviewed as part my research viewed their choice as a rational and prudent course of action, meant to increase rather than limit their opportunities. Though most courting couples are aware that social boycott and

FIGURE 2 A replica of the Eiffel Tower outside the Chandigarh School of Architecture testifies to global aspirations that must be realized in local settings.

Photo: Rama Srinivasan.

violence may follow an elopement, their efforts are geared toward securing social sanction or even ending the relationship if no viable solution is in sight.

An important feature of transgressive love in folktales—the engendering of a crisis or disorder—is a recurring motif. An eloping couple must find social sanction, which is not afforded through participation in a religious wedding ceremony. A licit relationship is one where wedding rituals are acknowledged by kin and community members. Where this acknowledgement is denied, such marriages occupy an ambiguous space even when the couples are allowed to live in community spaces. The unions are controversial only in particular times and in specific geographical locations; in the case of the Manoj-Babli murders, the fact that Babli's family was locally dominant and that one of the provocateurs had political ambitions played a fatal role.[2] But the ambiguity never bodes well for the couple, who could be subjected to minor and major social backlash.

When a particular relationship is not categorized as licit, the social crisis it provokes is persistent. Parents may extend their approval or even offer an option of cohabitation to the couple to ease the tension, but this may result in social boycott being extended to the entire family and kin groups. For example, in a case from Karnal district, a married couple was told that the match arranged by their parents had (inadvertently) violated incest taboos and their union was consequently invalid. As the couple and parents resisted this decision, their social exclusion steadily increased. According to the groom's parents, who spoke to me some time after the episode, tensions reduced significantly as the couple moved away from the region, but the parents continued to face aggression on an daily basis. In many ways, living in a community that feels threatened by the social crisis and thererfore subjects couples (and their families) to various levels of aggression is an understated but challenging endeavor. The glorified tales of rebellion and challenge to patriarchal order do not quite capture the everyday realities that extend beyond the particular event.

Though not valorized, conformity and acquisition of parental approval bring both momentary respite and a possibility of real change that is in no way less positive. Films that follow this plot line are treated as regressive by scholars when they appear on screens as urban romances, but they resonate with the aspirations of rural and small-town Indians who aspire to live in potentially unforgiving, rigid communities and optimize their opportunities rather than reduce them. For such couples, the romance of elopement does not necessarily lead to lives of isolation but rather fully realized participation in economy and society. Families often adjust themselves to changed realities, though they might appear to object to the match. During my interviews in rural Haryana, I often heard of families who had advised couples to elope and have a "court marriage" because they were unwilling to risk social exclusion themselves. Court marriage also afforded the couples more security as well as the "licit" label that their parents' approval and support might not. A couple I met in Chandigarh told me that after their court marriage their parents had decided to keep in touch with them through phone conversations or by meeting secretly. This performance, at least for a designated period, was undertaken in the hope that societal disapproval would eventually dissipate.

Where parents were unwilling or unable to approve of a wedding, court marriage became a respectable alternative for those seeking an end to the social rupture. Court marriage involves rebellious lovers who are willing to become docile subjects of the state; they are citizens who subscribe to notions of respectable marriage and consequently reduce everyday challenges. The act of elopement is indeed a challenge to patriarchal and kinship orders, but the lovers do not seek to live forever in the zone of rebellion.

Enlisting the state to ensure that the social crisis is resolved signals a *bureaucratization of desire and aspirations.* Elopement is no less defiant (or dangerous, in some cases), but I would argue that the state itself holds a romantic appeal for the couples. Dwelling in state spaces, which is at the center of society and community, with the possibility of becoming full subjects fuels the imagination in ways a lifetime in wilderness as social outcasts no longer does. Conformist love is also about claiming a space of one's own and occupying it instead of willfully disappearing into oblivion.

The introduction of the term *court marriage* into the local lexicon is one of the most fascinating developments in the rebellious love narrative. The origins of the term, and especially the space this form of legal marriage covers, are fuzzy at best. The Special Marriage Act is unviable for several reasons discussed in the previous chapter. Solemnizing or registering a wedding under the Hindu Marriage Act with a registrar, a phenomenon well documented by Mody (2008), is viable in urban regions but poses privacy and surveillance concerns for rural regions. When and how did court marriage in judicial courts become a viable civil marriage option? There are very few clues in popular culture and almost none in scholarly literature. In the next few sections, I outline my attempts at tracing the references to civil union in popular culture and how this informs the discussion on court marriage.

On the Margins of the State

In the Netflix India production *Love per Square Feet* (dir. Tiwari 2018), cross-community protagonists Sanjay and Karina pretend to be affianced to avail of a low-cost government housing scheme targeted at married couples. Their softhearted broker falls for the deception and provides them with bureaucratic assistance. Rehmanbhai arranges a marriage registration application, assuring them of the ease with which the marriage certificate would "travel" from the magistrate office to the housing department. Given that the protagonists belong to different religious communities, Rehmanbhai's fix must have involved the Special Marriage Act, though it is never referenced in the film. The solution will provide them with the legal paperwork to support a housing scheme application—here, marriage facilitates other aspirations.

Sanjay nervously assures Karina that the divorce office is right next to the marriage office, since neither of them had bargained on actually getting married. Both Rehmanbhai and Sanjay make an important observation on state

institutions, about how the proximity of the offices influences citizens' perceptions of bureaucracy and legality. Sanjay's father similarly evokes the cultural
imagination on civil weddings when he complains to Rehmanbhai that he cannot reconcile himself to this court-*kachehri ki shaadi* (court-tribunal wedding);
it is not the civil wedding itself that causes his distress but rather the space in
which it is conducted.

There are more striking examples of civil weddings of eloping couples in
films from other regions, but Bollywood has only a handful. In *Mr. & Mrs. '55*
(dir. Dutt 1955), which can be seen as an attack on the Hindu Marriage Act and
its divorce proceedings, the protagonists, a rich heiress and an unemployed
cartoonist, enter a sham marriage at an administrative office. Civil unions are
often viewed in this light—as weddings whose legal validity does not immediately translate to social sanctity and whose authenticity is shrouded in doubt.
In *Running Shaadi* (Running weddings; dir. Roy 2017), the protagonists come to
see law as an instrument when they run a successful web service to help eloping couples in Punjab. Through the help of an ambitious lawyer, the entrepre-
neurs learn to sift through the legal requirements of different couples, including
cross-community couples whose unions might require the Special Marriage
Act.[3] What this lesser-known film successfully illustrates is the widespread
trend of courtships and elopements in North India and how law can be instrumentalized for quick-fix solutions. In the film, the authenticity of the relationships is never in doubt, and most cases end simplistically with post facto
parental approval.

The clearest example of a civil marriage played out in the cinematic landscape is in *Ahiste Ahiste* (Slowly slowly; dir. Nair 2006), where a Delhi-based tout
beckons cautious couples into district court premises and offers himself as a
witness for furtive marriages. He ends up befriending a jilted woman whose
fiancé does not keep their appointment. Through recurring references to the
procedure that provides the protagonist with his remuneration, the film underlines the precarious situations of eloping couples as well as the routinization of
the procedure.

The film also recreates the architecture of the district administration complex authentically. District administration offices, including the magistrate's
court, are often grouped together in one complex or spread over a large campus
with narrow bylanes and corridors linking one office to another; the district or
sessions' judicial court enjoins these administrative offices. At the local levels,
bureaucracy and the judiciary are inextricably woven together in the popular
imagination due to this spatial organization.

In my travels across Haryana, the district administration complexes were
largely similar in their architecture. Notary public officials and lawyers, who
provide documentation and paperwork for different administrative functions,
occupy a huge, open hall with a makeshift roof and partitions to separate their

FIGURE 3 Legal mechanisms that may aid eloping couples are made accessible in this spin-off of the iconic film *Qayamat Se Qayamat Tak*, which also rehearses themes from timeless tales that resonate with its target audience.

Artwork: Namita and the Alternative Law Forum.

modest offices; desks and chairs are often chained to prevent burglary, and metallic or wooden shelves are also securely fastened. They beckon clueless and overwhelmed citizens, offering assistance in navigating the bureaucratic maze involved in a myriad of issues and problems. Computers and printing devices used for bureaucratic paperwork such as stamping papers and affidavits are located in small shops close by, which are more permanent constructions. The professionals instruct the technical help in these shops and, at times, offer tea and explanations to confused citizens (refreshments are class/caste dependent).

The confusion is often left unresolved by explanations that focus more on exuding confidence and charm than imparting information. These lawyers and officials provide paperwork without completely clarifying procedures or even explaining the legal import of the documents their clients end up signing and, the validity of the ones they take away with them. As Holden has noted, notary public officials attempt to provide closures in place of divorces (2016) and paperwork to ensure togetherness and cohabitation in new relationships, but these documents have little legal validity.

The Special Marriage Act does not figure in the discourses of lawyers in Chandigarh and Haryana. Professor Anil Thakur admitted that his law department in Panjab University, the largest and most reputable institution in the region, does not teach this law, and that the Indian legal system as well as legal studies have not adequately dealt with transformations in marriage. According to Thakur, research and innovation on marriage law is in no way comparable to other areas of litigation such as commercial law, which has innovated to keep pace with a postsocialist, globalizing economy. Ironically, significant uncertainties on finer points of marital disputes still send lawyers in search of an anthropological magnum opus, *The Hindu Law*, codified during a time when the field of anthropology was populated by jurists who were colonial agents seeking to understand the rules by which their subjects lived and governed themselves (see Rouland 1994 for a history of legal anthropology).

In the absence of adequate focus on legal challenges posed by transforming marital patterns, courts serve the function of adjudicating on a case-by-case basis. The Chandigarh-based high court does not share its premises with other administrative buildings, but notary public officers occupy designated corridors and more modest lawyers who cannot afford to lease chambers in the court complex fill out halls lined with assigned desks and shelf space; this is similar to the spatiality of district courts but within a concrete construction. The high court is reminiscent of a bureaucratic zone with which citizens may be familiar, providing a performative and ritualistic space similar to that of a district administrative complex. In both sites counsels hold out the promise of solutions for social problems via abstract bureaucratic paperwork and dialogue. But for couples to recognize a bureaucratic office or an administrative court as the right place to contract a civil union, there must be references in their everyday lives to recommend it. Yet, neither lawyers in the region nor popular culture media, including Bollywood films (with odd exceptions such as *Running Shaadi*), suggest this as an alternative.

In Haryana, until recently district courts were not seen as viable options for a civil wedding or a court marriage via protection petitions. When I conducted my research, lawyers in district courts as well as the high court expressed the belief that families and even police officers did not respect a district court order in the same way they adhered to the high court orders. By 2018 this situation had improved slightly, though the number of applications in the high court had not significantly reduced. The significance that couples and their families attribute to the high court is due, at least in part, to its bureaucratic spatiality. But courts are also imbued with the idea of sentimental justice, which means not only dwelling in the zone of justice but also recognizing that it exists.

Sentimental Justice

While the idea of rebellious love and the surveillance state can be traced through several cultural artifacts, the idea of justice and role of the courts is gleaned largely from media and cinema. Media reportage in no way inspires faith that courts will support the cause of justice, and yet in sociocultural spaces, courts are seen as the zone of justice. Indeed, the courts are burdened by this view to such an extent that four judges from the Supreme Court were recently in open rebellion to ensure the justice system does not collapse. As I have explained in the introduction, the popular faith in the judiciary had forced some judges into a transparent struggle for justice themselves, at the same time both shaking and confirming citizens' faith in the Indian judiciary.

Lauren Berlant argues that claims to the state are based on an optimistic attachment that the state had engendered through promises that go into subject creation (2011), promises that bind the citizen in an unfulfilling situation. As highlighted in the introduction, several feminist scholars on the Indian state would agree that the state is unable and often unwilling to fulfill citizens' expectations. A notable exception is Flavia Agnes, who has been involved several processes of legal reform on the question of women's rights. According to Agnes, with the passage of the Domestic Violence Act 2005, the feminist movement finally registered a success in placing violence against women into a sociolegal framework (2008, 3). Agnes shows how separating rights such as property rights from acts of criminal violence such as domestic violence and dowry deaths offers "new portals of hope" to matrimonial lawyers concerned with the rights of women (4).

On the issue of whether the law is hopeful, legal anthropologist Annelise Riles writes that law's potential for social change exists beyond its capacity to deliver (2010). Hirokazu Miyazaki states that this hope signifies "conscious negation one's own future agency" (1996, 156). Philosopher Hent de Vries offers a divergent perspective when he refers to hope as pragmatism, because realism without hope "leads principally nowhere, but merely brutally affirms whatever is and only strengthens the powers that be" (2009). In the context of Barack Obama's pragmatic politics, de Vries writes that hope goes beyond wishful thinking, with its realism providing an alternative to both utopia and cynicism. Similarly, investing in law can help us navigate the legal process better, despite the evidence of its bias toward patriarchal and kinship norms where the hope remains pragmatic.

In many landmark Supreme Court judgments, justice has come too late and offered too little. But the idea that justice would be delivered in the end is strong and persuasive, and the moral weight of the sentiment may finally uphold the demands of justice even in cases where procedural means repeatedly fail to uphold the rule of law.[4] This was evident in the case of Hadiya, an adult woman who, of her own volition, converted to Islam and later married a Muslim man. In May 2017, the Kerala High Court annulled the marriage and returned Hadiya to her parents to live under forced house arrest for eight months before the Supreme Court finally set aside the high court judgment and reunited her with her spouse.

Hadiya's case unfolded slowly. She was not even summoned by the Supreme Court to provide her testimony until the end of 2017. The court had instead ordered a National Investigation Agency probe into possible terror links in the case and reserved its judgment.[5] In later interviews, Hadiya revealed that her confinement and interactions with her parents in those crucial eight months were marked by psychological torture and physical abuse. The Indian judiciary had remained oblivious to this violence and therefore complicit in it. In February 2018 the Supreme Court finally allowed Hadiya to speak about her choice in a legal space, a right that had been denied to her repeatedly by both the courts. Subsequently, it ordered that she leave her parents' house where she had been incarcerated and move to her homeopathy college hostel to complete her studies "at state expense." A paternalistic, benevolent state is no stranger to feminist studies on law and marriage, as highlighted in the introduction.

Having heard Hadiya's side, the Supreme Court could have, and many would say should have, immediately reunited her with husband instead of sending her to a college hostel. My ethnographic research indicates that legal procedures on choice-based marriages often follow this pattern of moving the woman to a third-party site. In the event of a writ of habeas corpus, I have observed—and this was corroborated by lawyers—that women often but not always insist that they want to stay with the person (parent or husband) with whom they arrived at court. According to my ethnographic evidence and lawyers' experiences, testimony in favor of a parent may indicate psychological or physical torture.

In a video statement released by a Hindutva activist, Hadiya gave us a glimpse of the psychological torture endured by women at their parents' hands, which, I argue, regularly results in statements in favor of the parents in North Indian courts. Hadiya, however, had resolutely and repeatedly stated in courts that she wanted to be with her husband. She attributed this resolve to her religious faith.[6] State institutions, including the courts, which are otherwise anxious to ensure a women's well-being in the company of a partner of her own choice, often gloss over the violence encountered in family and kinship circles; the urban romances are also guilty of this.

Sending the woman to a neutral place (for what may be seen as a cooling-off period) is a practice with legal precedent, and a judge who follows established norms would choose this approach over sending a woman back to her parents. It is, of course, another matter that Hadiya was twenty-four at the time and did not need a guardian. Legally, it would have set a good precedent if the Supreme Court had immediately accepted an adult woman's statement and upheld her rights.

What exactly does legal precedent involve in this context? Ensuring the welfare of the woman and her financial security is at the heart of many litigations concerning marriage and family. The neutral location is designed to serve as a buffer zone where the woman would have time and space to consider her options without outside influence. This precedent provides further evidence for the contention the Indian state is paternalistic and struggles with the conflicting demands of sustaining liberal equality and addressing the violence in social relationships that it cannot reform. While upholding an adult woman's right to choose her partner, the state and its judiciary do not believe that the woman necessarily knows what is best for her, at least not as long as the men in her life may be coercing her to make a statement in their favor. Biswas, the law minister who had introduced the Special Marriage Bill, had strongly hinted that young people must be "guided" (by the state) to make decisions and warned of the possible consequences. Sending a woman to a neutral place such as a *Nari Niketan* (women's shelter) is standard practice for Haryana's district courts as well as the high court.

I perceive this legal practice of ordering women to temporary shelter as part of a narrative arc that is explicit in many films (across the world) that are partly or entirely constructed around courtroom scenes. In the moral universe of a film, an injustice must be perpetrated—an injustice that drives the plot and finally becomes the film's message, or the moral of the story. Indian films have utilized this trope effectively over many decades; notable examples include *Awaara* (1951), *Waqt* (1965), *Insaf ka Tarazu* (1980), *Damini* (1993), *Shahid* (2012), *Jolly LLB* (2013), *Pink* (2016), and *Mulk* (2018). While the aesthetics may differ, the films' plot devices and morals follow a similar pattern: marginalized persons in an unequal society (very often but not always women) are dealt a raw deal, and courts come to the rescue in the end. As film critic Baradwaj Rangan notes with reference to *Mulk*, courtroom dramas have been the best medium to deliver a social message.[7] The judge in *Mulk* lectures a wider audience, beyond the frame: "Instead of getting your information from echo-chamber WhatsApp groups, read up your history and the constitution." Rangan finds that this judge at first appears to condone the public prosecutor's excesses, but "gradually, we see that he is fair, that *justice* is fair" (italics in original).

Hadiya's story similarly began with a grave injustice but in the end we see that ultimately, *justice* is fair. First, the Kerala High Court annulled her marriage and sent her back to her parents, where she endured psychological torture and was drawn into an epic political battle that lies at the root of the BJP's rule in India. The Supreme Court at first appeared to condone the excesses, even ordering a terror probe on the issue. In many ways, the bogey of the Love Jihad depended on this one case that appeared to be going in favor of the Hindutva rhetoric.

For the aesthetics in a legal drama to work, there cannot be one big courtroom scene where all the important points are articulated and everyone is sent home to live happily ever after. The system of injustice needs to unravel slowly to be believable; a leap to justice cannot seem credible because judges, too, are integral parts of the system. Most observers, including conservative commentators, were forced to acknowledge Hadiya's confidence in her marriage after her first appearance at the Supreme Court.[8] By the time we, the audience, reached the climatic verdict, we had already come to terms with the conclusion of this story.

Hadiya's story, tragically, stayed faithful to its narrative arc, unravelling itself gradually, through an adherence to legal procedures and reached a conclusion that reinforces faith in sentimental justice. Despite previous miscarriages of justice and a formidable political machinery invested in the campaign, justice had ultimately emerged as fair. This classical narrative of a "fair justice" is not exclusive to South Asian films; see, for example, *12 Angry Men* (dir. Lumet 1957), *Philadelphia* (dir. Demme 1993), and *Bridge of Spies* (dir. Spielberg 2015). In Bollywood cinema, stories of young people in love, and stories where courts play a central role, the finale usually comes with an affirmative message. Bollywood films reify a pervasive moral code that holds that individuals who face many challenges due to their location in an unequal society will still find "justice" (legal or otherwise) in the end. In films across periods, courts adjudicated on individual cases of intimate relations while at the same time addressing larger social and political issues such as partition-related trauma (*Waqt*), rape and sexual assaults (*Damini; Pink*), persecution of minority communities (*Shahid; Mulk*), and class inequality (*Awaara; Jolly LLB*). Reunion of a couple or family torn apart due to larger social crises, including partition, is consequently a popular trope in Indian cinema.

One notable period when antistate and antilaw images were vigorously circulated occurred in the 1970s and 1980s. The outright rejection of law during the post-Emergency period in India is a topic Lawrence Liang takes up in an article on law and cinema (2003).[9] According to him, due to this "crisis of the state and legitimacy" Bollywood films of the period overlooked how people were working "their way around the law" (376) instead of operating outside or against the law. Liang directs our attention to "practices that resist being captured by the totalizing narrative of legality, but do not necessarily pose any alternative Utopias, they exist at the level of livelihood, tactical strategies and embody a certain irreverent playfulness in their negotiation of categories such as citizenship, modernity and the political" (376).

This approach to cinema, which Liang says reorients scholarship from representation to modes of experience, is instructive for the study of law as well. My focus in this book is on discourses generated in the courtroom as well as people's experiences and perceptions of the space. In particular, the experience of being wedded or emerging as fully wedded only after the courtroom episode, which is closely examined in chapter 5, provides key ethnographic insights. Melodramatic ideas such as "courts unite lovers" are part of a clichéd Bollywood template where in order to maintain its legitimacy the court must live up to a *narrative contract*, a term coined by Sudipta Kaviraj in 1991 and since used by cinema studies scholars.[10]

Over time, courts in India have acquired a reputation for being independent of the elected governments and have carved out significant power for themselves. This is due in part to the proliferation of public interest litigations in the high courts and the Supreme Court of India. While my interlocutors still see district courts as enmeshed in local hierarchies, the high courts have legitimacy that extends to the state itself. Though states cannot be extricated from the regime of the elected governments, my interlocutors still perceived the Indian state as an impersonal, neutral entity that existed behind the faces of the state agents, such as the judges.

Bollywood films that portray the courtroom space generously allow subjects to vicariously experience a "zone of justice" (to use a term from Biehl 2013a). My courtroom ethnography in some ways evokes the Bollywood template where this particular moral code of justice has assumed a life of its own, becoming a well-oiled legal machinery that puts the emotion into practice. Though Berlant's cruel optimism is more widely referenced in anthropological literature, I would rather analyze these processes through the lens of pragmatic hope offered by de Vries, which is better suited to the study of negotiations. As Liang argues, by studying negotiations, even irreverent ones, on "categories such as citizenship, modernity and the political," one can resist a totalizing narrative on legality.

A totalizing question about whether states manage to deliver on the desires and aspirations of their subjects would probably be answered with a resounding no. In studying this relatively small-scale, localized negotiation, I found that the experiences of hopeful subjects are often at odds with what state agents believe they are delivering. The "narrative contract" (Kaviraj 2010) allows for this creativity. In the case of folktales, a cautionary tale allows a space for fantasy where desires and even lust can find temporary fulfillment in bawdy performances. In the case of courtroom appearances, this creativity extends to interpretations that align popular faith in the justice system with the particular needs of eloping couples. The people who reject choice in marriage and couples who opt for a love marriage are not able to reject a court marriage without at the same time professing a lack of faith in the justice system. The narrative contracts bind them into accepting court interventions on elopement cases. Perhaps one of the best representations of this mode of sentimental justice, one forged by a binding narrative contract, came from a high court judge who was adjudicating on multiple protection petitions in 2008 in June, the vacation month when only urgent petitions are filed. While passing an order in the case of *Kumar v. B. Verma, A. Devi and S. Verma*, Justice Kanwaljit Alhuwalia made a series of observations that touch on themes raised in this chapter:

> It is a fact that from the last 4–5 years, this court is flooded with petitions where married couples come and seek protection. Times have changed but the response of the state has not changed. I have before me number of young married persons, who struck by cupid's arrow, have exchanged vows of marriage and promises to each other to live together, are running from pillar to post, chased by the musclemen or police. The law permits these young couples, who have eligibility of age on their side, to start their matrimonial lives and perform their marriage. . . . State is a mute spectator. When shall State awake from its slumber, till how long State shall allude permanent solution and till how long Courts can provide solace and balm by disposing such cases are questions which are abegging answers. . . . Time has come for State of speedily, evolve compassionate mechanism to redress the grievances of the young couples and their parents. Happy family life, social harmony, amicable and cordial neighborhood, should be concern of State and Society. (8–10)[11]

Conclusion

Hope and the experience of finding justice is, in some ways, independent of what state agents and documents articulate. The standard Bollywood narrative tells us that couples fall in love and face challenges to their unions from an unequal and unforgiving society, and courts come to their rescue by "enacting and transgressing caste-class conflicts" (Liang 2003, 369). Eloping couples are protagonists in their own larger-than-life narratives, transcending illegality (due the illicitness of their relationships) by entering the zone of justice. They shape their expectations and experiences of the space according to the vicarious experiences offered by Bollywood films, and in the process highlight the subjectivity and even malleability of the space of the state.

The romance that a court mediation might hold for courting couples is beautifully summarized by Payal, a young woman who married a colleague with the consent of both her mother and her spouse's parents. Although all surviving parents had agreed to the match (though her brother remained opposed), Payal confided that she had wanted a "court marriage," a desire that had remained unfulfilled. "Court se sab achcha ho jata hai," she explained. There are two possible translations of this statement in Hindi: either everything works out well after court intervention, or going through the court process makes it all good (*achcha*); that is, it is a filter that purifies marriage by removing all embedded ambiguity. While ambiguity regarding marriage (especially a potentially deviant one) may leave people feeling vaguely unsettled, court-facilitated marriages and reconciliations with family members provide much needed clarity, legitimacy, and perhaps finality.

3

Love, Marriage, and the Brave New World

Today Haryana is registering a shift in marriage norms on several fronts: there is a surge in the number of cases involving "trafficked brides" from poorer regions of the country;[1] various levels of incest prohibitions are being lifted by caste councils;[2] district courts are hearing a high number of divorce cases; and it seems that there is an explosion in the number of love marriages, and by most accounts, villages are leading the cities in this trend. These societal shifts have made it possible for my interlocutors to point out the inconsistencies among the dominant caste groups such as the Jats and Bishnois, which forbid intercaste and/or love marriages but allow matches that were previously considered incestuous and openly support the trafficking of brides from other regions. Baljeet, a Bishnoi man who married a woman from a lower caste, noted sarcastically: "These days all you hear is aan de, aan de [let them in, let them in]. How can incestuous relationships be better than intercaste ones? . . . And marriages with women 'bought' from elsewhere. . . . We all know a person who is bought and sold is a slave. How do you think people treat slaves?"

Baljeet's case is intriguing, for he was never allowed to forget his transgression. He has faced isolation and ill will as well as appreciation for his "conquest" (with elderly women admiring the exotic bride and often trying to snatch her veil to catch a glimpse) at a time when forced bachelorhood is a real possibility for men from his community, given Haryana's skewed sex ratios. His long experience with this hypocrisy has led him to muse, "If there is heavy traffic on the street, you will take your vehicle into the wrong lane. This is an offense, but you will do it." In his interview, Baljeet retrospectively reasoned that his deviation was a prudent one, but he has also learned that the society will never let him forget it.

Haryanvis marrying today not only have to wrestle with new social norms, they also face an uncertain economic future due to large-scale agrarian decline, which is discussed in chapter 4. Given the expectation that a marriage will remain a constant feature in one's life, decisions about it are based on ambitions and anticipations for one's future, which most people hope will be better than the present. In my analysis of the relationship between life and marriage, I am inspired by Husserl's concept of lebenswelt, which cannot be independent of our selves and our specific experience of it, according to Husserl (1970). Young women and men in Haryana, I argue, are able to create a different lifeworld (lebenswelt) for themselves than the one presented to them as the norm when they learn to view and inhabit the world differently. Even without moving away, geographically, from their familiar settings, some Haryanvis have transformed their lives by reconfiguring their own marriages.

In this chapter I describe certain symbolic and ideological continuities and departures with respect to the institution of marriage within this ethnographic context. With a focus on symbolic aspects and material culture and aspirations, my discussion evaluates the shifts in marital unions through the narratives of my interlocutors, rather than in relation to the benchmarks set by progressive circles in mainstream India, to which I myself belong.

Marrying Haryanvis: Ethnography from a Bishnoi Wedding

On the night of Rishi's wedding, after his wedding party had left for the bride's village, I sat with the women who had been left behind. I was told that in the past, women on the groom's side did not attend the actual wedding—"the men brought home the bride." But younger women had recently begun to defy this tradition, insisting on accompanying the groom and "enjoying" the party. Older women were habituated to staying back though, and they were preparing to enact the ritual of *aanta tutiya*, a satirical take on the actual wedding were women took on the roles of bride, groom, and their respective parties. I had been coaxed into agreeing to accompany the groom's party, but the aanta tutiya promised to be more intimate and fascinating from the perspective of my research, so I stayed. The performance had an in-built and self-aware critique of weddings in this region, including thinly veiled representations of grooms' relatives, who evaluated the length of the bride's veil and her dowry with a mixture of derision for the bride's family and approval of the many goods and jewels made available. The aanta tutiya resonated with one message that had emerged from many conversations during the course of my fieldwork: a wedding, an important rite of passage, was not to be taken seriously.

Weddings or *shaadis* were often described as impervious to changing times, but when the mock wedding was performed, recreating the familiar rituals with playfulness, the women not only adhered to tradition but also accounted for recent inclusions. The mock wedding was a representation of weddings in the community in general—not of Rishi's wedding in particular, which they had

FIGURE 4 *Rati joga* underway at Rishi's wedding.
Photo: Rama Srinivasan.

come together to celebrate. It provided historicity to the traditions associated with weddings but did not aim to capture the timeless traditions of Bishnoi weddings.

The ritual stood in contradiction to the claims of caste elders in Haryana who routinely resisted intercaste or intragotra marriages in the name of preserving local traditions and customs. Weddings in Haryana are continuously adapting and are open to additions both in symbolic and ideological terms. One hypervisible symbol is the dominance of what is locally known as "DJ music," or Punjabi pop music, which blared from loudspeakers every night before the night of the wedding, when the groom's party departed for the bride's village.

These loudspeakers nearly drowned out the women's tradition of *rati joga* (literally, awake all night), where women stay up all night, singing songs about marriage and life cycles. The rati joga, which took place the night before the wedding, appeared to be a cherished tradition for older women. It was a very intimate setting where women sang, applied *mehendi* on their hands, and gossiped intermittently (some even took short naps during the night) as figure 4 depicts. The songs were led by a respected artiste from a singing caste who was well versed in Rajasthani music, but as the young boys outside in the courtyard refused to lower the volume on the speakers, in the competition of sounds technology won out over custom—but only temporarily. As the drunk and exhausted boys gave way around midnight, the women's collective voices began to soar and continued into the dawn.

I do not wish to juxtapose the women's songs as timeless tradition, even if the women themselves might believe it to be the case, pitted in opposition to the amplified pop music, which could be seen as a symbol of modernity. Although the artiste sang old Rajashtani songs, there were other women, relatives and friends of the family, whose songs spoke to contemporary concerns and transforming societies. For example, one song performed by a Jat woman from Sonipat district detailed a mother's worries for her college-educated daughter about to enter wedlock and the daughter's soothing reassurances. The song, like most ritualist songs I had heard that night, used repetition for emphasis. Every stanza started with the line "Tu BA padh gayi" (You have completed your BA) before asking the daughter how she will adjust to her mother-in-law, father-in-law, brother-in-law, sister-in-law, and finally, her husband. The daughter's replies were also variations of a single idea—"main tika dungi/main sambhaal lungi" (I will fix them up, I will put them in their place, or I will manage the situation). Far from following the prescriptions of *nibhana* (making do), the bride with a BA was confident about holding her own even as her mother worried that her daughter's education might have rendered her incapable of negotiating the rigors of an arranged marriage and joint families.

The women who heard the song nodded gravely and made appreciative noises to compliment the singer's skills. As this example suggests, the tradition of rati joga could be inclusive of ideas of transformation. The educated girl as a plot device had struck a chord with the older women because many young women in their community were college educated or aspired to be. More importantly, a wedding had provided a platform to share these concerns regarding the viability of marriages when the priorities of both men and women had dramatically changed.

Central to the performances is the meaning of the Hindi word *shaadi*, which means both weddings and marriages. When I asked my informants about the institution of marriage, rather than the event that weddings really are, my question was often met with confusion. I wondered if this might be reflective of a certain North Indian sensibility where the two overlapped in people's minds, on a subconscious level. While witnessing weddings in Haryana I began to see the event and the institution as representations of each other. The event allowed invitees to vicariously live another individual's marital life before the fact, and relive one's own marriage and other invitees' marriages within a compressed period of time. Since the event preceded the actual marriage, the performances including aanta tutiya were not really about the shaadi at hand—no one knew as yet how Rishi's married life would unfold.

What I propose is a framework to explain older women's experiences and critiques that often were not discussed in interviews; instead, they were

FIGURE 5 Performance at a prewedding event in rural Haryana.
Photo: Rama Srinivasan.

communicated through performative knowledge, or what Judith Butler called "stylized repetition of acts" (1990, 179). There was something specific about this time and place, the ethnographic moment, but what transcended it was the idea that shaadis (both weddings and marriages) were supposed to be participatory, not just witnessed, and one's expected role (both in one's own wedding and in others') must be performed satisfactorily.

This pressure to participate in the wedding was something I, too, had keenly experienced. On the first few nights of this extended wedding celebration, I was expected to dance with the wedding party as the DJ music played. My inability to perform the role I was assigned was met more with incomprehension than with disappointment. One of the older women who was well versed in traditional music and dance forms took it upon herself to pull me into the festivities. She dragged me onto the makeshift dance floor, and once I had closely copied a few of her steps I sensed that I had satisfied many at the gathering. My tutor then started gesticulating earnestly, and when I failed to comprehend her body movements, she decided to drop subtlety and started bouncing her breasts vigorously. After a few seconds she looked at me expectantly without changing her serious expression. It was at this point that I understood that even my half-hearted performance had introduced another level of intimacy into the proceedings. My efforts were perhaps half-hearted but my inclusion had been nevertheless achieved—and it was signaled through a sexualized bodily act aimed at embarrassing me and exploiting what they perceived as my prudishness. This was first done through bodily gestures and later by spoken word, as the next section will highlight.

The creative expression of one's sexuality stems from the homosocial intimacy of the space, where speech acts about sex and sexuality are seen as legitimate and even warranted. Deborah Cameron and Don Kulick examine the "discursive construction of sexuality," where sexual experience is made meaningful through codes and conventions of signification (2006). What is significant in the literature on this subject is not only what sex talk tells us about the lives of the people engaging in it but also how sex is deployed as a narrative device, and often as a political instrument. Caroline Osella and Filippo Osella read in the performance of sexual joking, teasing, and flirting simultaneous processes of creating single-sex egalitarian communities as well as hierarchies, especially among young men (1998, 189). In the context of North Indian politics, Manuela Ciotti finds that women in homosocial settings used merciless teasing and gossip to scandalize the "other" while simultaneously constructing themselves as sexual beings and agents (2011). Sexually explicit conversations were also, in my experience, vital icebreakers that signaled that the outsider, a researcher in this case, had finally been included into the fold.

Embodied Ethnography and Intimate Knowledge Production

Despite my knowledge of the literature on sex talk and joking relationships, one particular conversation led by an elderly woman who spoke in a heavy baagri dialect (whom I will call BW) nevertheless caught me off guard. My embodied experience of discomfort with the attention of many participants, led by BW, and DG, another participant, devoted to the purpose of exploiting my prudishness for their enjoyment helped me to bridge the communication gap—that is, where linguistic gaps failed me, the intimacy of the moment acted as a conduit in carrying over the meaning.

In a previous interview, BW's comments on marriage had been restrained by the formalness of the exercise and the presence of her husband, but on this occasion the frivolity of the moment and the need to perform in a wedding produced an enriched ethnographic encounter. (A disclaimer: because BW spoke in a heavy dialect, a younger woman interpreted some of her words in standardized Hindi with a sprinkling of English, and her interpretation varied slightly from that of a translator in Chandigarh who worked on the audio recording at a later date.)

BAAGRI WOMAN (BW): Eh America ki kuddi, soni baat bolon main [Listen up, girl from America. Let me give you some useful advice / Let me tell you something good/beautiful]. Yahan kisi se setting mat kariyo [Don't have a setting/hookup with anyone here].

RAMA: Nahi. Aisa koi iraada nahi hai [No, I don't have any such plans].

BW: Nahi suno. Setting mat karna. Yahan ke mard aise hain na. Upar se harre barre par neeche se banjjar [Just listen to me. Don't hook up with anyone. About the men here—they appear green and fertile on the surface but are actually a desert below the surface].

[I ask if I can switch on my recorder]

     . . .

BW: Soni baat bolon mein beti, soni baat bolon [I always say something useful/important, daughter].

UNIDENTIFIED SPEAKER: Soni kisi na hai, naani [I would hardly call it beautiful/good, grandmother].

     . . .

DG: Rama! Shaadi karva le [Rama! You should get married here].

RAMA: Yahan pe? Magar yeh toh mana kar rahen hai [Out here? But she [BW] just told me not to].

DG: Mana kyun karen [Why would it be forbidden]?

     . . .

RAMA: Inhone abhi toh kaha. Setting mat karna [She just told me not to have a "setting" here].

INTERPRETER: Yeh toh without marriage ki setting ke liye keh rahe the [She was referring to settings out of wedlock].

     . . .

DG: Achcha laga yahan ka mahaul [You like it out here]?

RAMA: Haan. Mujhe toh achcha laga [Oh, yes. I do like it here].

BW [mischievously]: Aachho laag, Jee toh karen hai ["Likes" it. She does feel like it].

     . . .

BW: Jee karen nee? Mood karen thoda thoda [You do want to get married/get laid here, right? You are in the mood, at least a little].

RAMA: Nahi. Yahan pe DJ ka bahut shor hai. Jahan DJ nahi honge wahan karungi shaadi [Not really. This DJ music here is too loud. I will get married where there are no DJs].

BW: DJ lyay dei bo aaglo [He will bring a/the DJ for you].

INTERPRETER [*laughing uncontrollably*]: Yeh keh rahen hai DJ toh woh apne haathon se . . . [She is just saying that he [words lost] DJ with his own hands . . .]

RAMA: Phir toh main bhaag jaungi [In that case, I will run away].[3]

BW: Woh darr toh manne lage hain [I do have that fear with you].

Ekr bindhe bachh koni bhaajan de, tan laad ladai jinda bhaaj koni.

INTERPRETER: Ek baar setting ho jayen toh nahi . . . [After a "setting" you won't . . .]

BW [*interrupting*]: Laad ladayen nee toh bhaaj koni [No one runs away after their husband makes love to them].

BW: Laad kari tera! [He will make love to you]!

Laadan mein toh hu it reh gayi. Nahi hu it ke kru haar

INTERPRETER: Isi love mein toh yahan reh gayi varna chali jaati main bhi [She says, I only stayed back for this love. I would have left as well if it was not for it].

RAMA: Yeh toh inhone bataya hi ki inki toh love marriage hui thi [Yes, she did tell me (earlier) that she had had a love marriage].

BW: Bhaut laad karya mera. Jinda toh laad kariya, abhi ghurkaave hai [He used to make love to me all the time but now he only looks angrily at me].

. . .

BW: Jinda toh man aachho lagyo ho

INTERPRETER: Pehle toh mujhe achche lage the . . . [At first, I did like him . . .]

RAMA: Phir kab achche nahi lagne lage [When did you stop liking him]?

BW: Thaari umar mein achche lage the . . . [When I was your age I used to like him . . .]

RAMA: Ab nahi lagte [But not anymore]?

BW: Abi ke laage hai? Abi hoi adango dheelo hegyo, abi charkho ban gyo [What do I feel now? My vagina is now loose like a spinning wheel].

INTERPRETER: Matlab, inka neeche ka part toh bekaar ho gaya [That is, her sexual organ [vagina] is dysfunctional now].

. . .

[*BW then shifts to talking about my sexual life, but her exact inference was lost on me because the interpreter chose not to communicate her more scandalous imputations. The richness of this reference became more only with the translated transcript*]

BW: Charkho banne bachh aaglo kyun raakhi [Why will a man agree to stay with a woman when her vagina has turned into a spinning wheel]?

INTERPRETER: Keh rahen hai apka sexual part jo kharaab kar ke chodenge tab pata chalega [She says you will understand this when someone is done ruining your sexual organs].

BW: O charkho dheelo kar r rakh dei jinda aaglo raakh koni bachh [Once you elope with your lover and have sex with him, your husband will not be interested in you or your spinning wheel [i.e., a woman who elopes will have a vagina similar to that of an old woman]].

[*No interpretation provided*]

BW's joking testament was framed as a window into her own marriage, a succinct, playful representation of a long, well-lived married life. It is a skeptical and honest look at both her marriage and the society, in which she projects some of her disenchantments with her marriage not just onto men in the region but also onto the landscape and agriculture. Her dialogue is a perfect metaphor for the arid region in western Haryana where baagri is spoken. This region was one of the unlikely beneficiaries of the Green Revolution project. Lush green fields today stand next to parched communal lands used for grazing animals, and the species of trees that still grow in the region are typical of arid conditions and stand as clear indicators of the unnatural lushness of the agrarian farms. The baagri belt was an agrarian success only in appearance, part of the food bowl that the proponents of Green Revolution hoped Punjab and Haryana would become for the country. As beneficiaries of the Green Revolution, both states saw high rates of agricultural production and prosperity for individual land owners. As the disastrous effects of this unsustainable model for agriculture are recognized by Haryanvis today, farming, which was once a source of pride and prosperity, has become a site of disillusionment as dwindling yields engender a strong sense of betrayal in those who had grown accustomed to its fortunes.

BW, who lives in visible poverty today, looks at the changes in her personal and material circumstances with ironic disenchantment. The effects of the Green Revolution on the region's agricultural land overlap with the ravages of sexual intercourse on her own body. BW warned me in jest to not make the same mistake she (and Haryana?) had made—that is, build up hopes of a sexually fulfilling relationship based on the promise of love. Too much love can be dangerous; the "love" had consumed her body and what remained today were the signs of wreckage.

In many ways, the baagri region represented the love of its farmers for their agricultural land, and it had had too much *laad* (lovemaking) in too short a space of time. Even as the problems were becoming apparent, with growing demands for the promotion of organic farming, disillusionment had not quite forced farmers to give up their love for this increasingly unyielding land. But it

did, at least, prompt them to push the next generation away from this delu-
sional lovefest, resulting in a clamor for jobs in the government sector, which I
will take up in the next chapter. Community elders perhaps hoped that the
younger generation would not be left with a spinning wheel and little else.

BW discouraged me from a "setting" (hookup) because male virility in her
community (which she alluded to with her talk about green pastures and fertility) is a mirage, much like Haryana's agricultural prosperity. While her approval
of marital relations over hookups, as well as her warning against premarital
sex, resonates with calls to uphold a certain version of sexual morality, it hardly
does justice to her overall point. She had playfully dissuaded me from a marriage based on love or desire, which can be destructive in the long run, but that
advice was also based on her own experience, not just virtuous morality. In
many ways, it resonated more with Lila Abu-Lughod's analysis of the Bedouin
community she had studied, where women advised against a vulnerability that
comes from being in love with one's husband (1999). In *Veiled Sentiments*, Abu-
Lughod argues that emotions were restricted to the realm of poetry, where deep
affections were allowed as legitimate, whereas in the real world, emotions in
relationships signified weakness and could lead to a loss of honor, which
involved not just sexual morality but also strength of character (79).

In Haryana, marriage is often seen in a framework similar to what BW proposes: as a rational decision based on a realistic assessment of one's future
prospects. Even as BW seemed to follow the popular tendency of dissuading
young people from falling in love, she also underlined love's persuasiveness and
its ability to make people believe that the grass may indeed seem green on your
side. The voices that lined up against love marriages described them as lacking
rationality and foresight, but unlike BW, these informants rarely discussed the
contours of desire when they dismissed it for want of reason.

In several interviews, across gender lines and the urban-rural divide (albeit
more often in rural areas and among men), I heard that "affairs" that challenged social norms were acceptable as long as they were furtively conducted
and the couples did not decide to get married. "Making it public," especially
through the aspiration of marriage, was even dubbed "sheer madness" by Pul-
kit, who collects quantitative data for development agencies. Many interviews,
however, toned down this sentiment with a catchphrase of sorts: "love marriage
chalti nahi hai" (love marriages don't work). Both the young Haryanvis who
aspired to love marriages and those who were repulsed by the idea were still
reproducing their individual desires within this overarching narrative. What
they had in common with BW was that they were not following the virtues of
sexual morality but rather were claiming that love and desire belonged to a
realm different than that of marriage.

Sakshi, a Jat woman in her early twenties, reproduces this critique perfectly:
"Love marriages don't last because they are not well-considered decisions. These

couples later squabble and part ways because they did not know what they were
getting into." When I asked her if she knew any such couples she cited two cases
she had vaguely heard about, but her belief in the inherent truth of her claim
remained strong. Arranged marriage and love marriage are treated as binary
concepts, with the former standing in for traditions and customs and in opposition to the modern, liberal ideology that ostensibly promotes choosing one's
partner. Unfortunately, this is a sentiment often shared by upholders of traditions and by Indians/non-Indians who consider arranged marriage to be, by
definition, antichoice and a form of patriarchal control. I found these seemingly
contradictory groups to be intertwined in a complex web of aspirations. For
many young people, a courtship before the wedding was seen as ideal, even in
the scenario of an arranged marriage. The idea that one must know what one is
"getting into" was taking hold, even among young people who were against love
marriages.

Sakshi, for example, was very explicit in her preference for arranged marriage, and this was not aimed at upholding patriarchal values or local customs.
As I spent time in her company I noticed that during our conversations regarding the plight of women (financial or otherwise) in exploitative marriages, it
was clear that Sakshi was worried about her own uncertain future, and she
criticized the patriarchy with the English term "male-dominated society." She
and her family were adapting to the changes in their personal and social situations. Her family had already embraced and articulated the fact that matches
cannot be arranged as they used to be. Sakshi's mother stressed that the young
woman's consent would have to be ascertained before the match was finalized,
though she herself was never consulted when she was wedded as an adolescent.
"I was not asked because I was illiterate. I did not know anything. But Sakshi is
well educated," her mother explained. These were not empty words, for Sakshi
reported that on one occasion she had turned down a "good match," according
to her parents' standards, because the suitor's family owned buffaloes. "I cate-
gorically told my father [who was incidentally a veterinary doctor] that I cannot
work with animals," she explained.

Sakshi, who had completed her master's degree in English and another
program in education, would not have been able to refuse to milk animals had
the wedding taken place, but she was able to turn down the match. The young
woman was acutely aware of the gender division of labor in her community and
its nonnegotiability—as the only woman among several brothers and male
cousins, she performed a lot of household chores in addition to pursuing higher
education—but she had the option of aspiring for different horizons, a life far
away from home. "I want to get out of here. One keeps coming back to the same
circles and conversations," she exclaimed in frustration on one occasion. She
later added, in the same conversation, "I hope my parents can find a groom far

away from here." She had already told her father, to whom she felt closer, that she wants to leave the region.

Her aspirations for adventure and intellectual stimulation (signified by her need to engage in different circles) could be met, in her opinion, only by a government job that took her elsewhere or, more likely, by marriage. In her framework, marriage was a rational decision that should further her aspirations rather than circumscribe them. Falling in love was not an option she had given herself, but she did aspire to a companionate marriage where she would not be expected to perform certain traditional chores, her income would not be appropriated, and, more importantly, she would be able to venture out of her comfort zone.

Marriage as the Point of Exit

As I travelled from Chandigarh, where I had been conducting research, for another wedding in the same Bishnoi village, I was made aware of one of the scheduled stops of the bus I had boarded at Hisar bus station. The place was Mohabbatpur (Place of love), and though my ears perked up at the name I realized I was not going that far. I reflected, somewhat frivolously, given my travel-related fatigue, that most of my informants in Chandigarh and rural Haryana would not go that far either.

Mohabbat and *pyar*, words that could be translated as *love*, were very rarely used in interviews, where the English word had conclusively replaced them. While scholarly works on Bollywood films and queer nostalgia readings (Rao 2000) frequently used these terms as well as *yaar* (a gender-neutral term for lover or "best friend forever"), the terms *boyfriend* and *girlfriend* and their acronyms BF and GF are strongly preferred in Haryana today. *Mohabbat*, *pyar*, and especially *yaar* were loaded terms that indicated excessive passion, and most narratives of intimate relationships and marriages seemed to consciously avoid these connotations. Interviewees who resisted arranged marriages were not exactly pining for passionate relationships; what both women and men often dreaded was the idea of marrying a stranger. They would have liked to at least speak to their affianced partners once, even if only over the phone.

Rishi, whose wedding I described earlier in the chapter, told me that the question of whether the potential bride and groom should be allowed to meet or speak with each other is addressed when matches are initially discussed. It is usually the groom's family that brings it up, and if the bride's family rejects the request, no further questions are allowed. Rishi had been engaged twice, and while he had been allowed to speak regularly on the phone with his first fiancée, the family of the second bride—whom he eventually married—had forbidden any contact. Despite having certain doubts about the impending wedding after surviving a near-fatal accident in the previous year, he decided to go ahead with it because his orphaned fiancée, Sarita, had not liked the idea of being "abandoned again" (as she had been, she believed, by her parents).

Rishi's own chances of finding a spouse were diminishing because at thirty-two, he was past the average male age for marriage (around twenty-four) in a region with a skewed sex ratio. But when he narrated his story he emphasized that he had decided to proceed with the nuptials because he felt an obligation to the young woman. Indeed, he felt that it was his sense of responsibility to others that had prevented him from marrying his former girlfriend, who was Christian. He had been very close to his maternal uncle and grandfather who, according to him, were very conservative. But at another point in the conversation, he confessed that at twenty-five—considered as an appropriate age for men in the region to marry—he had not been ready to tie the knot with his girlfriend.

As I spent more time with his family, I realized that Rishi had lived under tremendous pressure from his mother (and others) to emulate the example set by one of his cousins, a high-ranking government employee who had achieved an impressive level of success by local standards. The family had constructed Rishi as a failure in comparison, and he responded to this situation by rationalizing his decisions as the fulfillment of his responsibilities toward his family rather than a matter of choice. On some level, the marriage had satisfied his near relatives when his professional accomplishments had not.

For both Rishi and Sarita, I could see that marriage had provided a means to make the best of their current situations. When I met Rishi again at Roop's wedding, he appeared to have made a remarkable recovery from his injuries. For Sarita, marriage had been liberating in more ways than one. She had set aside the master's degree in Hindi she had completed through a long-distance program and enrolled in a fashion-design course in Hisar city, and was commuting to classes without an escort. For someone who had been forbidden to speak to her own fiancé over phone, these were valuable perks that accrued from marriage. Like Rishi's wedding, where BW provided a humorous interpretation of her married life, Roop's wedding similarly offered a window into how Rishi and Sarita's life together might turn out to be.

Unlike Rishi, who approached his own wedding with a sense of responsibility toward his fiancée, Roop, the nineteen-year-old bride of the second wedding, had no such motivation. It was at Rishi's wedding that she had first come up to me and offered to apply *mehendi* (hand paint) on my palms. As she got to work, she started talking in a rush: "Rishi *bhaiya* [elder brother—they were second cousins] asked me to tell you my story. About why I wasn't allowed to study. He thinks it can be of help to you." Something of a storyteller, she started by telling me that she was everyone's pet, especially her maternal uncle's and Rishi's. "I have also obeyed everyone and I am being punished for this reason." She moved on to narrate a recent incident in the village. There was a family distantly related to hers that had sent one of their daughters to pursue higher education (the girl in question turned out to be BW's granddaughter). The young woman, SN, had had a "love marriage" with a fellow Bishnoi, which had a profound effect on the lives of many young women in the extended family. "She was the first one to attend college in that family, and she ended up having a love marriage. My folks told me, 'Usne BA karke yeh kamaal kiya. Tu kya karegi? Tere ko toh karwani hi nahi hai'" (That girl was up to such shenanigans in the name of pursuing a BA course, there is no telling what you will do. We are not going to send you to college).

Roop considered herself a promising student in high school and had hoped to complete college and find a decent job. But that one event (the "love marriage" in the village) had changed the course of her life. What hit her most was that the decision to keep her away from higher education was made not by her *dehaati* (ignorant, rustic) farmer-father but by her Chandigarh-based, government-employed paternal uncle. Roop articulated the hypocrisy in the fact that she had been thwarted in her dreams by an uncle who presumably was on the track of economic progress and had an urban lifestyle ("look at the mindset of these city-based people").

The "love marriage" and the backlash it provoked was specific to the time and place and not necessarily an attempt to safeguard tradition. Looking back at my notes from the interview with BW and her husband, it is clear that they acknowledged and defended their own "love marriage." The husband even said, in what could be a veiled reference to his son's (SN's father's) aversion to the love marriage, "Agar maa-baap shyane nahi ho toh mana karenge. Kehte hain apni marzi se karengi. Aaj kal bachche tez hote hain. Ladki court mein kara leti hain" (If parents are not smart they will forbid such matches. They will insist on imposing their own choice. But kids these days are quick-witted. Girls get married in courts). He was supportive of love marriages yet completely against intercaste marriages.

For SN's parents, though, even the (intracaste) marriage was a huge insult, and they severed all ties with the woman after hosting the wedding party. While caste had been important for the older man, his son had obviously prioritized his injured patriarchal values. Four women in the extended family, including the one who had managed to choose her own partner, had been wedded in the same wedding party, and one of the brides had not even attained the requisite legal age. The need to avenge the wounded patriarchy for the love marriage provoked was also apparent in how Roop's family reacted to the event. They made it clear to Roop and other women in the community that education was not their right but rather a reward for "good behavior." If it felt like a punishment to Roop, it was because it was meant to be one. The "punishment" continued, Roop alleged, as the family went about finalizing her match without providing her any information. "Can you imagine this: for a month after my engagement I didn't even know his [the fiancé's] name! I would have never agreed if my maternal uncle had not met him and told me he was a responsible boy. You know how boys are these days."

I asked her if she had been shown a photograph, a question she waved off with a scoff: "Yes, but even a *gadha* [ass] looks good in photos. I want to know what kind of a person he is. Can I adjust with him and his stepmother? What is his relationship with his stepmother like? [I want to know answers to these questions] if this is to be my life. . . . I am only nineteen . . . and I think my future looks very bleak." Roop was frustrated that her fiancé had made no attempt to communicate with her, because as a woman, she could hardly make such a request. "How stupid is he? He could have said he wants to see me. Banda soch kya raha hai" (What is the guy even thinking)?

Roop's commentary was poignant in that she viewed consent in the decision of marriage as nonnegotiable despite its complete absence in her own life. She expected and even demanded a say in her life decisions and was shocked to be denied that say. Arranged marriage in its most idealized form, where parents make all the decisions, was hardly the norm for her. According to her, the "bare minimum" required for her wedding to take place was that she should meet the prospective groom at least once, and with the few months she had at her disposal she meant to make this happen. Yet, regardless of whether she succeeded in this mission, the wedding appeared to be inevitable, if only because she had no other options—such as elopement with a partner of her choice. Though the planned wedding did not correspond with her own aspirations of studying and finding a job for herself, by the time of Rishi's wedding she had started to believe that married life would not necessarily be worse than her present family situation. "Sometimes I do think I should not get married but [if I do] at least mere khadoos family se peecha toh chuda lungi" (I would get rid of my perverse/intractable family).

When I returned for her wedding a few months later, she told me she had managed to find the groom's cell phone number but had decided not to contact him. When she finally met him—after the wedding—she was planning on asking why he had never made an attempt to contact her. Despite being visibly distraught, she was nominally hopeful about her future. "Till today my life has been about others. From tomorrow, I will take charge of it," she asserted. As the night of the wedding dragged on, however, her anxieties multiplied. During the wedding nuptials, her mother had to hold her head and back firmly to prevent her from swaying from her panic attacks. Her dread and its physical manifestations demonstrated that she recognized the rituals signify being wedded, but she clearly refused to perform the prescribed script of the coy bride.

I did not think I would meet Roop again, but in 2018 when I was visiting Rishi's family, she joined us for a short time. By this time, she had completed her undergraduate degree and was expecting her first child. She briefly consulted Rishi's father about examinations for some clerical jobs with the government, signaling that her aspirations had remained unchanged. When I tentatively enquired after her husband, she again deployed her creative skills in storytelling, finding a response that would answer my concerns about her well-being and happiness in a setting that afforded no privacy: "He is a technician at a pathological laboratory. Right now, he loves taking blood samples from me."

*   *   *

After their wedding nuptials had been solemnized, Roop and her spouse had been whisked away to the terrace to pose for photographs that suggested an intimacy and romance that was patently absent. The task was unmindful of the pain and anxiety felt by Roop (and possibly her husband, too, given that he had also wept through some of the ceremony). By contrast, the clinical act of taking blood samples conveyed to me an intimacy that she had been able to forge with her husband.

In Quest of Economic Rationale: Caring, Sharing, and Consideration in Relationships

As the previous sections suggest, there has been a generational shift in the understanding of the institution of marriage. Although the evidence shows that marrying Haryanvis seek to adapt and subtly alter the arranged marriage model to suit their individual needs and goals (with varying levels of success), what I have not seen is a significant deviation from the prescript of rational marriages. My interviews of young Haryanvis with different "relationship statuses" (to use Facebook slang)—dating, engaged, waiting for their parents to arrange their matches, recently married, or married for a while—revealed that their desires were not always paradigm-shifting but instead were framed as individualized economic rationales to make the existing options work better for them. Though many of these desires arose from the need to keep up with changing socioeconomic and personal situations, they have not yet found articulation in local idioms. Many Haryanvis were cautiously using select English words to communicate ideas still novel to them. Among them, *share*, *care*, and *friendship* were recurrent, and it is with these terms that I evolved a working definition for what the *love* in "love marriage" signified for Haryanvis. In describing how people perceived the term and the relationship it forged, I tried to stay cognizant of each individual's location and aspirations for the future and how these relate to changing socioeconomic realities.

Navjot, Baljeet's wife and a lower-caste Sikh woman, aspired to a more collegial marriage when she was still in high school. Friends her age had already been married and were reporting their discomforting experiences. In retrospect, she said, "I always knew I wanted to find a partner on my own. With love marriages, you know what you are getting into." Her conclusions were different from those of Sakshi, who believed that love marriages don't work, but what they had in common was the fear of marrying a stranger in an arranged marriage. This fear was already growing in her mind when she came across Baljeet. "It was so long ago," says Baljeet, as he recalls with some uncertainty that they had one meeting, after which they embarked on a primarily cell phone–based romance. But Navjot is confident that there was no meeting at first, just surreptitious phone conversations. When they did meet for the first time, Navjot insists, Baljeet proposed marriage. But fears about whether she would be able to adjust to a community different from her own prevented her from accepting immediately. She says it was almost a year before she finally came around to the idea. "I shared everything with him. He used to listen patiently and respond and advise. Eventually I realized woh meri kitni care karte hain" (He cares a lot about me).

Navjot employed an intriguing phrase that has resonance in the Hindi-speaking belts of North India—the English word *care* is followed by the Hindi verb *karte*, "to do," which suggests something different than the English usage of caring for or taking care of someone. Navjot and other women I met, including Radhika and Kusum, used the word *care* to articulate what they thought their partners were doing right to inspire confidence and trust. It was not just a feeling or emotion that people show with subtle gestures, and not the care work that is undertaken for the elderly or sick. For Radhika, it is the gesture of doing housework that endears her husband, Jeet, to her: "He supports me as I pursue my college degree and motivates me in every way; he even does housework. Bahut caring hai" (He is very caring).

Radhika was the first woman in her community (she is from the singer caste) to have started college, an accomplishment her parents were very proud of. "My parents only accepted his family's proposal when they assured us that he will not stall my education. They said nahi toh hum ladki nahi dete" (otherwise, we won't give you our girl). The fact that Jeet not only encouraged her to study but also supported her by doing domestic chores, despite the prevailing norm of rigid gender-based division of labor, convinced Radhika of his care. It demonstrated not so much what he felt for her but who he was—a man ready for a reciprocal and relatively equal relationship.

As a poet and research scholar, Jeet had come into contact with progressive circles in the region and expressed strong views on gender parity. Nevertheless, he felt obliged to marry within his caste, a trait I often came across in smaller communities with less political and social capital. Few people in such communities achieved professional success, and Jeet, a newly appointed junior lecturer in the public schooling system, was a highly valued suitor. As "one of the best" in the community, he was expected to marry "one of their own." He chose Radhika out of a strong sense of obligation that he explicitly articulated. At the time of our meeting, he was hoping to have Radhika enrolled in a master's program at the Chandigarh-based Panjab University, an opportunity he himself did not have. "I just want to set the child up for a good career," he told me. Jeet's use of the word *bachchi* (female child) for his wife suggested both the age difference between the two and the nurturing role he had taken on.

Rather than signifying romantic love in Jeet's relationship with his wife, his care reflected a social and political commitment to gender equality that translated into improving her individual prospects. It is a form of care explored in works by Angela Garcia (2010) and Clara Han (2012). For Garcia, care means dwelling in the shared zone of another person's vulnerabilities, whereas Han describes care as a form of social debt that accrues among members of a close-knit community. In regard to intimate relationships in a transforming Haryana, care serves the purpose of bridging a huge, socially sanctioned disparity between men and women. Given the existing inequalities, such relationships can tend toward a dependency caused by the power imbalance in the couple. This particular version of care offers an opportunity to establish a companionate relationship where men subvert patriarchal prescripts on how to treat the women in their lives, at times even using their relative privilege to ameliorate their partners' situations. One could define this care as an effort to reconceptualize a relationship based on notions of partnership between two unequal parties, in the absence of any existing vocabulary to define this shift.

For women from this region, who have been historically "under-valued" (Yadav 2001), the tendency among some men to treat them as human beings, to patiently listen to and engage with their aspirations, signaled a cross-gender relationship different from what they had taken to be the norm. They sought partners who would treat them as good friends, bestowing on them a special regard in a society notorious for its mistreatment of women via sex-selective abortions, malnourishment of girls and women in the face of plenty, and high rates of sexual crimes.

This hypothesis seemed to fall apart when I asked Kusum whether her (boy) friend's love is expressed through the "care" he performs. She replied slowly, "Not really. . . . One cares as a human being as well, right?" The poignancy of this statement did not register with me immediately: ideally, these Haryanvi women expected to be treated as human beings in their own families and immediate communities. Yet, some of them seek that treatment outside familiar zones, which was, to me, a clear indication of new political commitments. Finding care is a means for some women to experience what it is to be human, but this process also necessarily involves, for Kusum, taking certain universal human values for granted. It reflects what Geertz calls the dynamic process of making something commonsensical—it must represent "life in a nutshell" (1983, 75). Common sense is both that which "represents the world as a familiar world, one everyone can, and should, recognize" (91) and something that "lies so artlessly before our eyes it is almost impossible to see" (92). The vital act of doing "care" needs to have at least an appearance of the ordinary (despite conscious iterations). In this framework, care is presumed to exist in mutual relationships despite unequal structures and networks. Even when Kusum listed care as one of the endearing features of her partner, she sought to normalize it—as if its existence should not come as a surprise.

Given the level of surveillance in close-knit rural communities, many courtships are furtive and most likely conducted via phone conversations that involve sharing, caring, and an enduring friendship. On the rural college campus where I stayed for over five months, I witnessed many women engaged in long phone calls. When I interviewed some of these women on the topic of "love marriages," they described in great detail the telephonic intrigues of their peers. Most women and men spoke about it as something others, even close friends, engaged in, while they themselves did not. Despite the adage that love marriages are ill conceived, premarital affairs, conducted primarily through phone calls, were common.

Kusum, one of the few women who spoke to me openly about her phone-based romance, has had few occasions to meet her "friend" since she started attending college. The friend was a peer from her school days and they had remained together despite the distance and lack of opportunities to meet in person. "I like talking to him. I feel like I can share everything with him. . . . Yes, I would like to marry him someday, but that is far off in future. I must first complete my education and find a job," she explained in a narrative that had become familiar. When I asked her why she refers to him as her "friend," she replied, "Till we are married, we would call him my friend, right?" Would it be called a "love marriage" if she married him, I enquired. As she replied in the affirmative, I did not explain my tedious focus on terminology; though Kusum spoke in Hindi, the key words she used to describe her relationship were all in English.

In Kusum's narrative, which focused on her aspirations for a career, the friend constituted a vital support system but marriage was not the ultimate goal. She does expect to marry him some day and hopes that her parents would bless the match. "At the moment, they don't want to talk about it, although I think they suspect. If both of us are already set up in our careers, parents are less likely to object," she explained.

Seeing care in intimate relationships as a political claim does not necessarily suggest that such longings are always an indication of ill treatment or an unhappy childhood. Women who came from sheltered families sometimes did find love among their own. But as Roop's case showed, it was the kind of love that thwarted a woman in her life goals. What some women aspired to was not exactly romantic love, though "love marriage" was often used as a shorthand. While not exactly an escape from patriarchy, it was at least a rejection of the kind of circumscribing love they had experienced at home.

These narratives also challenge the other pervasive discourse surrounding "love marriage," the presumed irrationality. My interviews with eloping couples at the high court showed that in many cases, their affairs had lasted four or five years, based on the ability and interest of the women and men to have phone conversations for hours. Not all phone-based courtships result in marriage, but they do reveal a level of commitment to engage with each other, problematizing the claim that such couples are ignorant about what they are getting into. Even when phone-based courtships did not result in matrimony, the women experienced romance and entertained the possibility of a model for intimate relationships that was different from the one that had been presented as the norm. People who "fell in love" often appeared to have life goals and relationship goals similar to those of Sakshi and others who sought arranged marriages. Love marriages could be seen as a rational or prudent course of action based on what was already a long, sustainable relationship.

Conclusion

This chapter has examined certain shifts in symbolic, ideological, and phenomenological aspects of marital relationships in the baagri belt of Haryana. In this lifeworld, marriage is often approached through individual economic rationales, and although they are not entirely utilitarian, both family-arranged and love marriages reflect an attempt to make the best of one's situation when it comes to the "matrimonial game," following Bourdieu's definition of the term: "production of the practices regarded as 'reasonable' within the group and positively sanctioned by the laws of the market" (1977, 58). When we approach the institution of marriage through life history narratives, studying generational shifts and/or overlapping experiences within close-knit kin groups, we begin to see change not just on a universal scale of progress but as distances traveled within the realm of what is familiar. That is, these shifts in marital relationships signify a reworking from within, that of the lebenswelt, which finds ways to stay compatible with the material or socioeconomic world around it.

PART TWO

State and Subjectivity

Capacity to Aspire in Postagrarian
North India

4

Gender Trouble and a State of Illusions

The prevailing literature on Haryana, both the sparse academic works and the more sensational mainstream accounts about the region, has often led me ask myself: what have the men been doing when they are not contributing to or extending the oppression of women?. Despite Haryana's hypervisibility in the news due to the infamous "honor killings" in the state during the last decade, there is very little academic work analyzing Haryana's contemporary politics, especially its notorious hypermasculinity.[1] Chowdhry, a historian who has produced several acclaimed books about the region, has included some ethnographic work to complement her rich archival data. She traces the colonial roots of some of the trends we see today, especially the exploitation of women's productive and reproductive roles and the roots of the skewed gender hierarchies in the region. As discussed in previous chapters, her critique of North Indian patriarchy is key to understanding the nexus of the state and kinship in controlling women's sexuality, not just in Haryana but throughout the entire region. Scholars such as Bhupinder Yadav have followed with works on the state's severely skewed sex ratio, discussing the attitudes and social conditions that govern the strong preference for male children (2001). Thus, the scant literature on Haryana has focused on the prevailing gender inequality in the region, and I admit that my work continues this model.

With the slightly unorthodox question that I asked at the beginning of this chapter, I am still extending feminist research, because the masculinity of the contemporary male oppressors, its roots in agrarian/peasant politics of the region, and its links to the state are clearly underresearched in this context. When examining a situation where the oppression of women has dominated academic works and reduced men to the role of agents of oppression, a research project on gender and sexuality even demands a brief study of masculinity.

As discussed in the introduction, February 2016 events were a stark response to the process of unraveling layers of Jat masculinist privilege that was originally based on land ownership. That privilege extended to both the prosperity that the Green Revolution accrued to Haryanvi peasants, especially Jat men, and gender-based disparity in land ownership patterns. Bina Agrawal (1994), Prem Chowdhry (2011, 2017), and Smita Jassal (2012) have contributed to the literature on gender and land rights in North India from the perspective of women's dispossession.[2] In this chapter, I trace the gendered history of the region, the effects of the loss of land ownership on masculinity, and the aspirations of millennials, particularly women who are dislodging masculine domination in their own quiet ways.

As Arjun Appadurai has famously theorized, ideas of both past and future are embedded and nurtured in culture. The capacity to aspire is a "navigational capacity" (2004, 69), especially among those who do not possess the resources or opportunities to pursue their ambitions. In the context of Haryana, this has profound implications for the lives of women dwelling in disjointed ethnoscapes (Appadurai 1996) created through the recent ruptures in local cultures. At a time when the promise of globalization and neoliberal policies has lost its capacity to inspire, the fragile localities constructed by communities fail to recreate the material culture of the world that has already been lost and are unable to see the promised benefits of the new world order. The postagrarian North India is marked by a culture of aspiration that often eludes the affluent but has the capacity to inspire hope and to present pathways to the marginalized.

Green Revolution and Magic of the State

Haryana was one of only four states in India to benefit from the postcolonial state's Green Revolution project, which aimed to increase agricultural yields through the use of massive irrigation systems, chemical fertilizers, and pesticides. Peasants in Punjab and Haryana as well as parts of Uttar Pradesh and the south Indian state of Andhra Pradesh saw a massive surge in income and improvements in lifestyles, aided in no small measure by state subsidies in electricity and water supplies as well as minimum price supports for their produce. I argue that this seeming miracle in fertility and fortunes tied the people to the powers of the state, making it an integral part of their everyday life. The rising agrarian fortunes often feature in the life history narratives of the region's septuagenarians and octogenarians, such as BW in chapter 3.

The powers of the state were imbued, in the eyes of the people, with magical properties. The state representatives, Coronil wrote in the context of Venezuela, "appeared on state's stage as powerful magicians who pull social reality, from public institutions to cosmologies, out of the hat" (1997, 2). The Indian state had similarly transformed the landscape as well as the wealth and status of land-owning peasants in the region. Despite the post–Green Revolution age offering fertile ground (pun unintended) for a study of the transforming socioeconomic patterns, such a research project has largely eluded the state. Much of my knowledge on political economy is derived from works on states such as Uttar Pradesh that border Haryana (Jaffrelot 2003; Ashraf 2015).

Christophe Jaffrelot's book *India's Silent Revolution* (2003), an authoritative text on the rise of caste politics in North India, explains the growing dominance of peasant communities in Indian politics through the aspirations and consolidation of one bureaucratic category—Other Backward Castes (OBC). The category refers to groups whom the state has classified as requiring affirmative action in addition to the Scheduled Castes and Scheduled Tribes, which were categories introduced by the colonial government to make sense of groups outside the Hindu caste pyramid (also called the Varna system). Under the Varna system, these "OBC groups" belonged to historically marginalized groups, known as *shudras*, and were discriminated against on the basis of their traditional occupations.

As Jaffrelot describes in his book, numerical strength in electoral politics helped mobilize political sentiment among the peasant communities. Larger communities such as the Jats were turned into "vote banks" and oriented toward what is today known as "quota politics."[3] The feeling of historical injustice, coupled with confidence in their numbers, produced a potent political environment where peasant politics in Uttar Pradesh became a majoritarian, identity-based praxis, alienating other groups in rural, agrarian life.

Haryana has witnessed a similar churning, where the political interests of other castes, both upper and lower, have gradually aligned against those of the Jats. The community has repeatedly demanded inclusion in the affirmative action program, with a particular focus on securing employment in state institutions. Jat dominance in political and public life at the state and local government levels, combined with considerable control over state institutions, local resources, and the deployment of violence to achieve their demands, adds to the resentment against Jat groups. Given the Jats' affluence in the region, many have asked a question that also warrants our attention: Why do Jats want reservations (anyway)? Jaffrelot answered this in an editorial soon after the agitation in February 2016:

> These dominant castes do not see their future in agriculture because of the attraction exerted by the city and because of the crisis in village India. The 2014–15 Economic Survey showed that the wages of rural India were increasing at 3.6 percent only (when the inflation rate was above 5 percent), against 20 percent in 2011. Those who had land next to big cities could sell it to developers and even became rentiers sometimes.

But most of the migrants who left their village to try their luck in the city are disappointed by the job market. In contrast to the middle class inhabiting urban centres for generations, they have not received the kind of English-medium education that gives access to the services, the sector (especially in IT) offering opportunities. While they have sometimes run heavy debts to get some private, not-so-good education, they have to fall back on unskilled jobs.[4]

Jaffrelot goes on to note in the same article that while jobs in the private sector continue to be poorly paid, with average daily earnings of workers pegged at INR 249 (USD 3.73) in 2011 to 2012 and those of employees at large, at INR 388 (USD 5.81). By contrast, in the public sector, the figures for workers and employees were almost three times more, at 679 and 945 (USD 10.18 and 14.19), respectively. While government jobs are highly sought, especially after the wage rate revisions introduced by the federal government, an aggressive liberalization policy has resulted in the number of public sector jobs shrinking to 17.6 million while the population has climbed to 1.2 billion. At the same time, the extensive expansion of education at all levels in the past two decades further fuels aspirations for gainful employment in public sector. According to a 2018 survey conducted by the Centre for the Study of Developing Societies, between 2007 and 2016, the number of Indian youths who would prefer a government job grew from 63 to 65 percent.[5] While young people in big cities showed the highest rise, from 48 to 62 percent, 65 percent of the youths in small cities and 69 percent in villages today seek the proverbial *sarkari naukri* (government job). A whopping 82 percent of rural graduates have this aspiration. These conditions acquire distinctly caste-oriented overtones for Haryana and North India as the subsequent sections will outline.

Land Only in Name: The Burden of Entitlement in a Postagrarian Future

On April 19, 2015, the National Congress Party called for a national farmers' rally to protest the proposed Land Acquisition Bill Ordinance, which would have removed the mandatory requirement of landowners' consent in the acquisition process from the existing law. Due to Haryana's amorphous borders with the national capital, Haryanvi farmers were standing in for farmers from the rest of the country, but were also themselves enmeshed in complex local struggles. Jat men from the Rohtak region came to the rally in pink turbans, a symbol of their caste superiority (as it is worn by village headmen), and humiliated lower-caste leaders from their own political party who came from elsewhere in the state. A little less than a year after this "specter of pink," this aggressive posturing gave way to widespread violence in February 2016 for OBC status and reservations in government jobs.

The history of peasant politics in the region and the threat of losing land played a huge role in the agitations for affirmative action in 2016, but commentaries on land acquisition policy that focus on farmers' rights often do not adequately address the waning significance of agriculture in North India, which is pushing millennials from peasant families to explore employment elsewhere. In an in-depth piece on Jat men's aggression in North Indian politics, Ajaz Ashraf (2015) explains the extent of rural distress in the region, which finds expression in social oppression and communal violence by Jat men against Muslims, lower castes, and women. Ashraf quotes a paper from the National Bank for Agriculture and Rural Development that revealed that "landholdings in the marginal category (less than 1 hectare) constituted 67% of all operational holdings in the country in 2010–2011. Declining yields and rising cost of production has enhanced rural indebtedness. The National Sample Survey Office released data [2014] showing that more than 60% of the total rural households covered in its survey in 11 states were in deep debt (2015)." Ashraf draws a direct correlation between the shrinking landholdings and sites of social conflict, where violence against Dalit and Muslim communities increased as the size of landholdings and agricultural yields declined. In the article, Ashraf also mentions in passing that Haryana's Jats are "miffed" that BJP chose a non-Jat chief minister (CM) and "they fear the Land Acquisition Bill (2015)," but these two factors have more complex ramifications for Haryana.

In the field I encountered the keen sense of betrayal among Jats toward the ruling BJP government, which was especially intense because the party had installed a Punjabi in the role of Haryana's CM. The interests of non-Jat communities had collapsed into an unspoken alliance that had ensured BJP's victory in 2015, but many Jats, too, had voted for the BJP, identifying as "Hindus" and blaming Muslims—rather than the agrarian crisis—for their diminished social status. Jat interlocutors I spoke to before the state elections were invariably convinced that the "CM is always ours" irrespective of the political party in power. (Ironically, Bishnois were similarly convinced that one of their own would become the CM, although they had neither the numerical strength nor the panregional clout to support such an ambition.) Jat men's need to avenge themselves for their diminished political status—for having a Punjabi as CM—resulted in targeted violence against Punjabi businesses and property in February 2016. The agitation for affirmative action turned into communal violence, and neither the agrarian crisis nor the fear of land acquisition was adequately tackled.

My interviews with men across age groups shows that despite the acute agrarian distress, land is still central to identity formation for this peasant group. The thought of not having any land to one's name was deeply disturbing for the Haryanvi men I spoke to, especially those from Jat and Bishnoi communities. Many male students I interviewed in Haryana and Chandigarh sought nonagrarian jobs for the future but still hoped that their families would retain the lands they owned. "One should have at least some land" was a common sentiment, with one Jat man stating that "at least one acre (43,560 square feet)" was important, which seems reassuring only on a symbolic level. The subject of shrinking landholdings due to divisions among brothers also provokes emotional responses. Mahesh, a Jat man, said he argues with relatives who hint that he and his brother will eventually divide the land between themselves. For Abhay, a Bishnoi, who said he wants his family to stay together, not splitting the land was an indication of close family ties and the trust he had placed in his brother by leaving the family land in the brother's care. These men were suggesting that stalling the trend of shrinking land parcels required emotional labor.

Dividing the family land among male descendants is very common in rural Haryana and part of many life history narratives, and interlocutors commonly cited shrinking landholdings as the reason why agriculture had become unsustainable. Landowners were already moving away from farming even as they officially identified themselves as "farmers."[6] Sachin, an interlocutor from Fatehabad, was practical about the fact that parcel sizes will continue to shrink with every generation and that (male) members of his extended family needed to find alternative occupations. He was employed as a firefighter and he said he comfortably managed his farm-related chores in his spare time.

Students in Chandigarh recall lectures from their parents, who advised them to find occupations outside their villages because "there was no future in agriculture." In my observation, Haryanvis are already preparing themselves psychologically for life after agriculture, hopefully in government jobs, and are willing and at times even eager to sell their land for huge sums. In a frank conversation with me, a longtime social activist recalled an experience he had had with people protesting against a proposed automobile factory plant in the Gurugram district: "Many farmers arrived for the protests in SUVs and privately asked me to negotiate for one or two million more on their behalf." The activist's experience with a proposed nuclear power plant in Fatehabad was similar; it was not the fear of ecological disaster that triggered the protests, he insisted, although that was the ostensible reason. According to him, protests against land acquisition in Haryana were mostly aimed at securing higher compensation for landowners.

I realized over the course of my fieldwork that when informants referred to "some land" or "at least one acre" they literally meant that they hoped their family would retain a small farm as a matter of pride while selling the rest of their land to the highest bidder. Marilyn Strathern's *Partial Connections* (1991) is a useful reference for understanding Haryanvi men's relationship with land and how it mediates social ties. In the context of the Melanesian society, Strathern theorizes that aspects of one's composite self can be activated and externalized, creating "hybrids" that are then put into social circulation. Similarly, part of Haryanvi masculinity is externalized and entwined with family-owned land, and this land determines local networks and connections. Apart from determining key decisions, including political affiliations, weddings in North India were also primarily finalized according to considerations of land with its explicit purpose being the need to preserve and perpetuate ownership between certain groups and networks. Among men from dominant communities, lack of land ownership is, in turn, perceived as emasculating, and it determines the nature of their relationships and conduct with women and individuals from landless communities.

For Haryanvi men, the idea of remaking self/personhood in a postagrarian world is consequently a painful one, even for those who have already moved away from agriculture. The transformation can even lead to self-destructive actions, as Holly Wardlow's book (2006, 75–78) has highlighted, albeit in the context of a vulnerable group of Melanesian women. News reports from Haryana about drug abuse and farmer suicides, which the media and the state has attributed to crop failures, nonpayment of loans, and land acquisitions, need to be reassessed in this light.[7] There exists in North India a deep-rooted identity crisis generated by the transition away from agriculture, and self-destructive behaviors seem to be one of the responses to that crisis.

Loss of land is, however, an event that breaks long and deeply entrenched hegemonies. For women and individuals from historically landless communities, it can be liberating to move from an agrarian economy where their labor is both mandated and unrecognized. For these groups, although agriculture has been central to their everyday lives, they are not necessarily thrown into crisis by the loss of land. Women from the privileged communities have a more ambiguous relationship with land—they have no control over decisions regarding land use and indeed seldom hope to inherit land despite recent legislation in their favor.[8] Agricultural cycles still control women's lives to a certain extent—school and college teachers report more absences in particular months (figure 6)[9]—but as the cycles get shorter due to climate change and contract farming becomes widespread, individual contributions to farming have fallen. Women appear to be making the transition more smoothly because they do not inherit land and consequently their identites do not hinge on it. Families also often encourage women's outside employment, hoping to supplement farm income with their salaries.

Like all other groups, Jats (including women) seek security for the future, demanding affirmative action where jobs in state institutions in place of land as the resource the community can circulate among themselves. I observed that Jats often feel entitled to a dominant role in any possible postagrarian future society, expecting the state to dazzle them with its illusionary powers again. But

FIGURE 6 Cotton picking season (fall) means more labor for women and more absenteeism at colleges.

Photo: Rama Srinivasan.

some millennials have learned to look beyond entitlement and negotiate these transformations in political economy in their individual capacities.

Home and the World: Masculinity, Femininity, and Potential Futures

While agriculture determines the political economy in the region, dairy products often feature as cultural symbols, with many references to Haryana as the "land of milk and yoghurt" (Chowdhry 2007, 282). The emphasis on dairy products is not limited to the state; Punjab, Rajasthan, and Gujarat also have large dairy industries, though the material culture in these states depends on a greater variety of factors.[10] For Haryanvis, the powdery whiteness of milk represents a purity that can be embodied. Men, especially older men, prefer starched white attire that contrasts with the bright colors women traditionally wear. The purity of Haryana is also articulated in their "simple" needs that are easily met. Some (mostly younger) Haryanvis worry that they, as a group, do not have enough ambition. A middle-aged lawyer in Sirsa cited this to draw a contrast with Punjabis: "A Haryanvi will be satisfied with a dollop of butter on his *roti* (Indian bread) but a Punjabi would have at least four types of pickles at home to

FIGURE 7 Archived screenshot of Dushyant Chautala's Twitter page.

go with it," he claimed, before adding apologetically that Haryanvis probably "did not know how to live life."

The purity of Haryanvi life was sometimes presented as the fanciful quest for an uncomplicated, familiar life in an increasingly economically uncertain world. But I would argue that Haryanvis who emphasized their simplicity were not satisfied with less but rather satisfied *at home*. Older Haryanvi men from landed families, in particular, have preferred the comforts of home because being a farmer meant that the bulk of the agricultural work—cultivation and harvesting—was carried out by contract farmers (Jodhka 2014), while other farmwork and animal husbandry, including producing dairy products, fell onto the shoulders of women. Jat men's relatively easy life is best highlighted by the popular epigram "Jaat ke taath, hookah aur khaat" (A Jat's luxury is symbolized by his hookah pipe and cot), referring to the stereotype of an elderly Jat man smoking a hookah pipe while lounging outside his house on a cot in his long hours of leisure. Younger Jat men who do not share these interests still regard this image as a source of Jat pride and well-being. In figure 7, the profile picture from MP Dushyant Chautala's Twitter page shows him in the background as an older man in white smokes a hookah pipe. The cover image at the top of the page shows a group of men, all dressed in white, surveying chaffed wheat in a grain market, and significantly, this is not an image of farms or farm labor. Chautala was an MP from the Hisar district and is known for his soft, gentle political image. Although the young leader has moved to a digital platform, with these images he seeks to communicate that at least part of his validation is sourced from the older men in his community.

Jat identity at the local level is consolidated through visible symbols: purity, embodied in white clothes; peasant life, governed by an interest in agricultural production, though perhaps not the actual labor itself; and community elders' pride and well-being, expressed in material terms. Symbolic pride as well as the luxury of having one's needs met at home was available only to landowning men (predominantly Jats, Yadavs, Rajputs, and Bishnoi). But even in non-Jat families, I observed a strong feeling for home among men from families with small land-holdings. Jaynant, a Chandigarh-based student from a Punjabi family, explained his preference for home: "I am very attached to my home and parents. I certainly want to go back. But my own twin sister, who is in Delhi right now, will never return." According to him, girls born in the post-internet age ("digital natives") have known too much of the world outside and are too fond of the freedom they have found there to return home where that liberty will likely be curtailed. Of the twelve Haryanvi male students I interviewed in Chandigarh city, only two could imagine reconciling themselves to a life away from home, whereas of the eight women interviewed only one was convinced she would return—in order to provide her (future) children with pure milk and food.

Law student Kuljeet, a Jat woman from Hisar and a successful sportsperson, said she would not want to return to rural Haryana unless she reaches higher levels of judiciary. She believed this would allow her to help women plaintiffs in a deeply patriarchal society. Shivani, a Dalit woman from Kaithal and aspirant for a teaching post in the public schooling system, was similarly averse to returning to rural Haryana unless she was in a position to help women and people from lower castes. Because Jat instructors dominate in the schools and colleges back home, she was wary of how she would be treated by her future Jat colleagues, but also worried about Dalit students who have to deal with unsupportive and sometimes abusive Jat instructors, as she did.

Young, unmarried women interviewed in rural Haryana were more likely to be fascinated by the world outside, though escape did not seem to be an option for most of them. Sakshi wanted to move away from her native Fatehabad and familiar surroundings, even if not to a big city. She stayed silent when her male cousin Sachin claimed confidently that nobody in his extended family, including Sakshi, would want to stray too far from home, but later, in a private conversation, the young woman confided to me that she would like to get married to someone really "far away." In a slightly exasperated voice she said, "No one wants to leave their little cliques. Everyone is trapped in the same mindset." Some parents of educated young women, especially those from lower-caste landless families, also hoped their daughters would marry men in cities and towns, because according to them, life in rural Haryana did not provide a sustainable life for women.

The idea of "home and the world" in Haryana is a complex negotiation of opportunities and entitlement that turned Partha Chatterjee's argument on gender and cultural identity in colonial Bengal (1989) on its head. Haryanvi men had become placeholders for an idea of home and culture that signified masculine entitlement, whereas women, excluded from cultural identity markers, were looking outward into the world of opportunities.

In rural and semiurban Sirsa, Fatehabad, and Hisar, there is a distinct contrast between the restlessness of the majority of women and the listlessness of the majority of men. As the next section highlights, opportunities for higher education and employment have recently opened up for young women, and they are actively pursuing them. For the young men, especially those from land-owning castes, opportunities have to be really enticing for them to move away from home. Men who belong to lower castes find themselves in the same predicament as the women. Higher education is prized and they aspire to it, but not all of my male interlocutors from these groups showed the same enterprise the women from all caste groups did. The navigational capacity of aspirations that marks the journey toward an uncertain future was, at least during the period I studied, distinctly feminine.

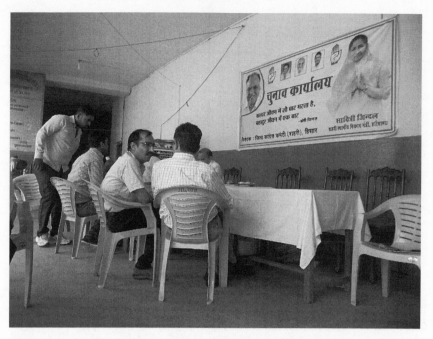

FIGURE 8 Congress Party candidate Savitri Jindal's campaign office in 2015 was dominated by men. Ms. Jindal, who stood in Hisar, the stronghold of her late husband O. P. Jindal, is one of the affluent women in Haryana who contest elections to keep the family's political fortunes together, but wield little power.

Photo: Rama Srinivasan.

Haryana's contemporary politics is defined, by women and individuals from lower castes and/or landless communities who push forward with their aspirations and men from the privileged classes who attempt to keep the status quo intact. A significant section of the population has aspired to government sector jobs since the very inception of the state (Sangwan 1991), but so far, men from certain communities and regions (for example, Jats from Sirsa and Rohtak and Bishnois from Hisar) have had the advantage. To a large extent, this advantage was determined by leaders of large landowning communities (including the extended Chautala clan in Sirsa, Bhajan Lal and his son Kuldeep Bishnoi of the Bishnoi community from Hisar, and the Hooda family in Rohtak and neighboring districts) who participate in a nepotistic politics that nurtures affiliations, encourages political loyalties through selective distribution of state resources and jobs, and the exclusion of women from political spaces (see figure 8). The next two sections explore the gradual dismantling of this distinctly masculine politics.

Breaking New Ground with Education: A Gendered Perspective

From 64.8 percent in 2001, India's literacy levels increased to 74.04 percent in 2011. With regard to higher education, sociologist Mary John notes, "While women constituted barely 10 per cent of the student body in higher education just after independence, by 2004–05 this figure increased to as much as 40 percent, and for the most recent year, 2010–11, has crossed 42 percent" (2012, 206). In 2015 the *All India Survey on Higher Education (2013–2014)*, released by the Ministry of Human Resource Development, estimated that total enrolment in higher education was 32.3 million, comprised of 17.5 million men and 14.8 million women (46%).[11] The report puts India's Gender Parity Index in higher education at 0.92 for all categories, 0.92 for Scheduled Castes, and 0.81 for Scheduled Tribes.[12] The survey's statistics pertain primarily to persons aged eighteen to twenty-three. Figures 9 and 10 show figures collated from the 207-page report.[13]

In the case of Haryana, the numbers present a fascinating picture for those willing to look beyond the "hard facts." Haryana's Gender Parity Index, at 0.90, does not vary a great deal from the national figure, but when it comes to Scheduled Castes (SC) it drops significantly, to 0.84. The Gross Enrollment Ratios (GERs) of women and men do not display a logical correlation to Haryana's skewed sex ratio (879 women to 1,000 men, according to the national census survey of 2011) or its literacy rates. More incongruent is the number of women completing degrees, diplomas, and certificates, which is significantly higher than the figure for men, even though all other numbers point to women's disadvantage. In India as a whole, which has a better sex ratio and women's literacy rate than Haryana does, men have a higher completion rate, but in Haryana fewer women than men dropped out or failed to complete their programs. The data on completion rates, which unfortunately do not include caste-based variations, hold some interesting insights for the state and its gender imbalance. First, Haryana's rate of completion (called "pass-outs" in the report) of educational programs is *lower* than the average India rate, though the GER is actually *higher* for the state than for India as a whole. Second, enrollment rates for women are higher than for men at the postgraduate level (MA, MPhil), while men enroll in undergraduate and PhD programs in greater numbers. But analysis of the completion rates shows that with the exception of PhD programs, women register consistently higher numbers of completions, irrespective of the enrolment numbers. For example, approximately 85,000 more men than women enrolled in undergraduate programs in Haryana, but approximately 3,000 more women than men actually completed their degrees.

Men's lower enrollment rates in postgraduate and MPhil programs may be explained in part by the fact that men who do well in their undergraduate programs often enroll in postgraduate programs outside Haryana, in Delhi,

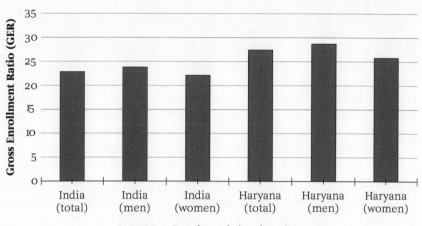

FIGURE 9 Broad trends in education.

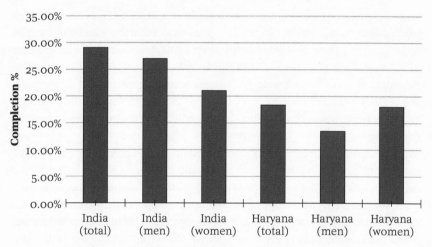

FIGURE 10 Rates of completion for degree and diploma programs.

Chandigarh, Rajasthan, or Uttar Pradesh; these opportunities do not always extend to women. Finally, with regard to PhD programs, the number of men enrolled was about 1,000 more than the number of women, but the gap between completion rates for women and men is only around sixty. The measure for PhD programs is probably not accurate because these programs (three to four years long) extend beyond the seventeen-to-twenty-three age bracket that was the survey's focus, but it gives us a clue to the social privilege required for men to outshine women on any measure of educational qualifications. As some of the life history narratives in my study detailed, for women, MPhil and PhD programs have to be negotiated with marriage and childbirth, giving men a distinct advantage.

In addition to the necessary task of factoring the discrepancies in numbers is the task of examining what is happening in Haryana that explains the statistics. The reasons for Haryanvi women's success in education, especially in comparison to men, is a script waiting to be deciphered. The figures lend statistical credence to my ethnographic observations that, by and large, young women appeared restless, seeking to attend more courses and pursue several centralized examinations, whereas the majority of young men seemed listless and unmotivated, lounging next to motorbikes at bus stops and markets. The ambitious among them had either already left their villages or were commuting great distances to regional cities in the hope of attaining a better education. Men who were enrolled in Panjab University, for example, said they needed to work harder than their Punjabi peers because their families had "sent them so far."

Young men who were left behind in the villages, including those from lower castes, waited for opportunities in unemployed or underemployed situations. My questions on education goals were received with interest by women in rural settings, who frequently sought my advice. Their male counterparts did not treat interview questions about higher education with the same eagerness or enthusiasm. Men who were willing to talk about their lives at college often listed their dominant interests as riding motorbikes with their peers and seeking to meet women. A former professor from my host college described his male students' approach to education as "a quest for teaching jobs that would ensure that they need not study any longer!"

For women, the relationship to education was a little more complicated, though aspirations for romance and teaching jobs also figured in their narratives. Their homosocial lives were restructured around the experience of commuting or walking to colleges together. To keep themselves and others safe, they forged and sustained bonds that extended beyond their kin and caste-based networks. Leaving for college or other classes (e.g., private instruction for recruitment examinations) was also a legitimate reason for escaping the domestic space. In interviews, some women expressed a desire to prolong the length of their education or to achieve more milestones in order to shake off the bonds of domesticity and/or delay impending weddings. Attending classes and commuting offered a chance to dwell in public spaces (see figure 11) and often their only opportunity to experience romance. But the most important factor in their quest for education, substantiated by numerous interviews conducted in rural Haryana and Chandigarh, is the self-confidence young women developed through holding a clutch of degrees and the respect they received for these achievements. Whether it was the regard of a previously dismissive mother-in-law or refusing to do certain domestic chores after finishing high school, stories in rural Haryana abound with examples of the "perks of education." Interlocutors also repeatedly expressed disbelief at the idea that I, then a

FIGURE 11 Women students from a rural college block traffic on a state highway to protest their low grades in a centralized university examination (2013).

Photo: Rama Srinivasan.

doctoral student, was interested in doing domestic chores, or even familiar with them.

Education also formed the basis for evaluation of modernity or progressiveness of a given family. Those who "allowed" their daughters to study occupied a high moral ground on the modernity scale than those who did not. The discussion on women's education revisits the classic binary of New Woman and Modern Girl. According to the introduction to the edited volume *The Modern Girl around the World*, the New Woman is seen as an empowered, socially and politically engaged citizen, while the Modern Girl is miscast as having "frivolous" interests such as clothes, cosmetics, and romantic experiences (Weinbaum et al. 2008, 9–10). In India, education is seen as a means to become empowered and employable, and the government mandate of *shashaktikaran* (empowerment) of women resonates in many quarters. Thus, support for women's education is driven both by expectations of jobs in the future and by political designs for a more "modern" Haryana. According to some interlocutors, "frivolous interests" associated with the Modern Girl such as cell phones (which were not discussed in Weinbaum et al. but figured in my data) and romance should be strictly avoided.

Employment in Public Sector: Securing the Future

Haryanvis' clamor for government jobs has existed since the inception of the state in 1966, according to a study by Nina Sangwan. When Haryana was carved out of Punjab, most of the administrative officials and teachers spoke Punjabi and opted to remain in the parent state, creating a vacuum in the administration that the less-educated local population was not immediately equipped to fill. Consequently, the number of government employees increased from 90,000 in 1967 to 230,000 in 1985 (1991,185). This fourfold increase explains the loyalties commanded by colorful male politicians from the state, as doling out jobs came easy and enhanced political clout phenomenally.

Local populations, especially the Jats, nursed resentment in 1966 against the Punjabi caste in Haryana (the group targeted during the violence of February 2016), who had migrated from present-day Pakistan during the partition of the subcontinent and were better educated than the locals. Their higher levels of education ensured the employment of the so-called outsiders, still known as refugees in some areas, and the local elites responded to this situation by aggressively seeking jobs for men from their own castes. In 1985 women's representation in the public sector was just 18 percent (Sangwan 1991).

When I was in rural Haryana, I observed that community elders were just beginning to recognize the discrepancy between the educational achievements of women and men. At least three older male interlocutors were especially concerned about the lack of motivation to secure jobs detected among Haryana's much-valued sons. The *sarpanch* (elected village head) of a large, Jat-dominated village waxed eloquent about his daughter's educational merit and self-confidence, expressing pleasure that her city-based parents-in-law have also acknowledged her accomplishments. In contrast, his son had incurred huge tuitions bills at a private engineering college but displayed no motivation for employment. He had refused to work in the private sector after only a week of employment because he disliked "taking orders," and now spent most of his time drifting about aimlessly. As a real estate agent and the owner of large farm holdings, the sarpanch could sustain his son's unproductive life. But he mourned the opportunities the young man had wasted and his lack of motivation even with regard to his father's existing business concerns. "He doesn't even know where our farms stand," he scoffed as he dismissed the subject of his son.

Many young men I interviewed had neither the desire to pursue agrarian life nor the motivation to create alternatives for themselves. Men from both landowning and landless families sought "office jobs" but spoke warily of the exploitation of poorly paid jobs with long working hours in the private sector. Jeevan, who had just turned eighteen when we talked about his future plans, had already worked in an automobile workshop as a young boy and said that although he liked cars, employment in a workshop was no life. He had considered becoming a chauffeur or taxi driver but decided against it due to legitimate concerns such as the long working hours and lack of respect from bosses and clients. His early experiences with an exploitative job had convinced him that a government job was the only logical course available.

His mother Nisha defended her decision to send him to work at an early age, after he had dropped out of school. She wanted to save him from the "bad company" associated with joblessness, but eventually she pulled him out of work when she found out that he had taken to smoking *beedis* (unfiltered tobacco) in the company of his colleagues. She hoped her sons would receive decent higher education but she was wary of unproductive periods in their lives. A few days after I interviewed Jeevan, Nisha informed me with great dismay that he had failed to clear the grade 12 (high school) centralized exams, throwing his future into greater uncertainty.

Jeevan came from a broken home and belonged to a lower caste, and the quality of education he had received at state-run schools had not prepared him adequately to achieve his goals. His elder brother, Rohit, had opted for an undergraduate course through a long-distance program and had started picking up small jobs whenever he could. He aspired to be a lecturer in a college, a job he felt commanded the respect that was currently missing in his professional life; this was a recurrent theme for the brothers. But Rohit's present was not held hostage to his future dreams. When I met him again in 2018, he had completed his undergraduate education and was preparing for examinations to select candidates for clerical jobs at state institutions. He spoke confidently about the techniques he had devised to crack the exam. His dream of bagging a government job had not faded over time, but he had become more realistic in his goals in the intervening period.

In the cases of Jeevan and Rohit I saw the results of the scarcity of institutional support and individual resources, combined with the widely held aspiration for government jobs. It could result in a lack of motivation conditioned by a state of hopelessness for the future, a hopelessness Rohit was trying hard to overcome. Unfortunately, the same could not be said about his brother. In the context of a rehab center in New Mexico, Angela Garcia describes a cycle of drug addiction where improving health is followed by more bouts of hopelessness (2010). Parts of Haryana, like many parts of Punjab today, are experiencing a crisis of drug abuse among men. Though this issue was not addressed in my ethnographic data, the state of hopelessness caused by uncertain futures and frustrated aspirations among Haryanvi men clearly intersects with the despair of some of the interlocutors in Garcia's ethnography.[14] One crucial difference between the situations I describe and those in Garcia's research is that in North India, the crisis has also affected affluent men.

The inability of wealthy landowning men from locally dominant communities to capitalize on available resources and opportunities was pronounced. When I asked a research scholar in Panjab University, who was originally from Fatehabad, whether he had noticed what I perceived as listlessness among young men of the region, he gradually came around to my view, sharing some stories from his own extended family and community. One of his young cousins, for example, had been unable to finish high school, unsuccessfully tried his luck at veterinarian courses, which would have secured him a coveted government job. According to the scholar, the cousin had not shown sufficient interest in veterinarian sciences—he had sought a government job simply because this is what most people around him did.

The contrast between some of these men of privilege and women from their own families was dramatic. Despite shouldering the burden of household tasks and farmwork from an early age and being constrained in their domestic spaces, women usually found ways to continue their education. If they were not allowed to attend regular courses, they enrolled in long-distance programs. Several private institutions had sprung up in the region to offer such women "non-attending" courses in teaching instruction or a bachelor's degree in education. Due to Haryana's policy focus on training some of India's best sportspersons, many women completed their degrees while enthusiastically opting for athletic training and availing of opportunities to travel to other parts of the country and participate in competitions. The sports instructor at my host college once joked in a casual conversation that these trips often presented opportunities for students' tentative attempts to experience romance. On another occasion, in response to a direct question, she claimed that the training did not significantly alter women's lives in their own homes and with respect to future marriages but it did make them fearless and equipped them to defend themselves against potential assaulters. More importantly, achievements in sports competitions led to greater chances of employment in the public sector, making the women ideal prospects in the marriage market. In summary, although women's educational accomplishments were checkered due to social factors, colleges enriched women's life and experiences, affording them hope for a better future.

A majority of the women students I spoke to in rural Haryana and Chandigarh also hoped to become school or college teachers in the public sector, which is considered a safe and appropriate profession for women because with its shorter, flexible working hours, they can also attend to housework. One economics student revealed that she had been trained to work in *aanganwadis* (village-level, government-run childcare units) but was pursuing her master's as she waited for her wedding. She had been betrothed for some time and explained that her career decisions would have to wait. In the meantime, she had already completed a bachelor's in education and one year of her master's program. Anita, who came from a modest Punjabi family, worked at an exploitative private school while she prepared for the National Eligibility Test, which is required for a job in the higher education sector. Though Anita complained regularly about her poorly paid job where she constantly suffered petty humiliation, she did not stay idle as she waited for a government job to come to her. Sakshi, who was her best friend and possessed the same qualifications, had chosen to not work, but she accompanied Anita to the city to attend coaching classes for the same exam. This was Sakshi's only legitimate excuse to travel to the city, as she was wary of being spotted there without a purpose by older Jat men from her village.

In India, education is widely viewed and promoted as a means to obtain a decent job and secure upward mobility, but for Haryanvi women in particular, it offers leave for free movement, social contact, and exposure to the outside world. Free movement considerations had no meaning to the unfettered sons in Haryana, and pursuing and completing degree did not automatically enrich their lives. Unless they secured "office jobs" in the public sector or secured admission to an institution outside Haryana, pursuing education for its own sake was not rewarding.

Haryana, previously a place known for its agrarian lifestyle and strong peasant identity, had become obsessed with government jobs. The unsustainable aspirations and the resulting desperation are today leading to caste wars, seen most recently in the February 2016 protests. Jat men, who feel entitled to both local domination and government jobs, are forced to compete with women as well as men from other castes, a predicament that provokes discontent and violence.

In summary, both statistical and ethnographic evidence shows that recently, women have taken the initiative to change their disadvantageous situation. They are motivated to work hard in a neoliberal ideology-driven India that demands individual effort and initiative rather than drudgery in the form of unrecognized labor. While non-Jat communities have challenged Jat men, women across caste lines are perhaps leading a "silent revolution" along the lines of Jaffrelot's claim regarding the political mobilization of OBC communities in North India. These women see pathways to the future where men may not.

Postscript

The hopelessness of some men and the immense hope of many women determines their individual approaches to marriage, especially love marriage. Aspirations for future careers and marriage are linked as marriage, social position, and prosperity almost always are. The discrepancy between the achievements of men and women helps us get closer to analyzing why some women might want to expand their horizons when it comes to finding potential spouses, either outside their castes or through an insistence on care in relationships. The story of Ravinder and Kavita, a Bishnoi couple, illuminates various themes from chapter 3, connecting them to the trends discussed here.

Ravinder, who had completed an undergraduate degree in commerce, claimed that he had wasted three years at a private college that had taught him nothing useful. For him and his friends, higher education had been about hanging around, riding their bikes, and for some of them, trying to court women. If Ravinder had been interested in the last activity he did not reveal this, as our interview had been set up by his fiancée Kavita. At the time of the interview, he was planning to start a dairy production unit because he believed that farming was not lucrative and his family already had many hands involved in that occupation, With dairy production, he was not deviating too much from the traditional family lifestyle but consciously resisting the other available, highly desirable option—a government job. He expanded on this passionately: "I am not scared of work [manual labor] or ashamed of it. I don't want to be like my college friends, who either want an office job or are willing to while away their time. If my dairy business does not work out, I am ready to go back to farming. The sun, the heat or hard work does not bother me." This was in fact my first interview with a young man from a large landowning family who was not deterred by the idea of farm work. When I asked if Kavita supported this plan, he replied that she was actually his inspiration. She regularly pushes him to not sit idle at home, living off his parents' money.

Like many young men in the region today, when his match was being finalized, he attempted to get to know his fiancée better. "I asked her brother for her phone number, which he refused despite being roughly my age. But I had many friends in their village so I made it happen anyway. Marriage is serious business, I needed to know what she was like, whether we will be compatible. Ab toh hadh se zyada love ho gaya hai" (Now I am madly in love with her). Ravinder initially accepted the match because his family is an important aspect in his life. And, although this was not underlined in his narrative, I could see that his aspirations required family backing. In addition to the space required for such a production unit, he needed a traditional family structure because regardless of caste, men in the region do not milk cows. He saw marriage as favorable in other material ways—he gleefully noted that a car in a dowry usually means a big one. There was also an expectation that Kavita would find a teaching job with a public school in the future. As a public school instructor, he believed, she would work fewer hours and could attend to domestic work and childcare even as she brought in a steady income to complement his earnings from the business venture.

That Ravinder did not present any threat to the prevailing social norms is apparent from his stated preference for a traditional division of labor and his hope that his wife would achieve the social benchmark of success that he had not—the coveted government job. But in their case, I had already learned that the match was advantageous from Kavita's point of view, too. Kavita, who was in her early twenties, had led a sheltered life because her paternal uncle had decided against her attending a college; she had enrolled in a long-distance degree course instead. When her paternal uncle had sought to finalize her match a few years ago, her older cousin, Hardeep, had intervened and argued that "our girl" was still very young. Though convinced of Ravinder's suitability for Kavita, he had insisted on a long engagement that would allow her to finish her undergraduate degree before entering wedlock. Kavita also joined Hardeep's wife in teaching at a private school for a miniscule salary. In this way, she had been allowed the time to experience adulthood and develop a relationship with her fiancé.

It was in this latter experience that she had made a radical departure, conducting a "secret" romance with Ravinder that all the women in the extended family were privy to and vicariously experienced. She included me in this privileged circle and while telling me about her first meeting with Ravinder, issued a strong disclaimer that I should not tell her male cousins. "He brought duplicates of my transcripts from the university to my school because I was planning to apply for another course. I kept chasing him away because I was afraid someone would see us and inform my family. But the next time I meet him I am not going to be so scared," she said, describing the event. In Kavita's case, romance and her goals for life, which dictated that she should not sit idle at home, had become entwined. Ravinder had connected her sheltered life with the outside world of opportunities.

Despite having some (legitimate) misgivings about Kavita's exploitative job and its future prospects, Ravinder was clear that he was not going to stall her educational goals. In fact, he disparaged the family's decision to enroll her in a distance-learning program and claimed that he was going to have her attend a regular master's program after they were married. It appeared that irrespective of the quality of his own education, which he complained about, he believed that the attainment of educational degrees was an important part of what makes a person whole and how they are perceived. Ravinder and Kavita got married in 2016.

5

Instituting Court Marriage

The Legal Fiction of Protection Petitions

Over time, cases of elopements and love marriages have consolidated into an established form of litigation: a petition for the protection of life and liberty. From ethnographic research conducted at the high court in May to August 2012 and January to August 2015, I noted subtle shifts in courtroom interactions that signal the existence and maturing of a legal morality that is discernibly distinct from other normative orders (including the kinship order). Even if they openly disapproved of elopements, several judges and lawyers claimed that every adult has a right to marry of their own accord. Despite strongly held and explicitly stated opinions on what was often described as evidence of eroding sexual moralities, many actors in this space were able to separate their support for social norms from their stated positions on the law and what it allows. By demarcating the boundaries between the realm of law and social prescripts, these actors have been able to create an established and socially recognized legal mechanism for eloping couples, providing a model for judicial intervention where actors both within and outside the legal space can facilitate trends that they do not necessarily endorse.

Protection cases are filed as writ petitions with reference to Article 21 of the Indian Constitution, which deals with the fundamental right to life and liberty, but this remains a source of great disquiet among some judges who uphold the right to protection without being able to reconcile themselves with the trend of elopements. One judge struggled to articulate his discontent on an occasion I was present in the court: "Everybody is approaching this court to get their [right to] life and liberty validated. As far as life is concerned, I understand . . . but liberty? . . . Should we be validating the liberty to . . . [elope]?"

The judge's words pushed me to probe the source of his confusion—it possibly comes from the application of a constitutional article in conjunction with the Indian Penal Code (protection cases are a criminal matter) for marriage-related cases, which are civil by legal definition. Whereas Article 21 refers to a broad range of issues, the Special Marriage Act directly addresses and guarantees the right to marry one's chosen partner, *under specific conditions*. Though Article 21 was widely used, in court proceedings it did not appear that the right to marry was a *fundamental or unalienable right*. That is, the Article 21 went only so far as ensuring couples that they may live their lives as they desire without interference or harm. And yet, many judges perused the paperwork carefully to establish the veracity of the claim of marriage. These efforts produced different dialogues in various courtrooms, but court orders of several judges contained a variation of the phrase "while not going into the validity of marriage . . ." (see figures 12 and 13). In my hypothesis, this discrepancy can be connected to the usage of Article 21 in such cases. Whereas protection of life was something almost all judges in the court were ready to guarantee in a majority of cases, the liberty of citizens (to choose one's spouse) was a more contentious issue for some judges.

In this chapter, I provide a thick description of the courtroom space that creates a legally tenable marriage through multiple, overlapping legal knowledge systems. *Court marriage*, a term that otherwise refers to weddings conducted at a magistrate's court and not in a judicial one, is also reproduced through courtroom interventions on elopements and love marriages. It has features that legal studies research often associates with a "legal fiction"—that is, a statement assumed to be accurate for legal purposes but which may be only partly true or even completely false. In the next section I discuss the phenomenon of court marriage as a procedure that involves multiple legal fictions.

Creating a Legal Wedding

Since at least 2010, an average of fifty couples from the states of Punjab and Haryana have visited the high court every business day. The court orders the state of Punjab or Haryana to protect the couples' right to life and liberty, often explicitly stating in the order that the judge does not comment on the validity of the marriage. Despite this disclaimer, communities in rural Haryana have come to refer to this process as a "court marriage." Interlocutors in Haryana's towns and villages brought up "the court in Chandigarh" in conversations about "love marriages" without any prompting. Sachin, a firefighter and part-time farmer, effectively summarized the dominant voices on the subject: "We don't approve of love marriages here. But if the couples visit the high court in Chandigarh that is another issue." A love marriage that has received court approval was, in his eyes, more acceptable. Payal (chapter 2), who had sought a court wedding for herself, similarly held the position that marriage was done right when it was done at the courts. A senior police officer in the baagri region communicated (indirectly, through a local reporter) that the police officers

In the High Court of Punjab and Haryana at
Chandigarh.

Crl.Misc.No.M-22617of 2012 (O&M)
Date of Decision:- 30.07.2012

████ and another   Petitioners.

        Versus

State of Haryana and others

                                          Respondents.

CORAM : HON'BLE MR.JUSTICE NARESH KUMAR SANGHI.

        Present: - Mr.Surinder Kaur Mamli, Advocate,
                   for the petitioners.

NARESH KUMAR SANGHI,J.

        Prayer in this petition, filed under Section 482, Cr.P.C., is

for the issuance of direction to respondents No. 1 to 3 to protect

lives and liberty of the petitioners from respondents No. 4 to 6. The

petitioners contend that they being major, have solemnized their

marriage in accordance with law. They further submit that the private

respondents are not accepting the marriage of the petitioners and

adamant to separate them from each other by resorting to illegal

means. They further submit that in view of the imminent danger to

their lives and liberty they have already moved a representation

(Annexure P-5) before the Superintendent of Police, Kurukshetra.

        Keeping in view the seriousness of the matter but without

FIGURE 12 Sample court order, page 1. The listed petitioner is the bride; "and
another" refers to the groom. On the respondents' line, "others" refers to family
members and kin (usually but not always) of the bride.

Crl.Misc.No.M-22617of 2012 (O&M)   **2**

going into the validity of the marriage, the present petition is disposed

of with a direction to the Superintendent of Police,Kurukshetra,to

take action as warranted by law on the representation moved by the

petitioners and in the meantime to issue necessary orders to

ensure that no harm is caused to the lives and liberty of the

petitioners at the hands of private respondents.

                                    (NARESH KUMAR SANGHI)
                                              JUDGE
30.07.2012
Anoop

FIGURE 13 Sample court order, page 2. The text of this order, which reproduces a standard document created by individual judges for protection cases, clearly states that the court does not "[go] into the validity of the marriage."

under his supervision had evolved an "efficient mechanism" to deal with such couples. The officers summoned the families of the duo and explained to them that no one, including the cops themselves, could "touch the couple" now that they had received the court order. Baljeet and Navjot, who lived in this region, confirmed that this had happened in their case. By "securing" the couples in a state where honor killings are widespread, the court orders were also ensuring conditional social sanction for their marriages and togetherness.

After my preliminary research at the high court in 2012, I interpreted couples' and community members' understanding of court marriage as an act of deliberate "misrecognition." According to Pierre Bourdieu, disposition to the sense of misrecognition could stem from "the delegation of authority which confers its authority on authorized discourse" (Bourdieu 1991, 113). Authority lies not in the intrinsic properties of the discourse itself but "in the social conditions of production and reproduction of the distribution between the classes of knowledge and recognition of legitimate languages" (13). Through the collective act of misrecognition, where authority to make pronouncements on universal rights is conferred on judges, the couples are able to negotiate the limited opportunities available to them to have their choices in intimate relationships "legitimatized." In many ways, the promise of court validation encourages some courting couples to push the limits of established norms.

Although the modes through which the courtrooms produce authorized discourse are pertinent to this study, the idea of perceiving the protection petition process as misrecognition had left me vaguely unsettled. It could be interpreted as suggesting manipulation and, worse, ignorance. In one sense, I had also been trapped within the stagnating question of structure and agency that is reflected in much of feminist scholarship on the Indian state and its laws today, where "misrecognition" can also signify *negative agency*—a term discussed by Holly Wardlow as she traced transformations in marriage and kinship relations in Melanesia (2006, 72).

The instrumentalization of legal space and its provisions could be more productively analyzed as "tactics" (as defined by Certeau in a 1998 translation by Mayol) where couples seemed disposed to accept a subject position—a curious docility for actors who have otherwise deviated from social norms. Investing in law, I argue, helps individuals, especially women, navigate the legal process better, despite the evidence of its bias in favor of patriarchal and kinship structures. The idea of tactics provides a means to escape the potential conclusion of negative agency or lack of agency. It suggests instead a maximization of opportunities when it comes to what Bourdieu calls a "matrimonial game," which involves the deployment of practices sanctioned by the laws of the market (1977, 58).

The protection petitions are usually premised on the anticipation of physical threat, which is conjectural in most cases. Many judges demonstrate—by either subtle or explicit speech—that they are cognizant that couples sought legal validations of their weddings, which neither the petitions nor the court could provide. During proceedings where the legality of a marriage is disputed by parents or relatives, judges often state that a protection petition does not address that question. This performance of obligations—of verifying the claim of marriage before issuing an explicit disavowal of any powers to bless couples—is now an established judicial practice where the meaning of the practice is not stated in legally binding texts and has to be construed, at times in contrivance to the court order itself. The threat of physical harm is accepted in principle by judges and validity conferred through court procedures is assumed by the couples when the protection order is passed. In this regard, the observation of a new judge on one of his first days at court was illuminating. As he learned his way around this line of litigation, which was typical to the court in Chandigarh though not as popular elsewhere, he said, "The court only states protection of life and liberty. Age [of the litigants] underlines validity for the wedding." To reiterate an argument from chapter I, the judge had espoused the idea that the role of the state was to facilitate rather than regulate marriage.

The lawyers who mediate this process are acutely aware of the role they play in creating and sustaining these constructed meanings, which can be seen as legal fictions. As Bruno Latour explained, "Lawyers can indulge a power to invent fictions, and to introduce what they call 'constructive solutions'" (2004, 110). But he warns almost immediately that the "special prowess of adjudication turns into a cynical nightmare of arbitrariness" (110). As I discuss toward the end of this chapter, on an occasion when there was a clear and visible threat of physical harm inside the courtroom and granting the couple state protection was essential, the legal fiction fell apart, providing little or no protection. At the time, I wondered if a necessary requirement of this process is the smooth rite of passage through the courts, with the couples finally emerging as married through a process that began with the elopement.

The court spaces very often afforded the sight of eloping women who appeared in wedding finery after visiting salons specializing in "bridal makeup." Even when the brides did not make such efforts, they still wore *chuddas* or red bangles (see figure 14), which in this region signify that the wearer is a newly wedded bride. Women who belong to communities where this practice is not as common, such as non-Punjabi–speaking Haryanvis and Muslim women, also appeared in court wearing wedding markers. This suggests that the court experience was an integral part of the wedding itself, rather than an ancillary procedure undertaken to have the claim of marriage legitimated in hindsight. My interviews with lawyers and ethnographic observations of courtroom proceedings (held in English unless specified otherwise) reveal the complex negotiation underway in the courtrooms that helps couples bridge the gap between articulation, connotation, and interpretation.

To understand this bridge better I turn again to the idea of the game, this time in Stanley Cavell's terms, where the intentionality of the actors is of less significance than what is at play. According to Cavell, the consequences of one's actions are limited a priori by the rules of the game. Instead of prefacing the courtroom proceedings with a morality question in which, as Cavell warns us, intentionality signifies individual actors' responsibility (2002, 233–237), I examine protection petitions as a literary effort—they are, after all, legal fictions—at coproducing legal meaning in creative ways.

Inventors of Legal Fiction

Manpreet pushed back her office chair and leisurely began to answer my questions on the phenomenon of elopement. Periodically, she gestured for me to stop and listen in as the junior lawyer at her law firm spoke on the phone to a couple who had recently eloped, instructing them on sundry matters such as where to have a quick religious wedding ("Does your family have weddings at a temple or a *gurudwara*?"), the evidence they will need from the religious

FIGURE 14 Because photography is not permitted inside courts, news reports in many nations publish sketches to depict the scene and mood inside the space. This sketch captures the occupation of state and legal spaces by newly married brides.

Artwork: Ranjitha Ramachandran.

establishment ("They do certificates and you have phones to take photos, right?"), and when and where to appear in the high court the next day.

As the parallel conversation on an imminent wedding case progressed over an hour, Manpreet told me about her past experiences dealing with elopements. "I think one of my first cases of this kind dates back to 1994. I remember . . . they came to the small, rented accommodation we used to have at that time," she recalled. The history of the trend was linked in her mind to her own situation in life and how she and her family had prospered in the years of her legal practice. She no longer takes up petitions for protection because they are a "routine matter." Her juniors take over clients who are referred to her, "unless it is a bail plea for a boy accused of kidnapping and rape [after a failed attempt at elopement]. Young lawyers get muddled if the judges ask too many questions."[1]

Manpreet's vast experience in criminal law had provided her a range of examples that added nuance to her interview. She described one interesting case she had recently come across: "We had, on an earlier occasion, fought a bail plea for a boy who had eloped. [After the police officers had caught up with them] the girl was sent back from the police station to her parents because she was underaged and, subsequently, kidnapping and rape charges were filed. We got the accused out and when the girl turned eighteen, she eloped again . . . with the same boy." The charges were still active though it was unlikely they would be pursued now that the couple had secured a protection order with Manpreet's help.

I obtained a copy of this case's file from her office and leafed through the several contradictory testimonies that had previously been filed on the bride's behalf, along with the most recent affidavit that accompanied her protection petition (to preserve anonymity, no citations are provided).[2] While many of the documents—pertaining to both the abduction and rape charges in the first case and the protection petition—were standardized texts, together they formed a pattern. As legal fiction, they were representations of self that determined the relationship of the citizen to the state. Consequently, their terms depend not on life situation but on different lawyers' impressions of what will be legible to the state. While abduction and rape charges, which often involve vivid descriptions of being drugged with a caffeinated beverage, are a preferred weapon for parents who want to delegitimize a wedding, protection petitions have emerged as a recognized means for couples to validate a wedding. Some lawyers rued that even when they advise against it, couples seek to file a protection petition, typically when the bride has not reached the required legal age for marriage and sexual consent.

Manpreet disclosed that she even gets calls from parents who want "court marriages" for offspring who have chosen their future spouses. "I have to frequently tell my friends and acquaintances not to send their children here.

Yahan shaadi nahi hoti" (We don't have weddings here). Another lawyer, Harvinder, had similar experiences: "I tell people weddings don't happen here. Only protection. If they want to go through the Special Marriage Act, that is a different, longer procedure. But people are told that the high court has weddings, which is simply not true. We [she and her husband, who are partners] never take up protection cases. I once fought a case where the woman later turned out to be already married. Humesha jhanjhat waala case hota hai [These cases are always hassle-prone]. If someone is in real trouble, we get another lawyer to do the case for them."

These experienced lawyers highlight that there is a perception that eloping couples who visit the court get married there. Manpreet and Harvinder may try to disabuse couples of this notion, but it appears to have already taken hold of the communities in Haryana and Punjab. Manpreet's role in contributing to this constructed perception cannot be discounted.

In making use of the right to life and liberty in this negotiation, couples and their lawyers are not necessarily displaying an ignorance of the fine distinctions between constitutional, penal, and civil law. Instead, they are voicing their demand via a discourse and a legal provision that is efficient and expedient in getting results. The court order is not a completely favorable result, in that the claim of marriage is not explicitly endorsed. But couples read endorsement and court approval into the text, and they are joined in this by various participants in the courtroom and the community outside. The modes through which legal knowledge travels between court spaces, where judges and lawyers explicitly state that courts do not conduct or sanction weddings, and the community, which believes that they do, are arguably a form of juridification, a concept I discussed in the introduction.

Despite their significant numbers, both inside and outside court spaces, eloping couples are not united by their aspirations or their decision to visit the courts. If there is something that links the members of this disparate group, it is that they have all heard what Eckert and colleagues call a "rumor of a just court," one recognized as neutral (2012, 148). District courts are assumed to function within the matrix of local hierarchies and networks of patronage, according to even some of the lawyers practicing in these courts. In contrast, the high court of Punjab and Haryana in Chandigarh is popularly understood as a neutral and fair institution. Several petitioners claimed in their interviews that they were impressed with the high court, describing it as "neat" or "straightforward," with one groom observing, "Achcha hai yahan ka system" (They have a good system here).

I observed that the litigation process in courtrooms went more smoothly when there were no caste or community-based affinities between the judges and the petitioners. As one of my courtroom examples will show, a judge's familiarity with the social location of the petitioners, especially the bride's, can result in circumvention of the rule of law. But incidents such as these have not dissuaded couples from visiting the court.

As discussed in the introduction, Eckert and colleagues emphasize that subjects are well aware of their vulnerability when it comes to legal processes—of the ability of law to "make people illegal" (2012, 150). Then again, as this chapter will show, courtrooms proceedings may also end in subjects *becoming legal*. Marriage as a rite of passage bestows adulthood and rights, where one *is* not but *becomes* legal. In the next section, I describe the modes by which court procedures and conversations symbolize a wedding ritual and consequently lead to the perception that successful couples have had a "court marriage."

"What Can the Court Do for You?": Adjudicating Contentious Marriages

Justice Ranjit (the names of all judges have been changed) was one of the few judges who presided over cases of elopements in both 2012 and 2015, the two years I conducted ethnographic research at the high court. He often managed to unnerve eloping couples by asking them rhetorical questions about their thoughts on the customs and traditions they were ostensibly defying. While his broader perspectives remained fairly consistent over the three years, subtle shifts in his positions were discernible when I returned to the high court in 2015. He also occasionally advocated in favor of the couples though his opinions on elopements had not changed. On one occasion, I observed him admonish a lawyer who had been negligent in preparing the petition with the following words: "Sir, please take pity on these couples. They are in great trouble. . . . They are on the run." Justice Ranjit's evolution, which in some ways is a reflection of the high court's, is best captured in an interaction I observed between him, a couple, the bride's parents, and the parents' lawyer in 2015:

JUSTICE RANJIT [*in Hindi*]: You must accept this change. What can you do?

[*Parents sob in reply*]

JR [*continues in Hindi*]: Parents of both [bride and groom] are unfortunate. But that is not the case here.

MOTHER: The girl has been brought here by force.

JR: The girl is right here. You can ask her.

PARENTS [*together*]: Please let us talk to her.

JR: Sure, you can talk to her.

BRIDE: I don't want to return to my parents. I want to marry him.

JR: You can get married but at least talk to your parents.

BRIDE: No, I don't want to talk to them.

JR: How did you manage to hate them so much over night? Why is there so much poison [in your outlook]?

BRIDE: I don't want to talk to them.

JR [*to parents' lawyer, in English*]: I have asked her. She is not willing [to speak to her parents]. What more can the court do for you?

PARENTS [*simultaneously, in Hindi*]: First you bring them up. Then you educate them. Why should we kill [them]? Other people kill their own children but we are educated people.

JR [*also in Hindi*]: The court has utmost sympathy for you. The court understands your pain. I hope that she will realize her mistake after a month or so and return to you.

PARENTS: What is the point then? Tab toh waqt nikhal jayega [By then it would be too late].

Several interlinked themes emerge in this interaction. First, the judge directly asked the parents' lawyer what the court could do for them. Second, in consoling the parents about the inevitability of change, he spoke of the trend of elopements as something he himself had learned to accept, and also clearly articulated that their emotions were not relevant to the case. Finally, the bride insisted that she wanted to marry the man she had eloped with, in an inconsistent reply to the urge for dialogue with the parents, which she subsequently refused to do. She hinted, with her choice of words ("I want to marry him"), that the marriage act—in particular, a wedding ritual—had not taken place. Or, perhaps closer to the truth, that the wedding ritual was not yet complete.

The stories of eloping couples from the region highlight all these factors that are collapsed into one definitive episode in which the high court plays a central role, and these factors are often confused with each other. Rather than trying to disentangle them, this book attempts to illuminate the different stages of this process—elopement, quick religious wedding, high court appearance, and return to the community, The judge's question, "What can the court do for you?," guides my efforts to trace what I have come to regard as a "liminal phase" prompted by an act of elopement.

In a piece published posthumously (1986), Victor Turner cited the wedding as one of the moments of crises, a liminal phase from which an individual emerges as a different person. The 'crisis' represented by elopements is additionally a precarious one, as court cases such as the one described above highlight only too well. But, with certain exceptions (discussed in detail below), court cases represent an effort at remaking meaning. Building on Turner's work, I argue that by performing a prescribed and familiar text, couples who petition for protection of life and liberty forge new modes of experiencing a personhood that is not just bound by kinship affinities and networks of relatedness but also connected to subject positions in relation to the state.

Enforcing the Legal Order

High dramas in which the parents of the bride appear before the court to plead for dialogue or allege foul play on part of the groom need to be seen as part of this contestation between kinship norms and rule of the state, where the latter ultimately takes precedence. The number of these episodes significantly increased between 2012 and 2015.[3] Many such cases roughly followed the pattern I observed in Justice Ranjit's courtroom. On some occasions, when there were multiple sets of parents present in the same courtroom, the cases tended to subtly influence each other, as in the following example where two elopement cases came before Justice Kishore. In both cases, his courtroom conduct played a significant role in consolidating the weddings; in the end, those present in the courtroom were convinced that he had validated both couples without reservations. This courtroom drama began when parents of Bride no. 1 started the conversation by talking about their honor.

JUSTICE KISHORE: Is there any honor left now?

PARENTS' LAWYER: Please just ask her to meet the parents. She is twenty; they cannot do anything [to contest the wedding].

BRIDE NO. 1 [*in Hindi*]: I will meet them later.

JK [*also in Hindi*]: Why don't you meet them now? Here? You can sit down right here [*gestures to some seats on the right behind his elevated desk*].

[*A young man aggressively steps forward*]

JK: I cannot let random people meet her.

LAWYER: I have checked [that he is bona fide]. He is her brother.

Kishore asked the bride if she wanted to meet her brother, and she refused. He then ordered that only a parent would be allowed to speak to the young woman. As the mother approached the bench, he addressed her (in Hindi) in a gentler tone than he had used with the lawyer: "You have to talk to her calmly. Don't fight with her now." As Bride no. 1 spoke to her mother in a spot behind the judge that was, for me, imbued with state power and protection, a discomforting scene unfolded in front of him. Whereas the legal counsel and the parents in the first case had appeared relatively respectful, the second case started on an offensive note, which made the judge brusque in his replies as the bride's extended family gathered in front of him.

PARENTS' LAWYER: They got married at some place and got the certificate elsewhere. It is not a valid marriage, my lord.

JUSTICE KISHORE: We are not here to give a stamp of approval for the wedding. The question here is of protection.

LAWYER: It is not a valid marriage.

JK: Even if there is no marriage. . . . There is no need. They are both majors [legal adults].

The parents then tried to force a conversation by getting physically closer to the woman. When other family members started speaking to the judge simultaneously, he ordered all relatives other than the parents to leave the courtroom before addressing the parents.

JK: The girl has taken a step she should not have. What can be done?

FATHER OF THE BRIDE: Aap humare chehre dekho [Look at our faces—please judge us by our appearance].

JK [over the father, who repeats the preceding sentence]: This is not trial court, sir.

JK [in Hindi and English]: Chehra dekhen kaunsa [Which face should I examine]? Don't say "chehra" [face] again. Do minute me dikha doge aap toh [It won't take you more than two minutes to show me your real face].

In a veiled reference to the phenomenon of honor killings, the judge appeared to be debunking the popular notion that only uneducated or rustic families indulged in such acts. He asserted that he was not taken in by the parents' self-perception (as urban, educated, or civilized) and indeed, does not trust them.

Even as the judge admonished the family for their misconduct, the mother shoved the bride roughly. At this point, Kishore was furious.

JK: Dakhkhe se nahi mil sakte yahan [You cannot push your way around here to meet your daughter].

PARENTS' LAWYER: Just ten minutes, please.

JK: I cannot force her. She is not interested.

LAWYER: Only ten minutes.

JK: I will not let her speak [to the parents] for even ten seconds. And you are asking me for ten minutes.

[The family members desperately allege that she is under pressure to say she won't speak to them]

PARENTS [in Hindi]: Let her meet us for four to five minutes and then it's her wish.

JK: Humare haath bandhe hai [We are bound by our sense of duty].

JK [to parents' lawyer, in English]: Knowing full well that a conversation is not possible you are still asking for one. See this girl sitting here? [gestures to the *first bride, who seems to be having a cordial conversation with her mother*] I cannot force anyone.

After finally passing the protection order in this contentious case, Kishore turned his attention to the first case, which he had pointed to to underline how his decisions are fair and just.

JK [*to parents' lawyer*]: Are you satisfied?

LAWYER: Very much so.

JK: Both of you [i.e., the lawyers representing the couple and the parents] should open a mediation center. Talk to each other about it. See if some mediations are possible.

In addition to holding up his own conduct as an example, Kishore credited the lawyers for handling the case to the satisfaction of all parties involved. His utterances on the loss of parents' honor and elopement as "a step she should not have [taken]" appeared to support kinship norms, but he had successfully separated those norms from legal norms. Kishore, like Ranjit, had upheld "the rule of law" over popular views on elopement, including the assumed loss of honor. With less empathy than Ranjit had shown toward the parents, Kishore also responded strongly to the disorderliness that had crept into the court proceedings. The second family had little respect for courtroom protocol, but in the exercise of his authority Kishore took back control of the court.

The legal process, too, evolved according to the judge's notion of best practices rather than any pre-existing rules. There are no provisions for parents contesting the claim of marriage during this stage of litigation, but in general, the high court tolerates and even indulges this form of intrusion. Kishore followed this unofficial norm. He did not seem averse to the deployment of emotions that exceeded the contours of the case. He was concerned with the individuals and what the court could do for them, evolving mechanisms and rules that he thought were just and fair as he proceeded.

Elopement cases present one of the few instances in which courtroom protocol is actively subverted. The disorder in the second case was the result of the exercise of a male guardian's rights over his daughter, with the active participation of the women of the family. In calling into the question the validity of the wedding, the family in the second case sought to emphasize that their authority over the daughter was still valid, and as such, not a matter for the court to adjudicate. Political scientist Pratiksha Baxi has argued that elopement cases often reduce women to objects—bodies with disputed ownership claims (2006, 62). But Kishore's conduct indicates that he perceived the adult woman as a citizen and not a ward who had strayed from the control of her guardian. Kishore also questioned the need for legally tenable weddings and stated that an adult citizen is entitled to cohabit with a partner of her choice. In chastising the parents and their lawyer, refusing to allow contact between the estranged family members, and rejecting the implicit need for a wedding in such cases, he did not employ the discourse of human rights but did still respect and protect the woman as an independent, rights-bearing citizen. His conduct in and of the court had an inbuilt mechanism of validating the couple as adults who can make their own choices, even without what he called a "stamp of approval."

A State of Exception

Observing courtroom proceedings in two different years presented the opportunity to record slippages, or the exceptions that strengthen the general rule, as Giorgio Agamben would put it (2005). The importance of how the court is conducted, rather than what the law allows for in such disputes, was brought home to me in another case, overseen by Justice Hardeep. Whereas Justice Kishore had affirmed the life, citizenry, and rights of the eloping couple, Justice Hardeep's conduct highlighted the precarity of a couple when the court sided with an "injured patriarchy." The case, which involved a woman from a wealthy Jat Sikh family from Haryana's Rania district, presented a rare instance in which a clear and imminent danger was visible inside the courtroom. As the case proceedings stretched over the course of the morning, the courtroom became chaotic. Ironically, in this case the presiding judge was concerned not with the matter of protection but with the validity of the wedding itself, an issue from which most judges, including Hardeep himself on other occasions, distanced themselves.

The proceedings started with a discussion of the question that often dominates decisions regarding marriage alliances in Haryana, especially among Jat families: how much land the bride's family owns. While I heard and scribbled in my notes that the bride's family said they had seven acres, I later learned that other people in the court heard different, much higher numbers. The mention of the figure produced a dramatic change in the judge's body language and the manner of his interaction with the petitioners' legal counsel, Nakul.

JUSTICE HARDEEP: Think of yourself as the father or brother of this girl. Not as a lawyer. What will you do?

NAKUL: But she is a major [legal adult] . . .

JH: Don't talk of advocacy. I am asking you to place yourself in this situation.

Nakul stammered over his legal vocabulary; the personal attack had rattled him. As he confided later in an interview, the deeply personal question continued to sting him in the days that followed. As his confidence waned under the belligerent attitude of the judge, the Rania family members and villagers filed in, seemingly occupying the whole courtroom space. Their formation faintly resembled a human fortification. After the judge decided to place the case at the end of the urgent petitions cause list, Nakul began consulting with other lawyers; I spotted some protection petition veterans among his advisers.

A woman occupied the seat next to me at this point and started asking me questions about this case, explaining that she was a journalist. The man on my other side, who was in his forties and wearing a Punjab police uniform, answered her questions eagerly on my behalf. Besides displaying a strong affinity for a family with whom, I believe, he was not previously acquainted, he also gave an inaccurate account of what had happened in the courtroom so far. It is possible that he, like the lawyers, had invented a fiction to support the Rania family. Speaking across me, he told the journalist, in Hindi, "They have hundreds of acres of land. This boy works on their farms. Jiska namak khaya" (He has eaten their salt). This is a colloquial expression that means one must remain loyal to an employer at all costs, but there had been no references to the groom being an employee of the family. Rather, it betrayed the police officer's caste prejudice that all men from lower castes are employees of the big landlords of any village.

At this point, the women of the Rania family were trying to surround the bride while continuously speaking to her, and the young woman held on desperately to her partner. I saw this as an attempt at self-protection but the policeman viewed it as immodesty and was emboldened in airing his views. A heated exchange between the three of us ensued.

POLICEMAN: Ladki ko sharam nahi aayi. Aise logon ko chad dena chahiye [This girl has no shame. Such people should just be killed or bumped off].[4]

JOURNALIST: You are proposing that they should be killed just because they fell in love. That is not done.

POLICEMAN [*under his breath*]: Journalist! [*scoffs*]

RAMA: If they get the protection order you will be responsible for protecting the couple, not killing them.

POLICEMAN: Woh toh baad ki baat hai, pehle judge-saab shaadi ki manjoori toh den [We are not concerned with that aspect yet. First, judge-sir has to approve the wedding].

RAMA: But you are still required to protect their lives. That is the law.

POLICEMAN [*heatedly*]: Kanoon saare galat hai [All these laws are just wrong]. We are suffering on their account. Siyapa hai [They just mean trouble].

When the petition was taken up again, Nakul presented a copy of the 2006 landmark Supreme Court judgment *Lata Singh v. State of U.P.*, which obligates state institutions to protect eloping couples from potential honor crimes. Hardeep immediately declared that the protection order could not be denied, which he could have said at the outset but had chosen not to. I left the court premises not at all convinced that this will turn out okay. On my way out, I passed a huge group of people in the corridor who seemed to be fellow villagers from Rania (Nakul later confirmed this) and I was not convinced that a protection order would mean much in this situation. Although Hardeep had passed the protection order, his court conduct had not provided an approval for the couple to stay together. As the police officer had said, he did not have to worry about protecting the couple *until* the judge approved the couple's wedding. Without an implicit validation of the wedding, an explicit order for protection would probably mean little to the officer—and to the couple's families.

Clearly, the protection of their lives and liberty was not concern for the policeman, as he himself had advocated the couple's cold-blooded murder. We cannot be sure that his behavior would have been any different if the case had been handled by Justice Kishore instead, but the officer had attached significant meaning to judges' approvals of weddings. It is possible that if the judge had validated the wedding in terms the officer recognized, he may have grudgingly agreed to protect the couple while complaining that he suffered on account of "unjust laws," but unfortunately that did not happen. The legal fiction had fallen apart, leaving the couple horrifically exposed.

Nakul later confirmed my cynical assumption that the protection order passed in the Rania case did little to help the couple, despite his best efforts. He requested that Justice Hardeep order forces under court command to escort the couple to a protection home in Chandigarh, but his plea was rejected. He then desperately appealed to the chief justice, and again encountered resistance, but that initiative rattled Hardeep, who passed a second order after 5 P.M., granting Nakul's request. By that time the court's administrative offices were already closed, and Nakul could not procure a hard copy of the order. He dropped the couple off at the closest police station in the hope that they would be safe there, but realized much later that he shouldn't have trusted anyone. The couple was finally cornered by the Rania family at a busy bus station while still under police protection. The groom was injured badly, and Nakul had reason to believe the bride was beaten up by her uncle before being taken away. "The guy [the groom] came to see me after a few days and I suggested that we could file a habeas corpus case that would obligate the family to bring the woman to a courtroom. He went back to think it through but I was never hopeful."

This exception to the general rule that the Rania case represents supports my hypothesis that the court procedure is a wedding ritual in itself, or at least part of a larger ritual where a smooth passage through the courtroom is critical for the couple to emerge as wedded. Even in declaring that the validity of a marriage is not a concern of the court, the judges implicitly validate a couple's togetherness and approve their wish for cohabitation. Justice Hardeep did not at any point state that the validity of this marriage was not a concern of the court—because for him, it was.

One could argue that when a judge says that the validity of a marriage is not the concern of the court, it is thereby construed by those in the courtroom as meaning that the validity is not in question or is not being disputed in court. Other state agents, lawyers, and litigants perceive court authority as such and sometimes try to engage the judge on issues they would like the court to take into consideration. This is especially relevant in cases where family members of the petitioning couples have disputed weddings on grounds ranging from critical legal issues such as the petitioners' ages or bigamous unions to unimportant, technical details such as inaccuracies on wedding certificates. The role of the judge becomes contentious in such a situation, but one cannot assume that the judge's personal biases and views will necessarily have a bearing on the case in question. Ranjit, for instance, routinely sympathized with parents but he nevertheless validated the couples' rights.

There is always a possibility that a judge will disentangle protection and validity, as Justice Hardeep did, thus removing the implicitness of the process. The creativity of the adjudication process, according to Alexandre Lefebvre (2008, 116), keeps the suspense alive. The couple, their lawyers, the court staff, police officers, and petitioners from different cases participate in this theater of a kind. Turner, in his discussion on liminality of theatric play, argued that though the script of a play is a familiar one, the potential for slippage exists in every performance (1986). In my analysis of the drama, occupants of the courtroom double up as both performers of their own play and audience for other petitioners' performances, witnessing how these multiple, overlapping plays turn out. In elopement cases, the audience serves as witnesses who construe not just the judge's personal biases for or against the phenomenon of elopement but also whether, despite these biases, an approval of togetherness can be interpreted. Despite the familiarity of the script, every performance holds the potential for a slippage.

The witnessing of the wedding ceremony is a ritualistic requirement and an integral part of the process. This conception can and has traveled from kinship spaces to state institutions. In court marriages, the judge presides over the ritual of witnessing as a facilitator or even a priestlike figure, while the audience in the courtroom (lawyers, police officers, other litigants, and perhaps even belligerent parents) perform the act of social witnessing. The earlier religious ceremony is part of the process, but the courtroom ritual transforms the claim of a wedding into an established fact and hence lends itself to be interpreted as court marriage in other settings. Here the petition and the dialogue it generates are acts in the extended wedding ritual drama and the resultant court order finally transforms the couples' matrimonial status. In social spaces, court marriages assume an importance similar to a civil union conducted under the provisions of the unwieldy Special Marriage Act, discussed in chapter 1. While, in principle, eloping couples can opt to register a religious wedding, the practice of registration, even in cases of arranged marriages, is not prevalent in this region. A visit to the courts, preferably the high court, has become an essential component of elopements. The juridification of love marriages in the form of court marriages fills a vacuum in law to provide a viable form of civil marriage by making relationships based on choice legally tenable.

Routinization and Bureaucratic Paperwork

By 2015 there was a prevailing sense that the extraordinary—that is, nonnormative—trend of elopements had somehow become the norm. So routine and mundane were some of the proceedings that whereas in 2012 several cases were followed up in a month's time, in 2015 cases were usually "disposed of," to use courtroom parlance, on the day of the first hearing. Typically, cases came up for review when bigamy could be proven; when the parents of the bride file abduction and rape charges; or when a husband filed a writ of habeas corpus requesting that his wife, previously forced to return to her parents' home, be brought to the court. A high court order served to deter criminal complaints against and arrests of grooms, and in many cases protection orders were sought simply to prevent harassment from police officers or kin groups.

The time spent on protection cases had gradually fallen because the court procedure had been streamlined and standardized and the emphasis was mostly on lawyers' preparedness with regard to documents. Especially in cases where parents did not show up to dispute the wedding, it seemed that in this process of producing documentary evidence, "bureaucratic formalism" (Weber 2002) had taken over the task of mediating the relationship. Different judges focused on different aspects of the paperwork and sometimes the lawyers could not predict the requirements in advance. As a young lawyer, Neeti, told me, "You got to have your paperwork complete. Judges will make comments [on the phenomenon of elopements] but you don't have to listen. We are only concerned with protection." Retired judge NK noted that it was only the document with proof of age that he was ever concerned with. "Every adult [citizen] has the right to make a choice. If you are not an adult then you have no business making choices," he said.

In addition to the document with proof of age, several other documents were at times essential to the petition only by virtue of being required. For example, there were affidavits, testimonies of self that were created by lawyers for many of their petitioners from different regions and years. They were also a means by which the state will read you at a later stage, as Manpreet's example has underlined. Affidavits are notarized, and falsified testimonies could be regarded as perjury if, at a later date, their contents are proven to be false.

In my observations there was only one judge who consistently focused on the affidavit. Justice Anmol put particular emphasis on affidavits from the grooms, rather than the brides. On one occasion she admonished a lawyer for not including this document in the case file, while waving off the proof of age document (which retired judge NK had said was most important).

JA: Where is the boy's affidavit?

LAWYER: The birth certificate is appended, my lord.

JA: I am asking you about the affidavit and you are showing me the certificate. . . . Please come back with the boy's affidavit.

Her consistent approach in ensuring that the groom's testimony was recorded and filed diverged from that of most other judges, who focused on the bride's age and ascertained whether she had been coerced to elope. Anmol, by contrast, invariably asked the grooms whether their parents and families had approved the match. In one case, when she learned that the groom was soon leaving for Dubai, where he had secured a job, she went to great lengths in asking about his family and whether the bride's well-being would be ensured while he was away. After a lengthy Q&A, she told the couple's legal counsel that she would strongly prefer that the bride accompanied him to Dubai.

Anmol's approach could be seen as as an example of benevolent patriarchy, where the state agent acts as an extension of the patriarch and the kin groups. However, her efforts also shifted the focus away from whether individuals, especially women, have the right to make life choices to whether their well-being will be ensured in their new situations; that is, she placed the onus on society to vouchsafe that couples are unharmed and unhindered. Specifically, the change from focusing on the woman's story to concentrating on the man's was a significant leap for both the judge and the court, as she sought to hold the man accountable for his end of the patriarchal bargain. As a legally binding text, the man's affidavit is "his word" on the marriage that he is obliged to uphold. Anmol had taken attention away from the hypervisible spectacle of women deviating from social norms and redirected it toward mundane details about life after the wedding. In this imagined future life, Anmol mandated that the man in the relationship, who has privileges that patriarchy affords him, must use them to ensure a better life for both of them.

Justice Anmol did not question patriarchy or patriarchal norms, but in her own way she redirected focus from the validity of marriages, which couples were expected to prove to the conduciveness of societies. Drawing on Cavellian ideas discussed in the introduction, Anmol was preparing society for its next stage by making sure that the petitioning citizens had consented to the existing society (through their affidavits) and were ready for the next stage—living in the society they were transforming. Like Cavell, she believed that forging societies of consent requires consent within marriage—consent that required articulation, reiteration, and documentary evidence. She came closer to answering than to posing the critical question Justice Ranjit had asked in his exchange with the parents of a bride, *what can the court do for you?* Anmol's approach appeared to be aimed at producing sustainable marriages, tailored to societal conditions, by insisting on bureaucratic paperwork that removed embedded ambiguity.

For their part, lawyers invariably offered me copies of case files when I contacted them, often stating that the petition itself contained all the information needed. Most law firms and lawyers recycled the same petition form for all the elopement cases they handled and sometimes were negligent about changing personally identifiable information. But the case files also included documents specific to individual cases, such as marriage certificates from a religious authority, identity documents that contained the ages of the marrying individuals, and court orders. I was intrigued that some lawyers were incapable of discussing couples and individual cases without reaching for paperwork of various kinds. Even if these were standardized texts, they mediated the conversation on the lawsuit *after the fact.* That is, after they were filed as legal documents in the court, these pieces of invented fiction found their own authority in the eyes of judges such as Anmol as well as lawyers and petitioners.

The legal paper is essentially a public document, and its intrinsic value lies in its exchange and its ability to mediate conversations and relationships. As Strathern argues, the role played by the legal technique in fabricating persons and things rehearses issues that have long troubled anthropologists studying marriage arrangements (2004, 202). At the high court, I saw this process of fabrication reflected in the paper trail generated by protection petitions.

Conclusion

The juridification of marriages and the legal fiction of protection petitions reflect the ability to both "fabricate" (Strathern 2004) and "fragment" (Strathern 1991) oneself and exchange one's partible, potentially fictionalized components in public and state spaces. As Strathern theorizes in *Partial Connections* (1991), partible aspects of self facilitate the creation of hybrids and networks where persons are defined through shared notions of belonging, and, as discussed in previous chapters, this can be belonging to one's immediate society as well as to the state. Belonging to the state is structured primarily by the legibility of documents that not only mediate social relationships but also create them in the process of making eloping couples legible to the community.

When couples return from courts with the orders, they also leave copies of their identity papers and affidavits behind at the court premises and in lawyers' offices. They leave with the realization that their testimonies and identity documents—part of their personhood—have been recorded and archived in state spaces. Court marriage and the legal fiction of protection petitions allow them to conceive themselves as newly minted subjects whose life choices have ostensibly received legal validation. The court visit, hence, has multiple functions—it completes the wedding ritual, institutes a court marriage, and validates couples as bona fide citizens who have successfully negotiated a state space and received legal approval to make life decisions. Bureaucratic procedures and paperwork at the high court provide a means to forge new forms of exchange, facilitating the creation of a different "set of hybrids" and networks within courts and elsewhere. Such hybrids are essential for the "fissured ethnoscapes" (Appadurai 1996) of a region where material relations as well as the aspirations of its citizens are rapidly transforming.

6

Consenting Adults and the State

Social Change through Conformity

The last chapter, on courtroom drama and legal fictions, revealed how the high court has remained a space to sustain legal procedures that do not strictly adhere to notions of "correct understanding of law" (Geertz 1983, 187). Ethical and moral concerns including adherence to the feminist movement, broadly defined, and imputation of individual intentionality obscure the fact that the courtroom drama is a game of sorts, and in Cavell's terms, actions are limited a priori by the rules of the game (2002). If Pratiksha Baxi's recent book *Public Secrets of Law: Rape Trials in India* (2014) is any indication, the courtroom game on cases of sexual violence is already set up for the complainant to fail. Ground-breaking legislations such as the 2013 Criminal Law (Amendment Act), discussed in the introduction, can function only within certain limitations and, while procedural moves undertaken to circumvent these limitations might not strictly align with either the letter of law or feminist efforts, they often invoke the spirit of law.

This chapter builds on my ethnographic work to approach the issue of consent through an angle different from that afforded by cases of sexual assault—through its exercise. First I discuss the law on age of consent and how it is interpreted in elopement cases. Next, I juxtapose my data alongside the discourses on rape and sexual assaults. Weaving into this discussion examples of philosophical works on the concept of consent, specifically with respect to the social contract that is discussed in the introduction, I show how cases of love marriages showcase the existence of organic modes of understanding, exercising and respecting the ideal of sexual consent in North India. The chapter closes with the story of Jaspreet and the challenges of incorporating notions of love, choice, and consent into one overarching narrative.

Age of Consent in Elopement Cases

In some ways, notions of sexual consent in India have been constantly mediated through a conversation on law. In May 2012 the Indian parliament passed the Protection of Children from Sexual Offences Act, which raised the age of consent from sixteen to eighteen years, ostensibly to curtail teenage sexual activity. This law was not debated at length or opposed; by contrast, when laws governing the age of consent were first introduced by the colonial British government they were resisted by independence movement leaders such as Tilak. According to their detractors, such laws intruded on the private sphere and threatened the fabric of the family because the institution of marriage itself was being altered by the law (Bannerji 1998; Tambe 2009).

As Gayle Rubin has noted in the context of age of consent laws and their enforcement in United States, legal texts can never completely cover the diversity in sexual behavior and relationships. Laws seek to make blurred boundaries tangible but are unable to make sense of diverse sexual practices. Rubin argues that laws and their enforcement gain potency only when they become objects of social concern and political uproar (1984, 289). By conceptualizing laws as a source of discourses, as she proposes, one can attempt to track the conversations laws and adjudication processes make possible, if only about the demarcations on sexual practices laws create.

When comparing my data from 2012 (May–August) and 2015 (January–August), the consequences of the 2012 act are not easily discernible. In 2012, proof of age had been an important criterion (as it had been in the years preceding my research, according to lawyers and a retired judge), and judges differed about which document was a more credible proof of age. On two occasions that I observed, judges ordered bone ossification tests to satisfy themselves of brides' ages, and either denied protection until the age could be "conclusively proved" or ordered only provisional protection, pending age verification.

Judges, hence, routinely conflated the requisite age of consent (which was sixteen before May 2012) with the requisite age for marriage (which was eighteen). Families and police officers, for their part, have filed and continue to file rape and/or abduction charges against grooms, though Indian women used to have the right to exercise sexual consent before they turned eighteen. There is a qualified distinction to be made between choice or consent as it pertains to marriage and sexual consent irrespective of marital status. As retired judge NK stressed in an interview with me, "Every adult has a right to make choices regarding his or her life. If you are not an adult, you have no business making choices."

In the case of Saima, a sixteen-year-old woman from the Meo Muslim community whose case hearings I attended in 2012, age was an intractable issue that was resolved only with time and not through legal arguments.[1] Her twenty-eight-year-old Hindu husband, Ajay, was arrested and jailed on charges of abduction and (statutory) rape after my interview with him on court premises, and Saima was placed in a government-run shelter home for women. According to his account of their relationship, Ajay had been reluctant to begin the affair due to Saima's age, but her reports of extreme ill treatment at the hands of her family members generated sympathy that "eventually led to love," he conceded. Yet he still was not ready for elopement and marriage, and according to him, she had coerced him into it with the threat of suicide. Saima was only fifteen when she got married and became pregnant.

Saima's case perfectly encapsulates Rubin's argument on the diversity of sexual practices that age of consent laws cannot adequately address. Witnessing this case unfold in the courtroom, I was conflicted on the question of whether Saima was capable of consenting to this relationship/marriage and whether her parents' legal rights on guardianship should be recognized. When I observed her interactions with family members during courtroom proceedings and in the corridors of the high court complex, it seemed that her fate would be bleaker if she were forced to return to her parents' home. Although Saima appeared to be vulnerable, she was not exactly without agential motivations. She had, if one is to believe the husband, blackmailed the latter into elopement and marriage; faked her own identity documents to file a protection petition in the Delhi High Court; and fearlessly expressed herself in the courtroom and elsewhere on the court premises. In my courtroom observations, Saima was both resourceful and assertive. For example, when she was bullied by her parents' lawyer in the corridors of the court complex in front of other litigants and lawyers, she yelled back at him, "Have I committed any crime by falling in love?"

Saima wore her emotions on her sleeve as she contested (and succeeded in overturning) a court order that would have forced her to return to her parents' home. She declared inside the courtroom (when the court was not in session but was still sparsely occupied) that "only my dead body" would be taken from the court premises, and she had to be held down by the police officers tasked with protecting her. Her statements and actions pushed her lawyer to meet the judge, Justice Kavitha (names of all the judges observed have been changed), in private to request a change in the order. According to the second order, she was ordered to the women's shelter. When discussing Saima's case with me, her lawyer reflected on the extent to which age of consent laws could be enforced when it was apparent that the litigant "knew very well what she wanted." The young litigant never wavered on whether she was in a position to consent to the relationship, and she appeared to be eminently capable of representing herself and her interests inside the legal space.

A resolution to Saima's case eventually came around through a complete nonengagement with the messy details of sexual consent. Her lawyer informed me in 2014 that a different judge, Justice Roshni, "had straightforwardly quashed the FIR [First Information Report regarding the kidnapping and rape] because Saima was pregnant." The couple were finally reunited, but not by the judge who had deliberated on the validity of Saima's marriage and of a court order of protection based on fake documents. In my observations, Justice Kavitha was usually positive and patronizing in her dealings with eloping couples (on two occasions, she good-humoredly advised the petitioners not to come back with a divorce plea), whereas Justice Roshni made apparent her distaste for other protection cases on several occasions (on one instance, she commented that the lawyer was too senior to handle "such cases"). And yet, the respectability conferred by childbearing and family life gave Saima and Ajay a resolution in Roshni's court and not in Kavitha's. It is worth revisiting my argument from chapter 5 regarding the consolidation of cases over time; most contested cases reached a resolution due to a lapse of time. Roshni's role was simply to provide much-needed closure. In Saima's case, although sexual consent remained a thorny issue, she had transformed herself into a citizen via her successful representation of her self and her self's interest, achieving a sort of legal emancipation in which she made her life choices count.

In 2015 I observed a case involving a young woman, Noor, again from the Meo Muslim community, which forms an interesting contrast to Saima's case.[2] Noor's age was never conclusively established, but there was general consensus in the courtroom that she had not reached the legal age for consent or marriage. Her partner's age, too, could not be determined in the absence of identification documents, but Justice Keshav, who presided over this case, brushed aside this issue, stating that he was "not concerned about the boy." Noor's parents did not participate in the conversation about her age; instead, they claimed that she was already married and therefore her second wedding was invalid. Consistent with the general position among judges in 2015, Keshav reiterated that age was pertinent only for establishing the validity of marriage, which a protection petition is not concerned with. In a curious choice of words, he said, "We are not at the point of legalizing marriage." I whimsically wondered if the court would ever be at the point of legalizing marriage in protection cases; he seemed to hold out this hope with his perhaps carelessly chosen words.

The argument put forward by the couples' lawyer in this case was provocative in that he sought to problematize the tendency of perceiving elopement cases only in terms of the age of consent law. He said, "They [the parents' lawyers] are concerned about her [legal] minority now, but she has been married before. If it is about marriage and age, then everybody will be on the dock."[3] After a series of arguments had been made, Keshav concluded that bigamy was not his concern either, stating that the first husband (who was not present in the court) could lodge a complaint if he wished. But Keshav remained ambivalent on the question of age. The lawyer's argument about the unfairness of using age as a deciding factor seemed to make an impression but had not completely

convinced the judge. He ordered a public prosecutor to have a private conversation with the woman, and, when he took up the case again later in the day, the
prosecutor stated that the woman preferred to stay with her current partner
and did not wish to return to her parents. In her "legal opinion," the prosecutor
said, an ossification test was warranted. Keshav decided not to order the medical test.

His slow and careful deliberation on the question on age confirmed which
issues were pertinent from the standpoint of the court; bigamy and the validity
of the current marriage were not among them. For him, age was a criterion not
for determining the right to choose a spouse but for establishing sexual consent. His approach revealed that the state cannot and must not stop being concerned about the question of consent, even if the legal guardians of the woman
had failed on that count. If required, the state is empowered and legally obliged
to take over as the guardian. But Keshav's statement on the bigamy allegation
nevertheless served to communicate that the grounds on which the parents
disputed the union were of no interest to him. In many ways, delegitimizing the
claims made by the parents allowed for the eventual return of the woman with
her chosen partner. The judge's long deliberation demonstrated that the state
itself, through its agent (Keshav), takes seriously its responsibilities to its
citizens—especially legal minors. He did not pass a judgment in this case but he
did take every aspect of it into account. He did, we might say, participate in a
conversation on consent.

Perhaps it is pertinent to also mention here that grooms like Noor's partner, who in all likelihood was short of the marriageable age of twenty-one years
set for men, often evoked amusement or disinterest but did not influence the
protection petition decision. In three cases I witnessed, the petition described
the groom's parents as threats while the bride's parents were said to support the
match. The age of the groom was not disputed in any of these cases.

On the whole, passing orders on elopement cases had become far more
streamlined and less contentious in 2015, even in cases where the legal age of
the bride was in dispute. Kishore, Anmol, and other judges passed protection
orders claiming that "even a minor was entitled to protection." As discussed in
chapter 5, the validity of weddings was not debated, and at times being younger
than eighteen did not result in separation from one's partner. On an occasion
when he was dealing with a seventeen-year-old petitioner, Justice Kishore gently
asked the woman, "Were you in any special hurry? You could have waited till
you turned eighteen." But he still passed the order without reservations. Justice
Anmol tersely cut off a lawyer representing the parents of a bride who was two
months short of the requisite age, snapping, "You want to create trouble for two
months now?" No ossification tests were ordered in my presence in 2015.

Unlike Noor and her partner, most litigants and their parents come armed
with documents to prove the petitioners' ages. Where the claims of the two

contesting sides were hopelessly at odds, judges were forced to pronounce their verdict on which document was better evidence. Justice Pratyusha, for example, pronounced that a "school certificate" produced by the parents was more reliable than the Aadhaar card presented by the bride, much to my surprise.[4] The idea that "even a minor was entitled to protection" had, by and large, overtaken concerns raised by the new age of consent law or the laws regulating marital ages.

The 2012 law was aimed at regulating teenage sexual activity outside the institution of marriage, but most protection cases involved cases where at least a claim of marriage has been made. According to lawyer Neeti, this may even be the reason for the high number of elopements. After a frustrating experience in Justice Keshav's courtroom in which the bride decided to return with her parents, Neeti observed, "The problem is that since childhood people have been told that physical relations are connected to marriage. If we can just delink physical relations from marriage these things [elopements] would not happen. Tell me something: do you think this is love? It is only physical attraction. Once the act is done, they lose interest. Aql aa jaati hai" (They have a reality check).

In the case Neeti was referring to, the bride made a statement on her nominal religious wedding that puts the entire conversation on consent into perspective: "Galti se marriage karli. Apni marzi se ki thi" (My marriage was a mistake but it was solemnized as per my wishes/choice). As she expressed her frustration with the case, Neeti told me that she had wanted the woman to take responsibility for her actions. But the litigant's words in the court suggest that she was indeed taking responsibility. A critical aspect of exercising consent as an adult citizen is to accept that some of your decisions may not be in your own best interest. This is especially the case in a society where there are severe constraints on exploring one's sexuality. In the subsequent sections I theorize sexual consent in the context of legally valid, consensual marriages.

The Conversation on Consensual Relationships

Taking John Rawls's *A Theory of Justice* as a point of departure, Stanley Cavell theorizes consent as the self's voice that lends recognition to a society. According to him, the idea of consent denotes a request "to make my society mine, one in which I am spoken for, where my voice may be raised in assessing the present state of society against a further or next state of society" (1990, 27). For Cavell, abiding by the law is a critical feature of this conversation of justice. Freedom, for him, is obeying the law "we give ourselves" (28). Criticizing one's society means criticizing oneself, because a compromised state of society signifies a compromised self.

Cavell brings the idea of consent in dialogue with the Emersonian idea of the "unattained but attainable self"—the self as a work in progress, one could say. Seeking moral perfection in a given society signifies the extension of the original consent that helped found the society in the first place. An invitation to one's next self and, consequently, the next state of society, reaffirms the consent to the current society and the one which will follow. It is important to note that Cavell does not discuss extensions to the next state of self or society through teleological modes but rather in dialectical terms.

Cavell extends the concept of the "conversation of justice" and the individual's consent to a given society to the institution of marriage in several of his works. According to him, the pursuit of happiness within the institution of marriage in the face of unaccounted misery elsewhere is an expression of consent to the society. This is especially true for people who are disadvantaged and cannot take care of themselves in an unequal society—their relative disadvantage distorts their participation in the dialogue on justice elsewhere. The eloping couples in my case studies, especially those from rural areas or from different castes, fit into this category surprisingly well.

There is a perception in Haryana and Chandigarh, even among interlocutors in progressive circles, that love marriages should somehow represent a positive development in society. Some feminist lawyers specifically insist that marriages based on the idea of mutual choice still continue on patriarchal lines, where the existing sexual division of labor is perpetuated. The search for more equal partnership through an invocation of the concept of care (discussed in chapter 3) signifies only a negligible or insignificant form of dissent for some interlocutors from progressive circles. Some "progressive" male interlocutors, especially those from older generations, have cautiously lent support to "love marriage" on the grounds that it represents a challenge to the caste system as well as the practice of dowry demands.

In principle, all these viewpoints are reasonable cautions for the project I have undertaken, but the implied (and at times, subconscious) expectation that eloping couples represent a higher cause in spite of their relative social and cultural disadvantage—that is, the point from which these couples enter the proverbial "conversation of justice"—seems overly ambitious. Furthermore, following Cavellian tropes, we can argue that by their willingness to work toward an as-yet unimagined future and an as-yet unattained self, the interlocutors quoted in this book have already contributed to the advancement of the society of consent without any professed claims on agency.

Cavell intriguingly calls the current self and its momentary perfection "conformity" in parenthesis (31), and embracing matrimony signifies for him a rejection of this conforming perfection. A recognition of the other in a relationship such as marriage signifies a readiness for the next state of self and, by extension, the next state of society. Within this relationship, articulation of mutual happiness becomes a point of conversation. John Milton's "meet and happy conversation," the end goal of marriage, represents for Cavell an extension of the "conversation of justice" and, consequently, the idea of consent in a given society itself. An unhappy marriage, where conversation has failed, represents a failure of the society as a whole.

Elopements and love marriages can arguably be seen as promoting nonconformity—not just in social terms but also in the way Cavell defines matrimony itself. Love marriages clearly register a rejection of the current, attained self—disadvantaged, in many instances. But for some men, giving up the privileges of patriarchy by deciding to elope and by investing in relationships of care represents a willingness to attain a different ideal of perfection. Both men and women who seek relationships that their current society does not support appear to be prepared for another state of society. That is, eloping couples consent to the given society through the mediation they seek from the court in their quest for a new, different society—in which their decision to marry a partner of their own choice will receive more support and approval. These couples' efforts signify a reinforcement of the social contract where they acknowledge their obligations to the state but also petition the state to provide them with a better contract than the one currently in place. That contract, presumably, would not limit sexuality to relationships deemed respectable by families and kin groups or curtail it through vehicles such as the age of consent law.

Cavell's discussion of marriage builds on an argument that runs through several of his writings that analyze the idea of remarriage (as represented in Hollywood comedies and melodrama) as an opportunity to re-examine marriage beyond what lies outside of it—church or state—and recognize the interiority of the relationship that cuts the couple off, for a temporary period, from the rest of the world. According to him, the trope of "get together again, back together" after a threatened or actual divorce initiates a state of conversation, often under the pretext of comedy, where finally agreeing to have the conversation constitutes marriage as an institution. Cavell stresses that in this sense, all genuine marriages are remarriages.

The dramatic episodes I observed in the courtroom reiterate this argument in intriguing ways. As I argued in chapter 5, the courtroom proceedings signify a wedding ritual with a state agent as presiding authority. The religious ceremony previously held is important only so far as it results in a certificate that can be filed as part of the paperwork required for the court case. Once the couple has passed through the court spaces, "court marriage" becomes the preferred term for describing the relationship. Instead of comparing the relative importance of the religious and courtroom rituals (as in chapter 5), we could analyze them as marriage and remarriage, where the second ritual, the courtroom one, signifies a conversation on consent that reconfigures the terms of the relationship. Through courtroom dialogue sometimes marked by melodrama, the second marriage of the eloping couples is consolidated and, in turn, extends the limits of the society of consent.

Contrary to popular perception, in my ethnographic analysis, love marriage does not function as a replacement for arranged marriage. Love marriage forcefully introduces the topic of consent into the larger conversation on marriage in India today. It promotes consent as an ideal that very few would actively argue against, even in Haryana. Even caste elders I spoke to in Fatehabad and Hisar were in favor of consent in arranged marriages, despite its problematic association with love marriage.[5] What the conversation on love marriages does, then, is problematize the norm of arranged marriages, especially through the difficulty of forging consensual relationships in them.

For couples like Navjot and Baljeet, arranged marriages signify bondage, which for them automatically represents unhappiness in marriage. Societies of consent, Cavell would also argue, cannot in good faith hold with unhappy marriages.[6] Ravinder and Kavita had an arranged marriage but they worked hard on creating the "meet and happy conversation" before the wedding date. Roop entered a marriage without her consent, but since then has forged a semblance of a happy conversation.

The increased dialogue on consent in Haryana and much of North India takes place against a backdrop of sexual crimes and honor killings reported in the news. Although justifications of rape appear in social media with more frequency than when I was in the field, these are not always universally espoused. Criticism of sexual crimes as in the "Nirbhaya" case in Delhi and cases in Haryana runs parallel to the criticism of love marriages. Simultaneously, creating a space for a conversation on consent within arranged marriages is seen as an ideal, though as yet unattained but attainable goal for society. This is where the theorizing of sexual consent, through its articulation, reconnects with previous discussions (by Baxi and others) that are prompted by cases of lack of consent— that is, rape cases.

Cavell asks us to understand sexual consent in correlation with the consent required by the social contract, where sexual consent depends on the social consent for its definition and the latter needs to encompass the former to eventually extend the justice project. This notion is most explicit in Cavell's discussion of a text by Heinrich von Kleist, *The Marquise of O*, in a lecture subtitled "Rawls and the Drama of Consent" (1990, 101–126). Cavell takes up Kleist's text to show how conversation on consent assumes a form of redemption where the protagonist, over time, forgives her former rapist and the two finally forge a relationship based on consent. Cavell argues that consent in this relationship is understood solely through its prior absence. Extending this provocative idea, we could argue that it is plausible that men and patriarchal societies learn to identify sexual consent by coming to terms with its nonexistence and having a conversation about it.

In Kleist's text, the conversation of justice is extended through its negotiation in marriage where the male protagonist redeems himself for his prior moral failings and acknowledges the importance of sexual consent in forging the happy conversation that is marriage. It signifies a willingness to give up an older, morally compromised self and aspire to be better and work for a (future) society where sexual consent is reaffirmed as a foundational aspect of marriage.

For people of Haryana and North India, the conversation on sexual consent is integral to the extension of the social contract and the conversation of justice. And this conversation continues to take place in elopement cases despite repeated assaults on citizens' rights and liberties elsewhere. The conversation in courtrooms that elopement cases initiate signifies a similar form of redemption for the society; indeed, the efforts of the eloping couples represent an advancement for every consenting adult in the society.

Ayesha, a battered woman who had escaped her alcoholic and abusive husband and entered the household of married man, summarizes the drama of consent in just two short sentences she repeated over the course of a long interview I conducted with her and her second husband: "Raazi hoon. Bahut kush hoon" (I consent to this. I am very happy). When Ayesha's family members—who had not offered her any help during the years of her abuse—started threatening Ayesha and her partner, Qasim, he approached the police. He claims that police officers chased him out of the station, telling him to either arrange for Ayesha's divorce or marry her.[7] Qasim was not sure how he could manage this (as she needed a divorce in order to marry him) and, in the end, he listened to the advice of an acquaintance who recommended filing a protection petition at the high court in Chandigarh. When I asked how he had resolved the problem of divorce and remarriage, their lawyer interrupted to claim that her alcoholic and vagabond husband could not be expected to participate in the legal process, but in the courtroom he had stated that some maulvis (men with religious authority in Islam) had heard the husband's divorce (talaq) testimony.

Ayesha smiled broadly throughout this entire discussion, appearing eager to interact with me. But her sole contribution to the conversation—and perhaps one of the most critical contributions to my entire ethnographic study—was her repetition of those two well-chosen sentences. Her use of an Urdu/Hindustani word, raazi, which translates as "consent," when most women prefer the word marzi (choice), underlines some key themes of this chapter. In some ways, as far as she was concerned, the only thing that mattered or was worth stressing was that she consents to this relationship and that she is very happy. For Cavell, Ayesha's continued entrapment in an unhappy and abusive relationship would represent a failure for any society of consent because the social contract requires that consent be extended to the institution of marriage.

Ayesha's ability to leave the relationship and find a legitimate and safe way to be in another one represents an extension of consent for the society in Cavellian terms. That is, her decision and ability to get away (without a legal divorce) and "get back together" (without a legal marriage) with another man by means of the protection petition represents that quest for the (as yet) unattained self and, consequently, the next state of society. Although her second marriage could not be termed legal, it was, I would argue, *legally tenable*. In a sense, this was the crux of the "drama of consent" that was played out through the protection petition story.

Ayesha and Qasim could fail in their endeavors (for all the interviews conducted in courtroom complex represent are hopes and plans for future), but their willingness to try to change the society that upholds staying in unhappy marriages as the norm over quitting them is a testimony to the consent they have given to the current society, their own place within it, and an attempt to transform it. The couple extended the conversation of justice by having the "marriage conversation" in the legal space, in what is literally a remarriage for Ayesha and a second marriage for Qasim. The high court may not have given them either the legal divorce or the legal marriage the police officers had demanded, but it did give them an opportunity to have the remarriage conversation and be heard.

The Melancholy of Love and Life

The conversation of justice in Haryana is still at a nascent stage. Some gambles end in hopeful trysts with the future. Others, as in the Rania case, are failures for the couple as well as society and its future, because consent both within and outside the marriage institution was delegitimized. Nakul's lesson from the Rania case is reminiscent of Socrates's experience with his own prosecution— "His quarrel was not with the laws but with the judges," as Hannah Arendt wrote in "Civil Disobedience" (1972, 59). According to Nakul, protection petitions where the threat of physical harm was minimal were more likely to succeed than cases where there was real danger. Drawing on his experiences with dowry harassment cases, he claimed that the "maximum number" of cases he handles were based on false claims. In the Indian litigation system, he had come to believe, cases (including dowry harassment cases) that genuinely required legal intervention fell through the cracks, while cases that manipulated the laws had a better chance at succeeding.

After endless reviews of his interview transcript, I began to get a sense that in separating the laws from the legal procedures they influence, Nakul was not merely highlighting the nihilism that had creeped into his practice and outlook. Instead, he was inviting me to analyze how law and legal procedures institute particular relations of power between people and the state and state agents. Laws can function as guides in the adjudication of cases that deal with the question of sexual consent but can never completely regulate and govern individuals' diverse sexual practices.

This is demonstrated particularly in cases that involve underage women in love. Jaspreet, a Sikh man in his early twenties originally from Fatehabad, has the same name as his former girlfriend, and a part of it (*preet*) translates as "love."[8] When I commented on this coincidence, he told me with melancholic irony that when he was being beaten up in a police station he overheard an officer say, "They both go by the name *Preet*. No wonder they fell in love." Jaspreet's girlfriend testified against him in the lower court, which led to his conviction on charges of abduction. She was seventeen and a half when they eloped, but Jaspreet maintains that "usko sab samajh thi" (she was a mature and knowledgeable woman). According to him, she was smarter than him on many counts and had arranged money for the elopement. He alleges that she coerced him to elope with her, despite the risks involved. Due to her age they had ruled out a "court marriage," and it was "all her idea" to travel to the Golden Temple, the Sikh religious site in Amritsar, Punjab, to get married.

When I asked him, as gently as I could, why he had gone along with her plans, he admitted that it was *paagalpan* (madness), before adding that for him the relationship represented "true love." He knew that she hated her family and was desperate to leave; elopement and marriage were a means of escape for her. Jaspreet himself had always wanted to have a "love marriage," or rather he had always wanted to fall in love. Despite his bitterness at her "betrayal" in the courtroom, Jaspreet believes that when they were together she felt the same way he did. He is still not sure what went wrong and why she "lied" in the court ("She knows why," he added cryptically). But after hearing her testimony, his love died. He said it did not affect him unduly when, after he was granted bail by the high court, he learned of her family-arranged wedding.

Jaspreet did not believe that his former girlfriend's age determined his guilt because she had seemed mature and a lot more knowledgeable than he was. Moreover, she hated her family and hoped to get away from it. The case files I secured from Jaspreet's high court advocate also trouble the question of establishing guilt beyond a reasonable doubt. In her first statement to the superintendent of police of their home district and to the magistrate's court, the young woman stated in clear terms that she had eloped with Jaspreet without having been coerced and that she still wanted to be with him. It was only after she was forced by police officers to return to her parents that her statements changed. The text of the district court judgment that convicted him itself spent considerable time discussing whether the woman had been coerced before arriving at the conclusion that it appeared that she had acted out of free will.[9] The conviction rested on the judge's determination that the guardianship of a legal minor does not end even if she leaves the guardian's care of her own free will. Thus, the judgment seemed to blame the woman for the turn of events even if she could not legally be held responsible. The conviction follows certain classic tropes in elopement cases (Chowdhry 2004; Baxi 2006) where women are condemned for the exercise of consent but the punishment is meted out to the man for not honoring the ownership rights of another man—the father, in this instance.

Yet, the district court judgment still engages holistically in a discussion of whether the woman exercised consent in the relationship and the decision to elope before it concludes that the legal guardian's rights over the ward do not end even if she rejects them. The judge did not deny the existence of consent or even state explicitly that a legal minor is not capable of exercising it; he merely sidestepped the issue when pronouncing the verdict.

Jaspreet declared in a sweeping statement that people in Haryana don't make a distinction between cases of elopement and rape. He has to come to believe that as many as fifty of every one hundred rape cases must be cases of love marriages "gone wrong." When he was held in the Hisar district prison he learned a lot more about the phenomenon of elopements, including the high court interventions ("I have learned enough if I ever need to elope again," he joked). At least twenty to twenty-five men lodged in the prison with him on abduction and rape charges were, he said, like him, "naajaayas phasse ladke" (boys who were unfairly locked up). Here, Jaspreet drew a nuanced and conclusive distinction between men like him and men who were imprisoned on rape and gang-rape charges. When a woman wanted to be with a man out of choice (apni marzi se) and because of true love (sacha pyaar), that was different from when they were abducted "on their way to school or elsewhere." "Woh toh galat hai na, madam?" (Wouldn't that be wrong?), he asked me rhetorically.

While discussing the issue of sexual consent in relationships and in sexual assault cases, Jaspreet did not mention marriage at all. Instead, he was speaking of sex without any defensive invocation of the respectability afforded to it by the institution of marriage. Although Jaspreet had been accused and convicted of abduction only—not rape, as many men "like him" were—he directly addressed the question of sexual consent in his conversation with me. In a leap reminiscent of Cavell's argument about the Marquise, Jaspreet understood the concept of sexual consent through the evidence of its nonexistence around him in Haryana. Through his legal struggles and incarceration, he had learned to distinguish between "men like him," who respected the idea of consent, choice, and love in intimate relationships, and men who denied women the same. Despite his heartbreak and humiliation, he held these three as ideal virtues that empower people to achieve something in life, a theme I will expand on in the next chapter. These may have seemed unattainable in his own life but they are still, according to him, worthy goals for people to have.

Conclusion

Building on my ethnographic research, I have described here the contours of this moral and legal prescript (i.e., sexual consent), its historical roots in liberal philosophy, and the potential role it can play in creating a more gender-just society in India. What my ethnographic examples conclusively suggest is that law and legal cases are and will probably continue to be an important avenue for the conversation on affirmative consent. While depending on the liberal roots of the concept and paternalistic collaborators might be a conservative move, as Janet Halley has argued (see discussion in the introduction), appealing to the rule of law may often be the only (though not guaranteed) avenue for those who lack the social capital to access rights, especially sexual rights.

My argument for the state's continuing role in adjudicating on consent despite evidence of its patriarchal biases (which are benevolent at best and regressive at worst) is based on the evidence from North India, where the Punjab and Haryana High Court plays a central role in validating choice in marriage but the discourses also suggest more engagement with universal notions on individual liberty. Entering into a contract with the state by consenting to the trial indicates both a willingness to assume docile subjectivity and a mobilizing of the state to expand one's limited options in marriage. The couples acknowledge the state and the rule of law as much as the state validates them as (adult) citizens and, thus, as a married couple, though the latter is only implied. The state nevertheless provides an important avenue for articulating the exercise of consent as part of a proverbial conversation on marriage, and it catalogues it on behalf of individuals who do not themselves have the social capital required to claim their rights as adult citizens.

In conclusion, while sexual relationships are culturally specific, certain ethical considerations may have universal or transnational signification. In protection cases, a resonant "yes" (often) means "yes," though litigants must always have the right to withdraw their consent to relationships at any point. Relatedly, a progressive judgment on individual liberty with regard to marital rape still eludes Indian law and society. A shared moral framework on "no means no" that encompasses marital and nonmarital relationships is vital for the justice project, but perhaps someday an acknowledgement of "yes means yes" both within and outside marriage may become shared and commonplace as well. An understanding of "yes means yes" and its articulation as it pertains to both love and court marriages could centrally inform and strengthen the #MeToo movement. The next chapter will deal with the contours of this shared moral framework, where consent and choice in marriage shapes and extends better, more livable lives for both women and men.

PART THREE

The Politics of Love, Marriage, and a Livable Future

7

Toward an Alternative Future

Eloping Couples, Citizenry, and Social Mobility

Our society cannot survive without the laws. Law is what is keeping us alive."
A retired police officer, originally from the Fatehabad district of Haryana and
now a resident of Chandigarh, made this unequivocal statement. The officer
was neither for or against elopements and he did not assert the primacy of kinship or tradition when he expressed his skepticism regarding elopements and
choice-based marriages. But he was explicit and affirmative when it came to
protection petitions and court interventions. According to him, there was no
conflict between legal and social norms; the terms of 'our lives' are set by the
Indian Constitution and no other normative order. Without the Constitution,
he claimed, "brothers would not remain brothers, parents and their offspring
would not stay together." Fascinated, I probed further, urging him to clarify his
position. "I have seen all sorts of people walk through police stations. When
it comes to property disputes, sisters would disown brothers and parents would
disown their own children." Our well-defined laws are what keep the society
from collapsing, and the Constitution holds everyone together, he further
asserted.

His work had taken him to almost every district of the state, and he had
seen the same story repeat itself in most places he was deputed for duty. The
suggestion that perhaps kinship ties were themselves dependent on the Constitution and laws that hold state institutions and legal processes together was an
unpopular view not only in community settings but also in scholarly circles.
Indian scholarship on the state has long subscribed to the idea of legal pluralism, where state and customary laws coexist in an uneasy harmony. The Indian
understanding of legal pluralism, unlike the Western interpretation, is concerned not so much with group rights, especially as they pertain to ethnic
minorities, but to living with and under multiple normative orders (Mahajan
2002; Bhargava 2011). My ethnographic evidence from the community as well as

FIGURE 15 View from the Punjab and Haryana High Court.
Photo: Janaki Srinivasan.

courtrooms reveal what Sally Merry described as the modes through which
"social groups conceive of ordering, of social relationships, and of ways of determining truth and justice" (1988, 889).

   According to the officer, in situations of conflict, the order of the state will
take supremacy over the kinship order, which provides an explanation of sorts
for how a protection petition creates an opportunity to forge marital unions
seemingly sanctioned by the state. As chapter 5 discussed, the juridification of
love marriages is a collective exercise of meaning making, a largely dialogical
process where marriage is conceived and legitimized through performative acts
that depend on multiple orders. In this chapter, I trace the life of the eloping
couple beyond the margins of the state and ascertain whether the citizen and the
society are indeed defined and regulated by law, as the police officer claimed.
How do the everyday lives of couples with love marriages transform social
norms and help a society facing an uncertain future cope with new realities?

Reordering Norms

Despite Geertz's early warning, discussed in chapters 1 and 6, customs continue
to be portrayed as a matter of habit and a cultural group is inevitably defined as
one with shared norms and values. For this reason, in legal pluralism literature
there is a persistent struggle centered on conflicts surrounding sexuality and

gender issues. Conflicts on sexuality are presented as empirical examples of the negotiations undertaken as part of multiple, overlapping normative orders, and not infrequently, theorization on issues ranging from legal arbitrariness and discretionary regimes are undertaken without an adequate feminist focus.[1] As I have previously argued, in Indian scholarship state law is not perceived as necessarily impinging on group rights. Empirical research has instead shown that the judiciary often acts as an extension of patriarchy, reinforcing kinship norms and the rule of the patriarch in the process. But as the last two chapters have highlighted, the judiciary plays a more complex and often contradictory role while adjudicating on a wide range of issues, and the consequences of judicial processes have to be parsed out beyond ideological dispositions. For this reason, the field of legal anthropology can benefit from phenomenological anthropology.

The experiences of people such as the police officer who do not support elopements but respect legal processes and state sanctions present a fascinating duality. We could call it a dividual personhood on the lines of Melanesian anthropology, where a person is defined not only by family and kinship relations but also through bonds forged with the state. This may indeed be as much a case of a false binary between custom versus law as it is about another misplaced distinction between person versus subject, where the former is defined by her goals and intentions and the latter by rule-following and obligations. As chapter 3 highlighted, the state is intertwined with aspirations for the future as well as memories of the recent past, and, as such, it is not extraneous to the experiences of a citizen.

As legal scholar Elena Loizidou argues, the notion that the legal/rational and the ethical/prereflexive subject are distinguishable is premised on shaky grounds. In her contention, our performance (as either or both) in legal spaces and/or with regard to perceived legalities can be better understood as negotiations toward achieving better and livable lives (2007). Haryanvis, who oppose the idea of love marriage but accept specific instances of it after court mediation, clearly register these enduring struggles.

NK, a retired judge who held an advisory position with the Haryana government when I interviewed him, offered a complementary view from the standpoint of the courts. According to him, passing judgments is a very small part of a judge's career. As a judge he had mostly listened to petitioners in distress to see how laws could be used to alleviate their lives. He was moved not only by his obligation to interpret laws faithfully but also to reflect on what people sought from the courts and how laws can help them to have better, more livable lives. At times, this may involve doing very little. According to Professor Anil Thakur, there is a strong tendency among North Indians to "bring facts to the knowledge of the state." Sometimes petitioners did not appeal for resolutions but rather sought to "inform the courts" of facts pertaining to their lives—possibly to ensure that they were still leading legitimate lives. According to Tim Murphy, legal recognition acts as an incision; a legal decision makes other decisions effective or creates possibility for further decisions (2004, 123–124). In this case, law is not just law, Murphy argues; rather, it "enable[s] decisions to intervene in the world" (124). According to him, decisions happen not just because of the letter of the law, as defined by jurists, but also due to a range of ancillary technologies that are constitutive of law (124). Personhood, gender, and family are legal categories that have organized thought and society, even if they evade the grasp of law (138).

Law in the context of my research is similarly not just a set of statutes that belong to the state but also the decisions that citizens make and the legal recognition citizens are afforded. Law belongs to social groups but it is also, I argue, constitutive of personhood. Given the ethnographic evidence and theoretical discussion from the previous chapters, we might reasonably ask whether state and/or court processes lead to a more gender-just world, given their implicit patriarchal biases. What the voices in my study highlight is that there need not be a cohesive social agreement on love marriages or elopements as long as legal recognition allows individuals to make decisions on and forge choice-based, livable marriages. Through a phenomenological approach, one can argue that law can provide opportunities to reimagine lives because law is already a constitutive element of self.

Here, the debate on law versus custom is not resolved, but the contestation on gender and sexuality issues does not persist as an unresolvable dilemma. Law and custom are both integral aspects of self, whose focus is on securing a livable life; for the retired Haryana police officer this involves upholding the law and the Constitution, even as an ethical subject. For some, such as the Punjab police officer quoted in chapter 5, kinship clearly superseded the law in that one instance, but he was nominally ready to re-evaluate his position if a judge were to approve the marriages. By and large, people in the community were less conflicted about the division. Kin networks are important for everyday life, but the law ensures survival through resolutions, closures, and new beginnings. Laws, in short, allow for perpetuation, especially after a rupture.

Gurmeet, a lower-caste man who belongs to the Sikh faith, realized this when his son expressed his desire to have a love marriage with Payal, quoted in chapter 2. Gurmeet sought a written statement from Payal and her mother that they were not being coerced to accept the match, and then had the statement notarized at the local court. Given the precedence of men being criminally prosecuted after eloping with women who later accused them of abduction or coercion, Gurmeet had strongly felt the need to take this precaution. He also stated that he strongly believed that all unions should be "legal marriages." "A legal marriage comes with responsibility. It mandates that people, especially men, take the bond seriously," he said. His beliefs aligned with those of Payal, who espoused faith in the courts' ability to make marriage *achcha* (right or good).

Gurmeet had reiterated what many judges at the high court had emphasized while adjudicating on elopement cases. Legal/court marriages ensure security, especially for women, as well as protection of the couple. The legitimacy or validity of the union is derived through an acknowledgement of these ideas. Benevolent or patriarchal as these impulses may be, choice-based marriages are validated and seen as validated through tropes represented in the Special Marriage Bill debates. Court-facilitated marriages (and divorces) are considered respectable and durable but they also require individuals to assume responsibility for their decisions. The following sections highlight how ideas of a future together are influenced by a couple's aspirations, which are connected to and yet divergent from kinship norms. As members of a civil society, their aspirations are closer to being realized after court adjudication.

Eloping Couples and Aspirations for Freedom, Legitimacy, and Upward Mobility

When I met Sonia in June 2012 she was planning to head back home armed with a protection order. She hoped that the court order would keep at bay her entire extended family, who had threatened to kill her and her partner. She declared that she wanted nothing to do with her parents in the future. But a month later, she was back at the court to withdraw her petition for protection as there was no longer any real threat. She was even in touch with her parents by this time. "They talk to me on the phone. My mom even came to meet me," she told me with some relief.

In 2015 I did not meet many couples back in court for a second hearing because most judges had "disposed off" the protection orders in the first hearing. But hopefulness for the future was a recurrent theme. Reshma and Ashish, for example, did not have encouraging life prospects. Ashish had dropped out of school after grade eight and worked as a construction painter, while Reshma had just completed grade ten. They had decided to visit the high court despite having meager resources because they had been warned by a lawyer from their home district, Fatehabad, that the district court's order would not be taken seriously by Reshma's family.

When I asked her if they had any specific plans for the future, Reshma replied with modest pride that she had passed her grade ten exams with good scores and her mother-in-law had promised that she would be supported in her efforts to acquire higher education. She expanded on this, saying, "I want to find a small job and then show my parents that I was not just wasting my time with this man. I will achieve something in life. Phir unhe bataungi ki jis ladke ko aap galat samajh rahe the ussi ne mujhe iss layak banaya hai" (And then I will tell my parents that the guy they distrusted was the one responsible for my success). On the possibility of meeting her parents in the future, she replied firmly that they would have to take the initiative to meet her and also accept the marriage. Her parents had promised to allow her to marry the man of her choice initially and then searched for a suitable groom on the sly. This still hurt her, but it was apparent that her dreams were not limited to making a marriage of her own choice; she had sought a marriage that would enable her achieve career goals that her parents may not have expected of her.

To be clear, I am only outlining people's expectations and hopes for their future after elopement. These hopes have not yet been realized, but they indicate disenchantment with the families these couples decided to break away from. Several eloping women spoke of being disappointed with their own parents who secretly looked for suitable matches after learning about their daughters' courtships. A woman who claimed that she filed a protection petition despite having received no threats (verbal or otherwise), clarified: "I told my parents about my partner myself and explained that I wanted to marry him but they started looking for another groom. *That* was the threat."

Other women and men were also often frank that their protection petitions were not in response to any direct threats. Their decisions to elope represented a desire for an orderly resolution to the problem of disapproving parents. Tanya, whose husband's family was against the relationship because she was a widow, and Kanika, a nurse from Central India whose parents disapproved of her Haryanvi partner, had similar views. Kanika said, "Anyone in their [parents'] place would get a little angry but they will come around eventually," but added that she wanted some distance between herself and her family. She preferred her husband's family and felt at home with them. About the future, she said, "I have a master's degree in nursing so I can get a position anywhere I want. My husband works in the television industry so he has to find a job in Delhi or Chandigarh. But I think we will be fine." When I asked Tanya if her in-laws would accept her match she replied, "We came to the high court because you can get a proof of marriage from here. We think they will accept it now. They will *have to* accept it" (emphasis added).

The sentiment that a court intervention would lead to (or rather would have to lead to) social acceptance was pervasive among couples. Qasim laid it out in explicit terms. As outlined in chapter 6, Qasim had been forced to elope and marry Ayesha, a battered woman he had taken into his household. Because Ayesha's family members—who had not offered her any help during the years of her abuse—had started harassing the couple, applying for protection was one of the few options available to them.

After receiving the court order, Qasim declared confidently, "Ab samaaj saath dega. Dena Padega" (Now the society will support us. It will have to). He added that the couple planned to stay for fifteen days at the district protection home for eloping couples, where he expected the family members to drop in and talk, eventually moving toward a resolution. He disclosed that his first wife and children were *raazi* (i.e., they had consented). Ayesha did not speak much during this conversation and was unsure when I asked her whether she would see her own children again. But she smiled broadly throughout the interview and repeated two sentences over and over again: "Raazi hoon. Bahut kush hoon" (I consent to this. I am very happy).

Ayesha's repetition as well as her use of an Urdu word that means consent exemplified some key themes discussed in the last chapter. Like other women quoted here, Ayesha had also left behind relationships, including an abusive marriage and indifferent parents who upheld the norm of sticking with an unhappy marriage rather than quitting it. Dislodging the centrality of the family—and particularly for young adult women, parental control—is one of the major shifts seen as part of the trend of court marriages. Adulthood and citizenship are realized here through a recognition from state agencies. This process may allow women to break the vicious cycle of guardianship between fathers and husbands and be seen as rights-bearing citizens in their own right.

Young women such as Reshma found that conversations with their families and parents could no longer proceed because of deceit or violence. As lawyer Neeti observed in her wide-ranging experience with protection cases, the women who are in more oppressive situations are the ones who are likely to elope. "A lot depends on the first reaction of the parents when they learn about the boyfriend," she explained. "If they are calm it could happen that the women lose interest in the courtship in due course. But if parents decide to crack the whip, women will definitely try and elope."

Neeti was not particularly convinced of the durability of these relationships. In two cases that involved acquaintances who had asked her to file protection petitions, she stayed in touch with them and learned that one had returned to her parents' home and the other often complained of disagreements with her mother-in-law. She wondered aloud why her acquaintances were not aware that love marriages will replicate problems witnessed in arranged marriages. In her cynical view, these elopements are about sex and the unfortunate consequence of attempting to keep sex within the confines of wedlock. While this view may well be an oversimplification of the situation, it does point to the realization among young women that at eighteeen they can legally consent to a sexual relationship; this is a universal right that they do not wish to be denied. Symbolically overthrowing the yoke of paternal guardianship by getting married and petitioning the high court might result in a renegotiation of the relationship with one's own family, creating a less hierarchical structure or even a clean break from the past. In contrast, arranged marriages in Haryana that I studied as part of this research did not offer an opportunity to challenge the hierarchy. The rule of the patriarch (benevolent or apathetic) is firmly lodged in this family structure, although the perks of conforming to norms have at times outweighed the longings for freedom in people like Ravinder and Kavita.

The high court holds the potential to initiate conversations with parents and communities afresh. This hope is underlined by the repeated refrain that a high court order forces communities or parents to accept matches and eventually opens dialogue. The high court order acts as leverage, working to the couple's advantage. After the court order, the couples learn to hope that they will be heard in the society as they were heard in the courtroom.

For many couples whose relationships lasted, their lives never seemed to normalize. Even when family ties had not been severed, isolation by family or community was widespread. Given the risk men faced of losing vital privileges that patriarchy ensures (diminished but not absent in the case of men from lower castes), when they did decide to deviate from the norm, they set themselves up for a challenging life. A couple based in Hisar city, Manoj and Asha, a Dalit man and Jat woman, respectively, were cognizant that their life goals differed considerably from most of their peers and acquaintances. Asha explained, "You see, we both have teaching jobs in government schools. Everyone wants government jobs but we are not satisfied with ours. We care about the work we do and whether it interests us."

Asha was just seventeen years old when she decided to elope with Manoj more than ten years ago. On the advice of a lawyer practicing at a district court, she falsely alleged that the man she had eloped with was planning to abandon her, a claim the groom refuted in court. Their lawyer had assured them that Manoj's statement of responsibility was enough to shore up their tenuous marriage.[2] Looking back at their courtship and elopement, Asha jokingly teased her husband for preying on a young child. She had certainly gained a different perspective on her decision as she completed her higher education and had been exposed to progressive circles, aspects of her life that she attributed to her husband's support. She also mourned the continuing estrangement from her natal family, while Manoj described his own parents' cold indifference toward them (despite being their neighbors). Life for them has not normalized after more than ten years of marriage, but while they hope to make peace with their past, the couple was unwilling to give up on their aspirations for a fulfilling life. Achieving the social benchmarks of marital and professional success that had proved the detractors of their union wrong was not a worthy enough goal in itself. Their nonconformity and the unusual life they led had broadened their horizons.

Baljeet and Navjot came to the question of life after the event (a love marriage) from different angles but underlined that there is no denying that both the marriage and everyday life itself requires more effort. Navjot and Baljeet visited the high court to file a protection petition in 2007 and remember it as a quick and hassle-free procedure. They left early in the morning and returned before anyone noticed their absence. Navjot returned to her parents' place, hoping to keep their secret for a little longer, but as Baljeet sardonically notes, surveillance in rural areas is "faster than 3G data connection." After spending a month holed up in an expensive rented accommodation in Sirsa city, they travelled back to Baljeet's village in the company of police officers. The police sternly warned his belligerent family against doing them any harm, physical or otherwise, because the couple possessed an order from the high court. When his mother informed the officers that she would rather die than accept the match, Baljeet recounted with his caustic sense of humor that they just told her to go right ahead. Everyday struggles, aside from the question of protection, began later.

According to Baljeet, in rural areas a love marriage marks you out. Every village has only a few such marriages—his was the first one in his own village—and the gossip networks train their eyes on those couples and quickly point out cracks in the relationship. Arranged marriages fall apart too, but they do not evoke as much interest because most marriages are arranged by families. Navjot contends that one has to work harder not only at making love marriages a success but also at having people perceive it as one. "If you have defied social norms you have to prove that you were right," she explains. Both theories highlight the social function their marriage serves—the collective will is to see such couples fail and it is the couple's enormous social responsibility to make it work despite outside pressures. Baljeet claimed in his interview that they never had disagreements, contrary to the popular belief that such couples squabble a lot, and Navjot backed this claim. But she also emphasized the effort, the emotional labor, that had gone into keeping things that way.

The conflicts in their lives had come from outside the marriage. Baljeet's locally dominant Bishnoi caste had not taken kindly to his elopement and marriage. His brothers were intent on evicting him from the family home and preventing him from inheriting ancestral landholdings. For Baljeet, who always knew there would be "some trouble," this still came as a bitter lesson. For Navjot, experiences such as building their own house after their eviction from Baljeet's ancestral home and farming the land herself while he was busy setting up his business enterprise signified for her a success that she believed had eluded the brothers' families.

Baljeet is today the only one of four brothers to have an income independent of agriculture; he owns a successful shop in the neighboring city and a small car that he says is not fancy but serves its purpose. He did not get a "truckload of dowry" or any family support during his years of struggle, but looking back at their personal and financial travails, he quipped, "Apne aap se kuch karna ho toh love marriage achi cheez hai. Par sabko paki pakayi khaani hai" (If you want to make something of yourself, love marriage can be a good thing. But everyone prefers precooked meals).

Jaspreet appears to hold a complementary idea that love can "make a man stand on his feet." When one has a love marriage, he says, family attitudes and the nature of one's relationships change. One can no longer depend on family and take life for granted. Jaspreet was pursuing a life of hard work and adventure, with plans to migrate to Dubai for work. Love had seemed to him a means to escape family comfort and the cushion it had provided him. Though his bid for freedom from patriarchal privilege had ended in bitter disappointment and he had had to lean heavily on his family to extricate himself from the crisis, Jaspreet still believed in the power of love to make people self-reliant. It was just not an option for him anymore. He looked forward to having a family-arranged marriage and being able to travel to Dubai one day. "When you fall down in life like I have, some things can just not be the same again. There is no place lower than the one I have been in," he explained.

In a region where most parents today encourage their male offspring to leave behind agriculture and the villages and "make something of themselves," Baljeet and Jaspreet seem to claim that love marriage can give you the sufficient impetus to do exactly that. Not everyone gets the opportunity to make something of themselves, as Jaspreet realized through his bitter disappointment. Ashok, a Haryanvi Jat bureaucrat who had married a Jat Sikh woman from Punjab after much family opposition, astutely observed that stories like his own are rare. He claimed that people who have achieved social and economic successes are careful not to lose their positions, especially if they have worked hard for them. "I notice that those who elope and visit courts are the most abject set. People without much education, daily wage laborers, etc. Once you have achieved something in life, the tendency is to conform to norms," he said, explaining the risks of deviating when one has already achieved normative standards of success. People with bleak future prospects who do not have much privilege or opportunity in the existing society find in love marriage the means to negotiate and make the transition to the as yet uncertain, postagrarian society—what Appadurai would call a navigational capacity.

These negotiations can often hold radical potential. In the district court of Gurugram, I met a lawyer who provided a notarized document to a lesbian couple from Meerut, Uttar Pradesh. After the couple's high-profile visit to the court, the parents of the women accepted their union and took them back home, acknowledging the notarization as adequate endorsement of the wedding. The affidavit, notarized or otherwise, is only a testimony of self and as such does not constitute marriage. Because same-sex marriage is not valid in India, the couple's relationship will remain legally ambiguous, but the bureaucratic paperwork made the approval of their kin groups possible, and the significance of this development cannot be underestimated. What the future holds for this lesbian couple's relationship within their community is unknown, but it is still an exceptional case. I perceive district courts as an important indicator of paradigm shifts that are already underway or recently concluded.

Whereas other state spaces for seeking redress are still deeply hierarchical, according to many informants in Haryana, district courts are at least ostensibly accessible to the public and have a mandate to "hear them out." For certain types of relationships, district courts that are open to hearing out individuals within the legal ambit provide a viable framework for the relationships to survive or be dissolved. These sites are interfaces with state institutions for people who sought alternative life arrangements that are frowned upon but permitted to exist. District courts usually do not support any paradigm-changing decisions or choices such as marriage equality but rather facilitate closures and inauguration of new chapters as an impersonal third party.

Such courts have especially become an enabling site for citizens when kin and family groups have walled them off. For example, Nisha, who had sought a divorce from an aging, alcoholic husband she had been wedded to as a child, found the experience at the local family court frustratingly long but otherwise trouble-free. Unlike her immediate social circle and natal family, who had denounced her for "abandoning" an ailing husband (who eventually died of alcoholism), the court was approachable and willing to help her. I also learned from interviews that customary methods of divorce and remarriage in the region such as *chhoot mel* (separation-union) were giving way to "tidy" court-facilitated closures, sometimes followed by regular weddings. Traditionally, not all wedding rituals were included in the ceremony for a second marriage, but in some cases legal divorces had led to a transformation. When I asked a woman in her mid-thirties why chhoot mel did not constitute a full wedding, she replied obliquely, "In a real wedding, the groom's party brings home the bride in broad daylight [after dawn], but as part of a chhoot mel, they bring the bride home at night, surreptitiously. You tell me, which one is more respectable?" As legal divorces become common, second marriages have become more respectable, with complete wedding rituals.

Jagdeep, a man in his forties, sought court approval for his wedding with a trafficked bride from Bihar, claiming that it was a case of elopement and that they required protection. His young wife, approximately twenty years old at the time of our meeting, admitted to lying in the district court that she had eloped with Jagdeep. "What was I supposed to do? Where would I go from here? I was cheated into coming here but I have nowhere else to go," she said with a hint of defiance, after explaining that her cousin had brought her to the region by deceit. The trafficking of women from poorer states such as Bihar, Jharkhand, Madhya Pradesh, and more recently, northeastern states, was widespread in many districts of Haryana, where the male-to-female sex ratios are dangerously skewed. These marriages are grudgingly allowed to exist. Minor ridicule and social disapproval aside, most Haryanvis accept that "importing" brides is a better idea than forcing men to remain celibate. One octogenarian Bishnoi woman refused to accept any trafficked brides or love marriages with brides from other castes for her own grandsons, but her staunch position was not shared even by her own sons and daughters-in-law.

Although an elopement of a couple from different castes (or even from the same caste) may be rejected after a district court order is procured, the validity of Jagdeep's marriage had been strengthened by court intervention. He eagerly showed me his documents, sheepishly recounted his deception, and encouraged me to speak to his wife. Though he had paid money to secure himself a bride, he believed that his marriage was both respectable and regular. Minor issues were smoothed out with the help of the court document. His young bride resented her cousin who had sold her more than the man whom she now considered her husband. The resources available in Haryana were certainly better than what she had known at home, she said, and her husband had come across as more humane than her own kin.

District courts were also frequented by families of couples seeking divorces, with long lists of dowry items—attested by the groom's family at the time of wedding—that needed to be returned at the court premises in the presence of lawyers. A young acquaintance-interlocutor informed me of her intention to reconcile with her estranged husband in the district court where she had filed cases of dowry harassment and domestic violence against him. She planned to withdraw these cases if he apologized to her in the presence of a judge and "took her home" from the court premises, but her plan had failed. For several rural Haryanvis I interviewed, there was something reassuring about these district court mediations—perhaps their presumed finality.

The courts gave certain forms of guarantees for relationships to survive (or dissolve) through the act of bringing them under the legal framework, the same way a civil union law does. The magical state offered a mystical route to achieve a desired life situation. Some of these life choices were not extraordinary, but even minor social deviations made the parties involved vulnerable in the face of rigid social conservatism. Law was not just law but rather a road map to the future and a means to navigate social and individual aspirations.

Pathways to the Future: Constitutional Validity to Existence and Survival

In their aspiration for legal validity, eloping couples do not come across as rebellious, and, I would argue, they are rarely agential. In the courtroom space, they appear as rule followers and law-abiding citizens, perhaps even conformists, since they seek a respectable marriage. In their own communities the couples are still seen as outliers, but the approval of the high court transforms

FIGURE 16 A sentimental car owner expresses the views "Love by Chance, Friends by Choice" and "One Life—One Chance." Not every courting couple seeks to fall in love, but many hope to find partners who can forge sharing, caring friendships.

Photo: Rama Srinivasan.

their position nevertheless. Love marriages and elopements may not appear to be decisions that signify agency, given the couples' eagerness to follow the rules in court and their tendency to fall back on social norms regarding the sexual division of labor. Yet, they still send out powerful messages about the state of the society. The pledge to be seen as married signifies a lack of social capital and agency (see figure 16), for the sexual liberation of young people in rural North India requires the respectability that the institution of marriage can afford them for survival and togetherness.

In prioritizing the normative order of the law over kinship order, couples signal that they are placing kinship lower in the hierarchy of institutions, and they have the audacity—kin representatives might say—to return and dwell in shared spaces. Outwardly, kinship structures maintain the semblance of a whole, but the memory of the rupture haunts some and is repulsively fascinating to others. Couples appear rebellious or nonnormative within social and kinship structures because of this collective memory of rupture. At times, this has resulted in honor killings, though sensational news reports of honor killings appeared more frequently in national media in the first decade of the twenty-first century than in the second. Yet, studies have suggested a sharp increase in honor killings in 2015, with Uttar Pradesh recording the highest number and Haryana a close second.[3] In states such as Tamil Nadu, where caste conflicts are as common as in Uttar Pradesh and Haryana, honor killings are occasionally reported.

Given the frequency of these crimes, I asked the police officer quoted at the beginning of this chapter whether the understanding of the Indian Constitution is uniform throughout the country. He replied in the affirmative before explaining that in his professional experience, even those who engage in unlawful activities—committing heinous crimes such as rape and murder—know they are "violating the law." According to him, laws are a moral code shared by society; even people who profess a lack of faith in laws know that their actions are illegal and subsequently without moral standing.

The interview was conducted in 2015 but by 2018, when I wrote this chapter, legal proceedings on some high profile cases of rape and murder (including the rapes of children and lynching incidents involving Muslim and Dalit men) had become more contentious and difficult to pursue. Simultaneously, a call to review the Constitution is under way elsewhere in the public sphere. If the police officer beliefs hold, these events indicate both an invocation of a future where shared moral frameworks will come unraveled but also a defiant assertion that this future is already here. In this period of contention between two competing worldviews, the Constitution offers a framework for mediating conflicts within communities, a framework that is not based on people's personally held views on elopements and crimes such as rape and murder. It dictates that the rule of law and not opinions determine the fates of people. Even when crimes go unpunished, there is a shared moral framework and the rule of law that holds society together. Recent political events validate the officer's prediction that the society and communities might collapse without laws and a law-abiding citizenry. This contest for the nation-state's future is essentially between two competing worldviews, where the rational and the ethical sides are not easily distinguishable.

For women, laws often offer the only protection, albeit not a strong one, because kin groups routinely ignore crimes against women, or even accuse women of provoking those crimes. A future where crimes against women will no longer be perceived as such and the Constitution can no longer uphold individual rights is indeed a bleak one. Hadiya's case provides a dramatic example to follow in rewriting this narrative, one that affirms that the constitutional framework can withstand severe attacks. In a joint interview conducted in Malayalam, Hadiya and Shafin Jahan offered a refreshing and radical perspective to challenge the tired binary of individual liberty versus collective rights, where law must curtail the onslaught of collective sentiments against an individual's rights.[4] Hadiya repeatedly emphasized her status as an adult and what she perceived as an unpardonable curtailment of her individual rights. The arguments against conversion and marriage were for her a form of disenfranchisement. While the Kerala High Court upheld her choice to convert to Islam, they had clamped down on her decision to marry a Muslim man. The rule of the patriarch extended to the state only so far as to reiterate its control over women's sexuality and to prevent mixed marriages. The decision to convert had troubled the state agent, but it did not invite the same backlash that the decision to marry did. In this instance, the courts had adjudicated in divergent ways on two issues that pertained to patriarchal authority.

In the same interview, Hadiya's husband Shafin was asked why he had not chosen a partner from a more traditional background, and he replied that he was a man of independent thinking and that his legal struggles were not only his own. He saw them as something he needed to do for the collective—for the imagined community of Indians, we might say, following Benedict Anderson (2006). For Shafin, upholding constitutional values as a version of group or collective rights was critical for the survival of both his own marriage and the nation-state. Together, Hadiya and Shafin fought and won a battle for both individual liberty and collective rights. Here, the Constitution had helped to forge an alternate community and protected individual freedom. In this framework, the state does not supersede community or kinship order, but merely upholds constitutional values as an example of shared moral values of an imagined community, a normative order that holds the individual and the collective together.

In 2018, there was still a shared framework on fundamental rights that the Constitution upholds. Hadiya's case stretched the limits of this framework, but the Supreme Court's judgment on the case not only highlighted the endurance of constitutional norms, it also upheld the right to choose one's spouse. Hadiya's case makes it easier for intracommunity couples who will likely face less political pressure.

When asked about her relationship with her father, Hadiya claimed that he had been misled by political groups but asserted that he still has great affection for her. That affection did not blind her to the psychological torture she had endured when she was incarcerated at her parents' home. In my case studies, consent-based marriages often required women (and occasionally the men) to make a choice between family and spouse, which is unsurprising, given the requirement to legally separate from one's family under the Special Marriage Act.

When the court orders a bride to return home with her parents, even for a short period before the next hearing, it often overlooks the possibility of psychological torture, which is less dramatic than reported instances of poisoning/murder but is still violence in which state agents are complicit. In a majority of these cases, the bride who returns to the court with her parents states that she intends to go home again with her parents because the decision to marry was a mistake. I did not witnessed any case where the bride came back to court with her parents and left with her husband, though Chowdhry found one such case in her archival research (2004).

When the bride is sent to a neutral location such as a women's shelter, her statement could possibly change by the next court hearing. Perhaps, given the evidence of psychological torture or even threat to life, at the Chandigarh High Court the disposition to send the women to their parents' place has been minimal. I witnessed only two cases where a judge ordered an adult woman who had come to court with her partner to return home with her parents, and these were only after she had explicitly stated that that was her choice. In one instance, on hearing that a magistrate's court had sent a bride to a women's shelter in spite of her stated preference to leave with her partner, the judge had strongly rebuked the attorney representing the state government of Haryana.

In light of the interviews I conducted, Hadiya's claims of psychological torture are not surprising. Incidentally, she was slightly older than the average petitioner from Punjab and Haryana, who is typically eighteen to twenty-two years of age. That Hadiya had the resolve to insist repeatedly that she wanted to be with her husband begs the question, must only the strong and independent women have the liberty to choose their spouses? The lawmakers who drafted the Special Marriage Act would probably say yes, but in court orders delivered each business day, the high court appears to be telling us that this right may be more universal.

Although some judges routinely show sympathy toward the parents, protection petitions force us to reconsider family as a legal category. The question of choice in marriage is also an opportunity for individuals to re-evaluate their relationships with kin groups and imagine a future that is not only qualitatively different from their lives with family but also different from what the mainstream upholds as normative. This future is both personal and political. The litigants whose adulthood and access to universal rights are recognized are allowed to live with their spouses but also as newly minted citizens who are not limited by their family and kinship ties.

In Haryana, aspirations for future are driven partly by large-scale socioeconomic transformations. There has been a tentative attempt by communities to reconcile themselves to the changes they have experienced in the recent past, as chapters 3 and 4 highlighted. The rise in educational levels across communities and genders has resulted in corresponding transformations in the marriage market. Although kin groups still encourage intracaste marriages even when arranged according to different criterion, young people are increasingly making decisions based on their own calculations and aspirations for the future.

In Haryana and other parts of India, the loss of the agrarian lifestyle is responsible for suffering that finds immediate expression in violence. But Haryanvi society has undergone a much longer period of social suffering on account of its severe gender inequality, with which it must also come to terms. Young women and men are in their own ways dealing with both the pain of the long-standing gender-based inequality and discrimination and the more immediate call to support society in this moment of crisis. Married couples who have been able to achieve choice in marriage seem to be more hopeful about the future, because they have had the opportunity to challenge family norms and the life kin groups hold as the normative ideal for women and men.

For some of my interlocutors, this hope uplifts them somewhat from the current state of uncertainty and social trauma. This is especially true for eloping couples, who are not only experiencing the upheavals in the socioeconomic sphere but also have fears for their immediate future, which may include social boycott and/or physical harm. Eloping couples readily answered questions I posed about the future, even when my questions about their relationships and decisions to elope caused embarrassment and reticence. In my ethnographic study, couples who eloped were almost always cognizant of the future, particularly with regard to the relationship they would like to have with their disapproving parents.

Through their collective moves, couples who approach state institutions to increase acceptability for their life choices signal that they are not necessarily defying social norms but rather aligning themselves more closely with the futures they hope for. Love marriage in Haryana signals a belonging to the imagined community that Shafin seeks to protect, a belonging forged despite Haryana's poor record in social movements and gender relations when compared to Kerala. Love marriage involves a recognition by the couples that they need to move away from the past and prepare for an uncertain future without the perks of kinship but with the recognition of citizenship and rights guaranteed as part of a rite of passage. Ironically, the critics who outrightly dismiss the trend of love marriage also subscribe to this idea of citizenship. The need to validate legal processes as part of their own claim on citizenship allows the critics to accept love marriage after mediation.

Conclusion

Closures, New Beginnings, and Happily Ever After?

The Hindu Mahasabha had promised to marry couples on VDay (Valentine's Day) if they saw any two people holding hands, cooing or even existing on 14th February. But when interested partners arrived outside the Mahasabha's office dressed in wedding gear and fully equipped with *Mehendi* (handpaint) cones, musical instruments, wedding props and of course *band baaja* (band music), they were left high and dry. The Mahasabha refused to come out except one Swami Omji who ordered around the police. . . . The Mahasabha hid behind the Delhi Police who in turn eloped with three buses full of protesters. The protesters were detained under Section 65 for about five hours. However, inside the Parliament Street police station too, the wedding ceremonies, right from *Mehendi* to *Sangeet* (ritualistic songs) and then the actual exchange of *Varmalas* (garlands) went on in full energy.[1]

On February 14, 2015, when the news media in India reported this Delhi-based protest against the moral policing efforts of a resurgent Hindu nationalist movement, some progressive observers in Chandigarh (where I was conducting fieldwork at the time) reacted with amused disbelief: who would have thought "marriage" could be radical? I held my peace, as I have for several years when both intellectuals and interlocutors in the field repeatedly questioned me with seemingly incredulous disbelief if I was *really* studying the trend of love marriage as part of my research, hinting that the topic was perhaps not worthy of my attention. One nineteen-year-old I met at a wedding in rural Haryana asked offhandedly, "Why are you in love with love marriage?" If the word *love* requires us to imagine scare quotes, as I argued in the introduction, then that is one loaded question.

My interest in love marriage runs parallel to the renewed efforts by feminist scholars in the West to make sense of the institution. In the light of marriage equality struggles, several feminist scholars have been forced to ask questions similar to the ones this book obliquely raises. Is love marriage in North India nonnormative? Is court marriage nonnormative, or conforming? Do either or both hold a radical potential?

First, as this book has shown, love marriages and elopements are coded differently under different registers. In seeking respectability and validity as well as state sanction, such couples come across as conformists and docile subjects. The contestations and negotiations that lead to a successful court marriage, however, underline the nonnormative aspects of this union. Through a performative and political act that is staged less defiantly than the protest described above, the radical edge of such marriages is smooth out. Moreover, these unions are the product of transforming socioeconomic realities and increasing mobility options as well as individual effort to secure one's future in a postagrarian society. Second, the ethnography also records the existence of romance, courtships, and sexual explorations that are not restricted to the institution of marriage. Without the respectability and social sanction nominally accorded to marriage, such relationships remain on shaky ground for an extended period before transitioning (dramatically) into a union with legal and/or social sanction. The question of whether sexual relationships outside marriage are radical is perhaps a topic for another research study.

I am humbled by the trust placed in me by interlocutors who shared confidences about sexual encounters, but these were few and disparate and did not form a definite pattern. The discourses on sexuality, consequently, inform my larger conclusions on (court) marriages and the material culture. Confidences about sexual encounters and gossip networks are important clues to the puzzle of social norms in general.

Given the level of surveillance in close-knit rural communities, many courtships are furtively conducted, most likely via phone conversations that involve sharing, caring, and an enduring friendship. I witnessed many women engaged in long phone calls, and during interviews young women described in great detail the telephonic intrigues of their peers. Most women and men spoke about these affairs as something others (even close friends) engaged in, while they themselves did not. Despite the adage that love marriages are ill conceived, premarital affairs were common, even if conducted primarily through phone calls (which did not rule the possibility of sexual encounters). These narratives of romance as something other people engaged in evokes the accounts collected in *The Secret*, an edited volume on extramarital affairs and the public secret (Hirsch et al. 2009). It is the secret husbands keep from their wives, the secret a couple keeps from the community, and a secret the community keeps from itself. That is, they refuse to see it in their own relationships, though they declare that adultery is widespread in the society they inhabit. Premarital affairs in Haryana may not always evoke shame, as Hirsch and colleagues claim

they do for married women with adulterous husbands, but they are nevertheless both widespread and a public secret.

As I argued in chapter 2, when a marriage is not seen as licit, the social
crisis it engineered persists. In contrast, romantic or sexual relationships that
cannot be defined in terms of the institution of marriage are seen as beyond
the kinship and community spaces, and for this reason often also beyond the
purview of kinship structures and moral policing. Furtive courtships and the
ambiguous status of a love marriage before or without court intervention thus
involve a certain straining of the concepts of licit and illicit. Because a conversation on premarital affairs does not take place, can they be presumed illicit? In
several interviews across gender lines and the urban-rural divide, I heard that
"affairs" that challenged social norms were acceptable so long as they were
secretly conducted and the couples in question did not seek to get married.
Young Haryanvis, who variously aspired to and were repulsed by the idea of
love marriage, were reproducing their individual desires within a normative
order that enabled courtships through its indifference, as long as an aspiration
for marriage did not exist.

Laura Ahearn (2001) and Caroline and Filippo Osella (1998) have discussed
courtships in the context of love letters in Nepal and flirting in Kerala, respectively, that straddle the space occupied by illicit relationships and have the
potential to subvert kinship norms. In North India, love marriages pose a
greater challenge to kinship than courtships do, creating a crisis that court
marriage strives to resolve. This testifies not just to the popular acknowledgement of the powers of the judiciary and the state, which this book highlights,
but also to the endurance of kinship structures and their unequal hierarchies.

Previously, kinship norms survived, as discussed in chapter 2, through
cautionary folktales that sought to dissuade young women from romantic
intrigues. Today, kin groups learn to both forgive and hold a grudge at the same
time, to validate and delegitimize simultaneously. Baljeet is well versed in this
duality, as he is both appreciated for his "conquest" and reminded of the infamous trend he pioneered in his village. Baljeet had forgotten that he was the
first in his village to elope, but he was reminded by a neighbor who appeared to
be in awe of Baljeet's decision to make a choice he himself would never make.
Sometimes the village and the kin groups will forgive men from dominant
castes, with time, but they do not forget. Forgiveness is still unavailable to
women from dominant castes, especially if they married outside their community. Contestations over marriages that involve women and men from lower or
upper castes are negotiated/resolved on an individual basis. Baljeet's wife Navjot has not met her own family members, including siblings she was fond of,
since her elopement.

Baljeet believes that society never changes in its regressive attitudes or
changes only in *majboori* (reluctantly, under pressure), but he also noted that

things are always changing around him. The duality of his experience is an ideological versus symbolic tension. His experience with a nonnormative, unforgettable wedding reveals a stubbornly unforgiving society and a constantly adapting world, demonstrating both a constant state of the present and the lifelong journey toward the future. As discussed in chapter 3, given the expectation that marriage will remain a constant feature in life, decisions surrounding it are also based on ambitions for one's future, which most people hope will be better than the present. Baljeet's married life is lived in the present but also speaks to the hopes he has for future—hopes that had a bearing on his original decision to deviate in his marital choices.

Haryana has been experiencing a rapid transformation that could be called a time-space compression (Harvey 1999). The situation in this region is in flux due to uncertainty in the political economy and social unrest caused by caste-based conflicts. Such uncertain conditions make mutations in interpersonal relations plausible, but it is a difficult personal and political process. Kinship structures and networks, though weakened, persevere through these changes and challenges, forging new hybrids, hierarchies, and normative orders to stay relevant.

Decisions before and immediately after elopements and court marriages present something of a crossroads situation for both the couples and their communities. It is easier to perpetuate the public secret on courtships and live in denial than to confront the dilemmas posed by these deviations. According to Bedi, quoted in the introduction, many couples had not even spoken to their families about their intentions to elope and did not know whether the wedding would be opposed. Couples who spoke to me believed that after the court visit, their parents, whether they were estranged or blissfully ignorant of the elopement, would have to reconcile themselves to the new reality. Both in the courtrooms and in rural Haryana, I was told of couples who were not able to make the decision to elope and had subsequently parted ways. The secrets and denials allowed those individuals to survive within kinship spaces and for the kinship to present its norms as sacrosanct. On one occasion in 2012, I observed a woman's father and kinsmen insist in the courtroom that they had no clue that the woman was in a relationship. The groom's uncle rubbished this claim, insisting that "the entire village regularly spotted them together on motorbikes for two whole years." In a society where, as Baljeet joked, surveillance is faster than a 3G data connection, such a denial is striking. Marriage had allowed the groom's uncle to reveal a secret that her kin groups were still unwilling to admit.

In the case of Manoj and Babli, a young couple who were brutally murdered in 2007 even after they were granted protection by the high court, how they had kept their courtship secret bewildered journalists such as Geetanjali Gayatri.

Gayatri wrote, "Their story of togetherness goes back to 2005. There's no date because love usually happens just like that, without provocation or planning. . . . Little is known about how the affair blossomed under the wary eyes of the village fanatics and the moral police."[2] D. R. Chaudhary, a veteran political commenter from Haryana, would have scoffed at this report.

In 2011 Chaudhary told me his own experience at a caste conclave that had been convened after this double murder. He declared to the conclave that the entire village had known about this affair for years (multiple reports substantiate this claim). Taking the caste elders to task, he asked them why no measures had been taken to separate them during their years of courtship. Why had they chosen instead to react after the elopement? And why in such a brutal fashion? After conducting ethnographic research for years since 2011, I have come to realize the radical potential of Chaudhary's intervention at the conclave—he had outed the public secret the kin groups had carefully kept from each other and even themselves. He had discredited the dominant narrative as based on willful ignorance, and thereby exposed the modes through which kinship survives such challenges.

This paradox of allowing premarital relationships to thrive but reacting strongly when they are made public by a wedding act may run counter to what some theorists on honor have proposed (Wikan 2014). It is perhaps not romance or sexuality that is a problem in kin circles in North India, but the act of going public. When elopement, court marriage, and return to the community are undertaken by conformists and docile subjects, they are exposing the community to challenges and adaptions already underway. In this sense, marriage could be viewed as radical, as it functions as a mirror for socioeconomic transformations underway and does the vital act of ensuring that sexual relationships remain public and political. Following Rubin's work, this book contends that while the legal text can never completely cover the diversity of sexual behaviors and relationships, conceptualizing laws as a source of discourses and legal procedures as opportunities allows us one possible framework to contextualize the public and political nature of sexual relationships.

The ritual of a high court visit transforms both the couples and the kinships in irrevocable ways. When the couples return to community spaces, they not only have undermined kinship norms but have also had an opportunity to realize and reconstruct their selfhood in more complete ways. The ensuing emancipation is a defiant attempt to participate in democratic processes. Whereas family, kinship, and community refuse to follow democratic practices such as allowing conversations on one's own marriage and future, the state is mandated to do just that. What is at stake is not just individual freedom and sexual rights but the endurance of democracy itself. Freedom, Cavell tells us, is obeying the law "we give ourselves" (1990, 28).

The Long Road (Back) to Democracy: Individual Freedoms, Sexual Liberties, and Marriage Equality

Over the last few years civil liberties in India have increasingly become constrained, and it would not be surprising if, in this conservative political landscape, sexual rights were gradually withdrawn. The Supreme Court recriminalized homosexuality at the beginning of 2014 before the national elections in April to May 2014, foreshadowing the heightened contestations around the Love Jihad and anti-Romeo squads, which the BJP pushed with renewed vigor in Uttar Pradesh. But the LGBTQI communities have also continued the legal and political struggle since the setback in 2014 (see figure 17).

In 2018 the Supreme Court again issued a slew of judgments, ahead of the 2019 elections. With these decisions the Court upheld individual liberty but did not adequately address the allegations leveled against it—charges of political compromise and bias toward the ruling party.[3]

Some of these landmark judgments pertain to gender and sexuality. They deal with the decriminalization of homosexuality and adultery, Hadiya's reunification with her husband, and women in their menstruating years being allowed into a temple from which they had been barred (Sabrimala, in the state of Kerala). But in the midst of open rebellion among the ranks of the judges as well as threatened impeachment proceedings against a former chief justice on grounds of political bias, the Supreme Court has exemplified the contradictory role played by the judicial institutions, a theme extensively explored in this book. At the very least, the arbitrary and discretionary modes through which the judicial institutions function warn us against sweeping studies of the postcolonial state's ideological dispensation and inherently patriarchal structures. In spite of instances of judicial bias or miscarriage of justice, the courts have persevered as sites where citizens will be heard and assisted. The sentimental attachment to the courts serves to hold judges accountable in ways that even elected representatives, who provoke cynicism and disillusionment, are not.

Court petitions and adjudications become a mode through which apolitical citizens can participate in democratic processes. In effectively utilizing the right to life and liberty in this negotiation, eloping couples voice their demands through a discourse and a legal provision that is efficient and expedient in getting results. The resultant court order does not necessarily signify a favorable result, in that the claim of marriage is not explicitly endorsed, but couples read endorsement and court approval into the text, a leap in which they are joined by various parties in the courtroom and the community outside. The modes through which legal knowledge travels between court spaces, where judges and lawyers explicitly state that courts do not conduct or sanction weddings, and the community, which believes that they do, is a form of juridification that allows

FIGURE 17 Pride parade 2015 in Chandigarh city passes a Hindu temple.
Photo: Rama Srinivasan.

for citizen participation in ensuring individual freedoms at a time when political praxis does not.

One of the key contributions these case studies offer for the survival of democratic rights and processes is the articulation of consent. As I argued in chapter 6, litigation is a mode through which citizens reiterate their consent to the social contract and also, simultaneously, hold the state to its end of the bargain. Existence of sexual consent in relationships is, to draw from Cavell, a vital extension of the social contract. The cases I witnessed centrally inform the discourses on sexual consent, though their significance is underemphasized in comparison to cases of sexual assaults. Sexual consent as it is understood in the cases I observed is crafted, articulated, and validated (or not) through an exercise of consent, not through its previous usurpation. The woman's role is directly under scrutiny here, as it is in rape cases, but what is different is that the woman (represented by lawyers but often also speaking for herself) can take control of her narrative and emphasize the exercise of consent (which is independent of but connected to choice in marital decisions).

A case of rape is pursued by the state (with or without an official complaint from the survivor or the family) as an offense committed against the state. Thus, a rape or sexual assault is a moral affront to the state, to its laws, and to the society that it claims to protect and for which it acts as conscience keeper. Sexual consent and its absence in certain cases are, hence, notions deliberated on by a state and the level of affront citizens and state agents feel toward a case of rape. A case such as the "Nirbhaya" case dominates the national imagination because both the society and the state experienced the affront intimately due to various temporal and class factors. In the Farooqui judgment, the state apparently did not sufficiently experience the affront.

At least in the initial stages, the legal narrative on court marriages is constructed not by the public prosecutors but by couples in partnership with their legal counsels, though neither has any power with regard to authorizing the discourse—that power rests with the judges alone. What the process allows for is an articulation of consent in a space and context where its exercise can be validated or reaffirmed, reducing the fear of social persecution and shaming. The failure of the process in some individual cases has not resulted in a decline in the number of eloping couples who try their luck at this unpredictable and potentially dangerous game.

The act of elopement is indeed a challenge to patriarchal and kinship orders, but the lovers do not want to live forever in the zone of rebellion. Enlisting the state to ensure that the social crisis is resolved signals a bureaucratization of aspirations, as discussed in chapter 2. Elopement here is not less defiant or dangerous in some cases, but the visit to the courts holds out the promise of becoming full subjects. Hope and the experience of finding justice make real the idea that "court comes to lovers' rescue" because couples see justice delivered. Court procedures both uphold the right of an adult citizen to marry a person of their own choice and provide a ritualistic framework where the court visit can later be coded as a "court marriage."

Even if couples' futures are enjoined, it appears that both the bride and the groom feel validated as individuals. A woman's statement in court that she had eloped of her own *marzi* (choice) is a statement of consent, and recognition of that is a validation of their adult citizenship. Whereas women get to articulate their choice in many courtrooms, men were not often called upon to do so. Courtroom performances also sometimes have unpredictable outcomes that depend on a variety of factors. Not all trysts with justice end in hope and affirmation. Cases such as Jaspreet's are reminders of how this book cannot end in a metaphorical "meet and happy conversation." But it can end with cautious hope; even Jaspreet, who failed in his efforts, holds on to hope.

*   *   *

Less than a month after the Supreme Court decriminalized homosexuality in September 2018, a lesbian couple from Rajasthan petitioned the Delhi High Court for the protection of their life and liberty, which they insisted was under threat from their families.[4] The petition included a statement that the women wished to marry each other and that the family of one of the women had forcibly engaged her to a man, with a wedding date set for November. They allege that after the couple's elopement to Delhi, police officers refused to protect them and even threatened the couple's lawyer.

The Delhi High Court, which had made the landmark decision to decriminalize homosexuality in 2009 (which the Supreme Court reversed in 2014), in passing the protection order once again upheld the constitutional rights of the queer community. The momentum initiated by the Supreme Court judgment has enabled members of marginalized communities to present in legal spaces their aspirations for marriage that existing laws may not be able to fulfill. In invoking the litigation procedure regularly utilized by eloping couples in Haryana and Punjab—that is, the protection petition—this case highlights how the struggles of heterosexual and homosexual couples to forge relationships and marriages of choice and consent are intertwined.

Some of the cases discussed in this book were concerned with couples who planned or had already solemnized weddings that may never be fully validated. In the Rania case handled by Nakul and the case in which Neeti's client confessed that her marriage had been a mistake, the religious weddings already conducted were ambiguous and disposable. The religious wedding never became a court marriage. In Ayesha and Qasim's case, the validity of their marriage could never be implicit. In bigamous relationships where petitioners pleaded loss/unavailability of divorce certificates, abandonment by spouses, or invalidity of the first marriage, protection petitions were a mechanism of extending the cautious legitimacy courts regularly grant to eloping couples in cases where the judges can only ensure togetherness. For women like Ayesha, even such adjudications were welcome.

In courtrooms and in rural Haryana, I heard about numerous cases where previously married women had eloped with another partner, but these petitioners usually withheld the information about the prior marriage at the first court hearing. When such facts were brought to the court's notice after the protection order had been passed, the couples did not return to court spaces. One judge actively advised state governments to pursue bigamy cases against the women, but others refused to get drawn into the affair. Justice Keshav, for example, declared that it was up to the first husband to file a bigamy case.

Keshav seemed to have made peace with legal fictions created for people in precarious positions. In another bigamy case where the petitioner had withheld information about her first marriage, he brushed aside the question of a false affidavit: "Sometimes one has to pretend these things. If you are under pressure or worried about your life and liberty you do such things." Although it seemed that perjury had been committed, the judge took a lenient view, choosing to focus on the question of protection. He ordered that the protection order previously passed would remain valid, ensuring that the woman could leave the court with the partner with whom she had eloped.

Such cases straddled the precarious terrain between licit and illicit, never quite making it to the other side. At least three lawyers told me that bigamy cases are necessarily different from elopement cases involving two eligible bachelors, but I would argue that these cases represent attempts by individuals (especially women) with few opportunities to recraft their life situations. Although they might desire a legally tenable marriage, divorce is a much longer and uncertain process for women from marginalized or vulnerable backgrounds. Juridification of intimate relationships offers them an opportunity the legal text itself may not, and that opportunity might be extended to lesbian and gay couples, too.

Marriage equality is the next stage of this struggle, another long battle for inclusive and representative frameworks for the institution. As discussed in chapter 1, the narrative of any legal struggle must complete its designated arc to reach its logical resolution. Meanwhile, the protection petition offers citizens such as the Rajasthani lesbian couple an opportunity to solemnize a wedding and experience cohabitation and togetherness that may not be a legal marriage in the strictest sense of the term, but will be, as it is for heterosexual couples visiting the high court in Chandigarh, legally tenable. Perhaps, as in the case of the word *love* in its heterogenous form, the gradual inclusiveness of marriage could go a small way toward salvaging the institution from its problematic aspects.

The other, larger question of gender equality and the persistent sexual division of labor in love marriages must be left unresolved as far as this book is concerned. My ethnography offers a window into a region that is deeply hierarchal in terms of gender, caste, religion, and class. For this reason, the attack on farmers' rights and the land acquisitions by big businesses operating with the backing of state power is a cause for concern. But one cannot fail to note that a breakdown in the cycle of land ownership, masculine domination, and political privilege has also afforded a space for women across communities to aspire to a more livable life at some point in the postagrarian future.

As an ethnographer, it is inevitable that I empathize with the pain of men from dominant communities who must make a difficult transition, but I also remain cognizant of gender inequality in the region and the social suffering that is part of this lifeworld of violence. The incredible journeys women have undertaken, often leaving men behind in their educational and employment achievements, perhaps skews my narrative in their favor. Yet, we must remember that regardless of their aspirations, women still return to an unequal society and experience everyday violence that an ethnographer like me has the luxury to quit. In considering these narratives of constant social change and yet not enough change, I am reminded of a Gramscian summation of the situation in contemporary North India, offered by a retired professor in Fatehabad: "The old is dying and the new cannot be born" (Gramsci et al. 2001, 556). This immensely popular and often misattributed quote continues: ". . . in this interregnum a great variety of morbid symptoms appear" (556). Some might maintain that a proliferation of sexual desires with explicit legal sanction at the cusp of a new economic order represents a morbid, dangerous symptom. As a feminist scholar, I am allowing myself a cautious (some might say naïve) hope that relationships based on the idea of consent will become more ubiquitous.

APPENDIX

TABLE A.1
Broad Trends in Education

Measures	India (men)	India (women)	India (total)	Haryana (men)	Haryana (women)	Haryana (total)
Literacy rate	434.763.622	328.875.190	763.638.812	9.794.067↑	6.804.921↓	16.598.988
Population aged 18–23, 2013–14	73.254.717	67.546.809	140.801.526	1.730.366↑	1.454.917↓	3.185.283
	12.543.284 (SC)	11.534.001 (SC)	24.077.285 (SC)	368.266 (SC)	306.546 (SC)	674.812 (SC)
Gross enrollment ratio (GER)	23.9	22.0	23.0	28.8↑	25.9↓	27.5
	17.7 (SC)	16.4 (SC)	17.1 (SC)	18.9 (SC)	15.8 (SC)	17.5 (SC)
Total enrollment	15.349.137	13.057.003	28.406.140	482.571↑	369.286↓	851.857
Completion rates (degrees, diplomas, certificates, etc.)	4.154.656	2.748.577	8.235.852	64.811↓	66.507↑	155.658

TABLE A.2

Completion Rates of Degree and Diploma Programs

Degree level	India (men)	India (women)	India (total)	Haryana (men)	Haryana (women)	Haryana (total)
Enrollment at undergraduate level	13574434	11925891	25500325	389.582	304.894	694476
Completion of undergraduate degrees	2911349	1921741	5926096	43.236	46.720 ↑	109284
Enrollment at postgraduate level	1249719	1294879	2544598	29131	45215↑	74346
Completion of postgraduate programs	663466	508692	1332083	8481	11987↑	24063
Enrollment in MPhil programs	13632	17748	31380	303	382↑	685
Completion of MPhil programs	9027	9257	21954	145	155↑	310
Enrollment in PhD programs	64772	43118	107890	1570↑	1473	3043

ACKNOWLEDGMENTS

To me, all good academic work is what Judith Butler would call a "stylized repetition of acts." To this end, this book has been a felicitous enterprise for me, and I hope those who read it perceive it in a similar way. I would like to acknowledge and thank some of the people who have been associated with my research and facilitated this speech act in intimate ways.

This project would not have been possible without the generous support and guidance from many people in Haryana and Chandigarh. They not only welcomed me into their homes and social circles but also contributed substantially with suggestions about themes, ethnographic questions, and research angles. The following list is not exhaustive, especially because many persons have been quoted in the book and cannot be named. But I am extremely grateful to Haryanvis from the districts of Fatehabad, Sirsa, and Hisar and the city of Chandigarh who offered their time, affection, and hospitality in addition to providing illuminating interviews that have enriched my research and life in multiple ways.

I am humbled by the generosity of my hosts in rural Haryana, Meet, Satyam, R. K. Sharma, and Madhu Sharma. They included me in their everyday lives, relationships, struggles, and joys. I cannot thank Meet and R. K. Sharma enough for the nourishment of mind and body I received in their company through our shared love for culinary and literary delights. They have influenced my research and my personal growth as an intellectual in countless ways.

In Chandigarh, I would like to thank the following in particular: Rajeev and Divya Godara, Daljit Ami, Arjun Sheoran, and Harish. I thank Kuldeep for introducing me to his extended family in Fatehabad and Hisar as well as his network of friends and acquaintances in Chandigarh. In Fatehabad: journalists Sushil Manav and Hardeep; Krishan Kumar and the staff at his school; and Professor Harbhagwan Chawla and the staff at his college. In Hisar: Manoj and Dipti, junior lecturers at government schools. Special thanks to Priyanka, who provided excellent translations for my audio recordings of conversions conducted in heavy *baagri* dialect.

I cannot thank Professor Jyoti Puri enough for her generously extensive and far-reaching feedback on my doctoral dissertation; she helped me envision an actual book out of what now appears to be a fairly rudimentary text. I am also grateful to my advisers at Brown University: Lina Fruzzetti, who always prioritized the person in the scholar and taught me to do the same; and Kay Warren, whose strong belief in my scholarship has not wavered since day one. I also thank the following professors at Brown and elsewhere for their invaluable contributions to my development as a scholar: Nivedita Menon, Gopal Guru, V. Geetha, Gayle Rubin, Livia Holden, Laura Prieto, Adia Benton, Bhrigupati Singh, and finally, Prem Chowdhry, whose work on North India and Haryana provides the essential background for any scholarly writing on this region.

It is difficult to imagine anyone with as much patience and perseverance as Pat Dickson; her mission to bring discipline into the lives of people as scattered as I am and her training in the last eight years has been one of my most valuable life lessons.

I also thank Péter Berta, the series editor, Jasper Chang and the team at Rutgers University Press and Westchester Publishing Services, and Anne Davidson, my rigorous copy editor, for their resourcefulness and support throughout the publication process.

The last few years have been a great test of faith for those of us who believe in social justice, plural societies, and democracy, all of which are under threat in several parts of the world, especially two countries in which I have spent most of my life: India and the United States. I am lucky to have forged alternate kin groups that have supported each other through all the shared pain and fear. These enduring friendships have also helped me focus on the writing process through despairing times and even weave a hopeful message throughout this book. I thank the following in particular: Magnus Hansen, Andrea Wright, Sa'ed Atshan, Brenda Sanya, Kaushik Das Gupta, Anusha Chandrasekharan, Parita Patel, Sanchari Bhattacharya, Liani Tlau, and Yana Stainova.

On the family front, I thank my late grandmother Alamelu, who was the first woman in her family to complete high school, and all the women on both sides of my family who have consistently pushed the envelope on all fronts. I am grateful to my uncle and aunt M.G.R. and Padma, who have always been invested in my success, scholarly and otherwise; my cousins Ramya and Ranjitha, who have supported me emotionally through long periods of uncertainty and self-doubt; and my *schwiegermutter* Katharina and my entire family by marriage, who have allowed me to grow as an anthropologist and humanist by patiently waiting for me to overcome language and cultural barriers and find common ground.

I cannot separate my achievements or life journeys from the following: my parents, Kamini and Srinivasan, who taught me that no life goal of mine can equal that of higher education; my elder sister Janaki, who as a prodigious young adult laid out the intellectual and political path that I have always followed; and my partner, Martin Ulirsch, whose sensible, practical, and ambitious approach to life gives me a sense of purpose every day and the necessary energy to always hunt for new projects. As I argue in this book, marriage can be, for some, a hopeful tryst with a more livable future.

NOTES

INTRODUCTION

1. See Padmaparna Ghosh's in-depth report on the transforming nature of *khaps*, "Haryana's Khaps Are Gradually Reforming—but Their Motives Are Far from Progressive," *Scroll.in*, February 25, 2015, https://scroll.in/article/709075/Haryana%E2%80%99s-khaps-are-gradually-reforming-%E2%80%93-but-their-motives-are-far-from-progressive.

2. See the inter-state comparison compiled by a researcher from the Centre for Advanced Financial Research and Learning, Sujan Bandyopadhyay, "A Closer Look at Statistics on Sexual Violence in India," *The Wire*, May 8, 2018, https://thewire.in/society/a-closer-look-at-statistics-on-sexual-violence-in-india.

3. Reservations for Jats were stayed through judicial intervention at a later date. But a new 2019 law, passed on the last day of the parliamentary session (ahead of national elections), aims to provide 10 percent of reservations to the economically backward sections in the society. Though aimed at facilitating the already well-represented upper castes, in states such as Haryana it is likely to benefit the locally powerful peasant communities not included in the OBC category. It is also likely that the judiciary will scrap this law on constitutional grounds.

4. See Betwa Sharma, "Jat Policemen Deserted Posts, Backed Protestors, during Violent Agitation in Haryana: Report," *Huffington Post*, April 18, 2016, https://www.huffingtonpost.in/2016/04/18/jat-agitation_n_9717806.html.

5. See Nishita Jha, "'They Say We Did This to Get Attention': Rohtak Sisters Struggle to Get on with Life," *Scroll.in*, March 7, 2015, http://scroll.in/article/708776/'They-say-we-did-this-to-get-attention':-Rohtak-sisters-struggle-to-get-on-with-life.

6. Though masculinist domination is not exclusive to Haryana, the state's singular lack of strong women as political figures or public personalities, despite women's reasonable representation in the legislative and local bodies, demonstrates and contributes to the exclusion and invisibility of women in popular culture and as identity markers. By contrast, Haryana's immediate neighbors, Uttar Pradesh and Rajasthan, have produced strong women leaders and public and popular culture figures. Though Punjab's politics is dominated by the religious establishment, the Sikh faith has allowed women to occupy several positions of power, and there is no dearth of women role models and female imagery in popular culture, even at the national level, when it comes to Punjabi women.

7. See Varinda Bhatia, "A Wedding, Two Funerals, a Rogue Cop and a Runaway Bride," *Indian Express*, June 3, 2013.

8. Ashwaq Masoodi and Nikita Doval, "Rohtak: No Place for Women," *Livemint*, February 28, 2015, http://www.livemint.com/Leisure/MPYNL7dIDwWfbIplJu6xDK/Rohtak -No-place-for-women.html.

9. After spending three decades with the Congress Party, Rao Inderjit Singh joined the BJP ahead of the 2014 elections, ostensibly because he had been rendered powerless by the former (Jat) chief minister, Bhupinder Singh Hooda. His move transferred Yadav votes en masse to BJP. See Dipak Kumar Dash, "Cong's 3-Time Haryana MP Inderjit Singh Defects to BJP," *Times of India*, January 21, 2014, https://timesofindia .indiatimes.com/india/Congs-3-time-Haryana-MP-Inderjit-Singh-defects-to-BJP /articleshow/29176879.cms.

10. The university's spelling of the name of the state, *Panjab*, is in line with the colonial institution located in Lahore.

11. For the full judgment on Mahmood Farooqui v. State (Govt of Nct of Delhi), see https://indiankanoon.org/doc/160377045/.

12. An Indian man in Australia was acquitted of stalking charges after his counsel argued that Bollywood films had taught the accused that stalking was a legitimate means to find a partner. See Jonathan Pearlman, "Australian Man Accused of Stalking Escapes Conviction after Blaming Bollywood," *Telegraph* (UK), January 29, 2015, http://www.telegraph.co.uk/news/worldnews/australiaandthepacific/australia /11377511/Australian-man-accused-of-stalking-escapes-conviction-after-blaming -Bollywood.html.

13. See G. Ananthakrishnan, "Hadiya Case Didn't Warrant Probe by NIA, Kerala Government Tells Supreme Court," *Indian Express*, October 8, 2017, http://indianexpress.com /article/india/hadiya-case-didnt-warrant-probe-by-nia-kerala-government-tells -supreme-court-4879826/.

14. *Gendering Human Development Indices* (2009), a report from India's Ministry of Women and Child Development, placed Haryana's Gender Development Index and Gender Empowerment Measure at 0.63 and 0.53, respectively (12 and 15).

15. The then president of the Jawaharlal Nehru University Students' Union, Kanhaiya Kumar, was attacked by a Haryanvi Rajput lawyer inside the court premises. See "'Lawlessness' Continues in Delhi Courts, Journalist Beaten up Again," *Deccan Chronicle*, February 17, 2016, http://www.deccanchronicle.com/nation/current-affairs/170216 /jnu-row-student-s-union-president-kanhaiya-kumar-to-be-produced-in-court-today .html.

16. Four judges of the Supreme Court held an open press conference in 2018 raising concerns regarding the judiciary's impartiality. See A. Vaidyanathan, "Democracy at Stake, Things Not in Order: 4 Supreme Court Judges—10 Points," NDTV, January 13, 2018, https://www.ndtv.com/india-news/for-first-time-ever-4-senior-supreme-court -judges-to-address-media-1799152.

CHAPTER 1   CIVIL MARRIAGE IN POSTINDEPENDENCE INDIA

1. The Muslim Women (Protection of Rights of Rights on Divorce) Act of 1986 was repealed, but a new (2017) bill bearing the same name was passed by the lower house of the parliament in December 2018. It awaits passage by the upper house.

2. Arya Samaj was the product of a Hindu reformist movement in the nineteenth century that simplified religious prescripts, rituals, and ceremonies. Unlike the Brahmo Samaj from East India, Arya Samaj emphasized the integrity of Vedic texts

and sought to bring Hindu societies in line with the principles of ancient philosophies. Although the movement and the sect it forged propagated several progressive ideas in the nineteenth and twentieth centuries, such as widow remarriage and intercaste marriages, today the community is regarded as conservative with puritan impulses. Nevertheless, the Arya Samaj offices allow for quick wedding ceremonies for eloping couples and conversion options for interfaith couples who decide against a Special Marriage Act wedding. The popular belief that an Arya Samaj wedding facilitates registration or is valid in court ensures a steady clientele for the sect.

3. I worked out a version of this argument in "Science of the Secular," *From a Corner of the Academic Field* (blog), April 1, 2018, http://whenindoubtramble.blogspot.com/2018 /04/science-of-secular.html.

4. For more on incest taboos, see women's rights activist Jagmati Sangwan's piece, "Khap Panchayat: Signs of Desperation?," *The Hindu*, May 7, 2010, https://www.thehindu .com/opinion/lead/Khap-panchayat-signs-of-desperation/article13796344.ece. *Gotra* is best understood as a hereditary line or lineage; in large parts of North India, alliances typically cannot be forged with the lineages to which one's father, mother, and maternal and paternal grandmothers belong. Additionally, subcaste groups may have brotherhood ties with different lineages and/or villages, forbidding another set of alliances. In some regions of Haryana, marriage alliances are sought in distant villages to avoid potentially consanguine marriages but in the districts where I conducted my research, incest taboos are more simplified. Marriages even within villages were possible for some caste groups where no gotras were shared, and brotherhood ties were also less common. One of my informants from the Bishnoi community had married someone from her grandmother's gotra, but her family members did not raise any objections to their union.

5. See Rohan Venkataramakrishnan, "Muslim Women and the Surprising Facts about Polygamy in India," *Scroll.in*, July 8, 2014, https://scroll.in/article/669083/muslim -women-and-the-surprising-facts-about-polygamy-in-india.

6. See the full judgment at "Modify Court Marriage Check List to Promote Inter-Religion Marriages Instead of Hampering Them: Punjab & Haryana HC to State [Read Judgment]," *Livelaw*, August 1, 2018, https://www.livelaw.in/modify-court-marriage-check -list-to-promote-inter-religion-marriages-instead-of-hampering-them-punjab -haryana-hc-to-state-read-judgment/.

7. The Hindu Marriage Act, which offered the option of legal divorce to Hindu groups, was passed only in 1955, after the Special Marriage Act came into effect. Customary forms of divorce have existed in different Hindu communities, as shown in the introduction's discussion of Livia Holden's work. Marriages under the Muslim Personal Law were similarly dissolvable.

8. According to several court judgments that have interpreted the Hindu Marriage Act on the question of Gandharva marriages, these are not included in the set of recognized weddings for Hindu couples. One notable case that has set precedent in this regard comes from the Calcutta High Court. See Ram Chandra Bhattacharjee v. Manju Bhattacharjee, https://indiankanoon.org/doc/1284806/?type=print. For other notable cases, see https://indiankanoon.org/search/?formInput=gandharva%20 marriage.

9. The legal age of consent was raised from ten to twelve in 1892, to fifteen in 1949, to sixteen in 1983, and finally to eighteen in 2012. I discuss age of consent law of 2012 in chapter 6, which deals with sexual consent in elopement cases.

10. Pandit was a powerful diplomat who held the position of the president of the United Nations General Assembly in 1953. Her intervention here is from 1954. She was also the sister of the first prime minister, Jawaharlal Nehru.

11. The Delhi-based NGO Dhanak actively promotes the utilization of the Special Marriage Act, especially (but not only) for interreligious marriages. Dhanak's Asif admitted in a conversation with me that catering to Haryana's eloping couples complicated matters because couples often sought protection petitions in addition to marriage under the law, highlighting that this document/instrument was familiar to them and their communities.

CHAPTER 2   OF REBELLIOUS LOVERS AND CONFORMIST CITIZENS

1. Although it is a relatively young city, Gurugram, formerly Gurgaon, contributes close to 1 percent of the GDP, compared to Delhi, which contributes 4 percent. For details, see Swati Ramanathan, "Gurgaon's Millennial Magic Is Fading Fast. But We Can Stop That," *Hindustan Times*, January 28, 2018, https://www.hindustantimes.com/opinion /is-gurgaon-a-doomed-city/story-vunipHHRnTWNoVvo6dhr6M.html.

2. See Chandan Suta Dogra's investigative book *Manoj and Babli: A Hate Story* (London: Penguin, 2013).

3. There are some instances of misinformation in the film. For example, a Hindu-Sikh couple does not necessarily require the Special Marriage Act, although the film's protagonists operate on this assumption. But the film works well as a reflection of an ill-informed citizenry eager to avail of legal help when it is available.

4. Justice as a moral sentiment appears in the works of the eighteenth-century scholars David Hume and Adam Smith, but this chapter is not inspired by them; instead, it is firmly rooted in phenomenological anthropology traditions.

5. For a timeline of Hadiya's case, see Richa Taneja, "Hadiya's Story: A Timeline of Kerala 'Love Jihad' Case," NDTV, November 27, 2017, https://www.ndtv.com/india-news /hadiya-case-a-timeline-of-kerala-love-jihad-case-1780500.

6. For a subtitled version of her interview, see "Hadiya Shafin Jahan," YouTube, March 15, 2018, https://www.youtube.com/watch?v=-rXoZ9CIzjI&feature=youtu.be.

7. Baradwaj Rangan, "'Mulk' . . . A Smashingly Effective Return to Hindi Cinema's Social-Potboiler Roots," *Baradwaj Rangan* (personal blog), August 24, 2018, https:// baradwajrangan.wordpress.com/2018/08/24/mulk-a-smashingly-effective-return-to -hindi-cinemas-social-potboiler-roots/.

8. Twitter, an ideal site for surveying right-wing discourses, registered a high number of posts that claimed there was no hope for Hadiya. One verified conservative Twitter personality with 161,000 followers who in December 2017 emphasized trumped-up reports of links between Hadiya's husband and ISIS ended up decrying the waste of state resources on investigating the links. See Anshul Saxena, Twitter posts, December 4, 2017, 3:32 A.M., https://twitter.com/AskAnshul/status/93764586293043 2000?s=20, and March 8, 2018, 1:52 A.M., https://twitter.com/AskAnshul/status/97168 4991292858368?s=20.

9. Between 1975 and 1977 democratic institutions were suspended, leading to large-scale civil society unrest and state-sponsored violence.

10. Liang references it in his article but also credits Ashish Rajadhyaksha (1999) for introducing the concept into cinema studies.

11. Alhuwalia, Kanwaljit S. Ashok Kumar v. Bharat Verma, Asha Devi and Suraj Verma, Criminal Writ Petition No. 555 of 2008 (High Court of Punjab and Haryana).

CHAPTER 3   LOVE, MARRIAGE, AND THE BRAVE NEW WORLD

1. Given the severely skewed male-female sex ratio in the state, compulsory bachelor-hood is a reality for many men. Women are also being trafficked from Bihar, West Bengal, Jharkhand, Assam, and Kerala to make up for the paucity of eligible brides in the state. Also see Deeksha Sharma, "The Ugly Truth of Bride Trafficking and Agrarian Labour in Haryana," *Feminism in India*, September 14, 2017, https://feminisminindia .com/2017/09/14/bride-trafficking/.

2. For details, see Deepender Deswal, "Haryana Khap Relaxes Norm on Same-Gotra Marriage," *Times of India*, March 5, 2013, https://timesofindia.indiatimes.com/india /Haryana-khap-relaxes-norm-on-same-gotra-marriage/articleshow/18804988.cms.

3. Eloping couples are also popularly known as "runaway couples," so from BW's perspective, my response was a loaded one. A young and presumably well-educated girl is stereotypically cast in this role.

CHAPTER 4   GENDER TROUBLE AND A STATE OF ILLUSIONS

1. There have been a few research projects on "honor killings" but I have not yet seen published work on the subject.

2. Also see Sumi Krishna's collected volume, *Women's Livelihood Rights: Recasting Citizenship for Development* (Los Angeles: Sage Publications, 2007).

3. Defined as politics aimed at getting a bigger share of state subsidies and affirmative action initiatives.

4. Christophe Jaffrelot, "Why Jats Want a Quota," *Indian Express*, February 23, 2016, http://indianexpress.com/article/opinion/columns/jats-reservation-stir-obc-quota -rohtak-haryana-protests/#sthash.xPcgYqrn.dpuf.

5. Sanjay Kumar and Pranav Gupta, "What Young India Wants: 'Sarkari Naukri,'" *Livemint*, August 22, 2018, https://www.livemint.com/Industry/Ic7wicj8vnoT9BMj0Mj5TJ /What-Young-India-wants-Sarkari-Naukri.html.

6. Surinder Jodhka (2014) examines the widespread trend of contract farming in Punjab and Haryana, where the owners collect a percentage of the revenue from tenants without actively participating in cultivation.

7. On drug abuse, see Ajay Sura, "Drug Abuse: Haryana Catching Up with Neighbour Punjab," *Times of India*, August 14, 2017, https://timesofindia.indiatimes.com/city /chandigarh/drug-abuse-haryana-catching-up-with-neighbour-punjab/articleshow /60053870.cms. On farmer suicides, see Sanjeeb Mukherjee, "Big Rise in Farmer Suicides in Four States during 2016, Says NCRB Data," *Business Standard*, March 23, 2018, https://www.business-standard.com/article/economy-policy/big-rise-in-farmer -suicides-in-four-states-during-2016-says-ncrb-data-118032300025_1.html.

8. Conversations with young women revealed their knowledge of the provisions (though not the name) of the Hindu Succession (Amendment) Act, 2005, which gave Hindu women a right to ancestral property. Governmental incentives such as rebates on property tax and electricity bills for houses owned by women have led to changes in legal titles. But a real sense of ownership eludes the young women who told me that when they get married they will have to sign away their rights in favor of their

brothers. Still, their legal ownership rights gave them a sense of power over these brothers, and a few admitted to using that power in everyday bargains and negotiations.

9. When I was living on a college campus during the fall, attendance thinned because it was the season to pick cotton, a chore for the women.

10. Rajasthan and Gujarat boast rich cultural heritages, while Punjab dominates in popular culture, including cinema and performing arts. The region that today constitutes Haryana was historically a buffer zone for great Delhi-based empires, and it has not developed a distinct political or cultural identity (Kumar 1991).

11. I use the quantitative report published in 2015 because I conducted major portions of my fieldwork in 2014 and 2015. Regarding the categories, since the 2014 Supreme Court judgment in favor of the transgender community, institutions are mandated to include a third option on applications. Data on this would enrich such studies. The 2011 census puts Haryana's transgender population at 8,422, with a literacy rate of 62.11 percent. Census 2011, accessed on January 21, 2019, http://www.census2011.co.in /transgender.php.

12. The Gender Parity Index (GPI) is calculated by dividing the female Gross Enrolment Ratio by the male Gross Enrolment Ratio, at each level of education.

13. For the tables these graphs are based on, as well as the the population numbers and literacy rates mentioned here, see the appendix.

14. Because of my gender, my interactions with young men did not produce confidences on this subject. But doctors, journalists, and professors, among others, emphasized the widespread drug abuse in Haryana.

CHAPTER 5   INSTITUTING COURT MARRIAGE

1. Although I would use the word *abduction* rather than *kidnapping*, when interlocutors used English words, I have retained them.

2. Court orders are public documents and can, in principle, be cited, but in cases that involve sensitive personal information, the researcher is responsible for ensuring that individuals are not identifiable from references in a scholarly text.

3. I attribute this to increased knowledge of and familiarity with the high court procedure—due to the rise in the number of couples who have "succeeded" through court interventions—as well as the phenomenal growth in cell phone data coverage in rural India, which makes accessing high court websites and cause lists easier.

4. While he spoke in Hindi—possibly for our benefit—he did slip in a few Punjabi words such as *chad* and, later on, *siyapa.*

CHAPTER 6   CONSENTING ADULTS AND THE STATE

1. Due to ethical concerns that arise from Saima's legal age, this discussion is based only on what I observed at court premises (a public site) and what I learned from interviews with the legal adults involved in the case. Although Saima was a central figure in this episode, I include only my observations of her public conduct and public statements.

2. The case selection here is not intended to give the impression that the marriage of legal minors is a community-specific problem. There were also several Hindu and Sikh women who had not reached the requisite age of eighteen at the time of their

petitions. These two cases generated illuminating conversations and presented a useful comparison because they involved members of the same community. In general, however, cases involving fifteen- or sixteen-year-old women were rare.

3. In a sense, this is a statement on the elopement phenomenon as a whole; in popular conception, the age of the bride is an issue only in the case of a love or court marriage. Teenagers in relationships, who know that they cannot elope and have a court marriage before they turn eighteen, also fear the prospect of a family-arranged wedding. This is an indictment of the legal apparatus that requires attainment of legal age to petition the court as a citizen but does not afford adequate protections for legal minors still under the guardianship of their parents.

4. The Aadhaar card is a form of identification that allows for high levels of surveillance by linking many forms of government records, including the Indian versions of social security numbers and driver's licenses. It is fast becoming the preferred form of requested identification for both private and public entities.

5. My identity as an urban woman could have had something to do this.

6. Here, Cavell discusses Milton's theory, according to which the commonwealth suffers when one suffers in such a marriage. This leads Cavell to wonder whether the covenant of marriage is a miniature of the covenant of the commonwealth, where participation in a happy conversation of marriage is an obligation to the commonwealth.

7. According to the Muslim Personal Law in India, Qasim is allowed to have a second wife but Ayesha would have had to secure a divorce in order to remarry.

8. Jaspreet is not his real name (all names have been changed to protect identities). *Preet* is a common suffix for names of Punjabi-speaking women and men in both Punjab and Haryana.

9. The judgment is not cited here because its title would reveal the interlocuter's real name.

CHAPTER 7   TOWARD AN ALTERNATIVE FUTURE

1. This was seen most recently at a three-day conference, (Re)designing Justice for Plural Societies: Accommodative Practices Put to the Test, June 14–16, 2017, at the Max Planck Institute for Social Anthropology, Germany.

2. Prem Chowdhry mentions such cases in her article on runaway couples (Chowdhry 2004).

3. Nirmala George "India Records Huge Spike in 'Honour Killings' in 2015," Global News, December 7, 2016, http://globalnews.ca/news/3111543/india-records-huge-spike -in-honour-killings-in-2015/.

4. See the subtitled interview here: "Hadiya Shafin Jahan," YouTube, March 15, 2018, https://www.youtube.com/watch?v=-rXoZ9CIzjI&feature=youtu.be.

CONCLUSION

1. Jaspleen Pasricha, "V-Day in Photos: From Protest to Sangeet & Mehendi inside the Police Station," *Feminism in India*, February 14, 2104, http://feminisminindia.com /2015/02/14/v-day-photos-protest-sangeet-mehendi-inside-police-station/.

2. Geetanjali Gayatri, "A Love Story with a Full Stop," *Tribune India*, March 30, 2010, http://www.tribuneindia.com/2010/20100331/khapdiktat.htm#2.

3. See Sruthisagar Yamunan, "One of India's Most Controversial Judges Has Retired," *Quartz India*, October 2, 2101, https://qz.com/india/1409917/dipak-misra-indias-controversial-chief -justice-retires/.

4. Press Trust of India, "Police Protection for Lesbian Couple Who 'Fear for Life' from Parents," NDTV, October 1, 2018, https://www.ndtv.com/india-news/police-protection -for-lesbian-couple-who-fear-for-life-from-parents-1925251.

REFERENCES

Abu-Lughod, Lila. 1999. *Veiled Sentiments: Honor and Poetry in a Bedouin Society.* Berkeley: University of California Press.

Agamben, Giorgio. 2005. *State of Exception.* Translated by Kevin Attell. Chicago: University of Chicago Press.

Agarwal, Bina. 1994. *A Field of One's Own: Gender and Land Rights in South Asia.* Cambridge: Cambridge University Press.

Agnes, Flavia. 1995. "Hindu Men, Monogamy and Uniform Civil Code." *Economic and Political Weekly* 30 (50): 3238–3244.

———. 1999. *Law and Gender Inequality: The Politics of Women's Rights in India.* New Delhi: Oxford University Press.

———. 2008. "Women's Rights and Legislative Reforms: An Overview." *International Journal of Legal Information* 36 (2): 265–270.

Ahearn, Laura M. 2001. *Invitations to Love: Literacy, Love Letters, and Social Change in Nepal.* Ann Arbor: University of Michigan Press.

Ambedkar, Bhimrao Ramji, and Sharmila Rege. 2013. *Against the Madness of Manu: BR Ambedkar's Writings on Brahmanical Patriarchy.* New Delhi: Navayana.

Ami, Daljit. 2016. "*Mirza Sahiban*: Cinematic Journeys of a Lesson." PhD diss. proposal, Jawaharlal Nehru University.

Anderson, Benedict R. 2006. *Imagined Communities: Reflections on the Origin and Spread of Nationalism.* London: Verso.

Appadurai, Arjun. 1996. *Modernity at Large: Cultural Dimensions of Globalization.* Minneapolis: University of Minnesota Press.

———. 2004. "The Capacity to Aspire: Culture and the Terms of Recognition." In *Culture and Public Action*, edited by Vijayendra Rao and Michael Walton, 59–84. Stanford, CA: Stanford University Press.

Arendt, Hannah. 1972. *Crises of the Republic: Lying in Politics, Civil Disobedience on Violence, Thoughts on Politics, and Revolution.* Boston: Houghton Mifflin Harcourt.

Ashraf, Ajaz. 2015. "Why BJP and the Rural Distress Are to Blame for the Violence of Jats." *Scroll.in*, June 9. https://scroll.in/article/732464/why-bjp-and-the-rural-distress-are -to-blame-for-the-violence-of-jats.

Bannerji, Himani. 1998. "Age of Consent and Hegemonic Social Reform." In *Gender and Imperialism*, edited by Clare Midgley, 21–44. Manchester, UK: Manchester University Press.

Basu, Srimati. 2015. *The Trouble with Marriage: Feminists Confront Law and Violence in India.* Berkeley: University of California Press.

Baxi, Pratiksha. 2006. "Habeas Corpus in the Realm of Love: Litigating Marriages of Choice in India." *Australian Feminist Law Journal* 25 (1): 59–78.

——. 2014. *Public Secrets of Law: Rape Trials in India.* New Delhi: Oxford University Press.

Baxi, Upendra. 2012. "Epilogue: Changing Paradigms of Human Rights." In *Law against the State: Ethnographic Forays into Law's Transformations,* edited by Julia Eckert, Zerrin Özlem Biner, Brian Donahoe and Christian Strumpell, 266–285. Cambridge: Cambridge University Press.

Berlant, Lauren Gail. 2011. *Cruel Optimism.* Durham, NC: Duke University Press.

Bhargava, Rajeev. 2011. *Multiculturalism, Liberalism and Democracy.* New Delhi: Oxford University Press.

Biehl, João. 2013a. "The Judicialization of Biopolitics: Claiming the Right to Pharmaceuticals in Brazilian Courts." *American Ethnologist* 40 (3): 419–436.

——. 2013b. *Vita: Life in a Zone of Social Abandonment.* Berkeley: University of California Press.

Bourdieu, Pierre. 1977. *Outline of a Theory of Practice.* Cambridge: Cambridge University Press.

——. 1991. *Language and Symbolic Power.* Cambridge, MA: Harvard University Press.

Butler, Judith. 1990. *Gender Trouble: Feminism and the Subversion of Identity.* New York: Routledge.

——. 2015. *Notes toward a Performative Theory of Assembly.* Vol. 1. Cambridge: Harvard University Press.

Cameron, Deborah, and Don Kulick. 2003. "Introduction: Language and Desire in Theory and Practice." *Language and Communication.* 23 (2): 93–105.

Cavell, Stanley. 1990. *Conditions Handsome and Unhandsome: The Constitution of Emersonian Perfectionism.* La Salle, IL: Open Court.

——. 2002. *Must We Mean What We Say? A Book of Essays.* Cambridge: Cambridge University Press.

Certeau, Michel de, and Pierre Mayol. 1998. *The Practice of Everyday Life: Living and Cooking.* Vol. 2. Minneapolis: University of Minnesota Press.

Chatterjee, Partha. 1989. "Colonialism, Nationalism, and Colonized Women: The Contest in India." *American Ethnologist.* 16 (4): 622-633.

——.2004. *The Politics of the Governed: Reflections on Popular Politics in Most of the World.* New York: Columbia University Press.

Chowdhry, Prem. 1994. *The Veiled Women: Shifting Gender Equations in Rural Haryana, 1880–1990.* New Delhi: Oxford University Press.

——. 2004. "Private Lives, State Intervention: Cases of Runaway Marriage in Rural North India." *Modern Asian Studies* 38 (1): 55–84.

——. 2007. *Contentious Marriages, Eloping Couples.* New Delhi: Oxford University Press.

——. 2011. *Political Economy of Production and Reproduction.* New Delhi: Oxford University Press.

——. 2017. *Understanding Women's Land Rights: Gender Discrimination in Ownership.* New Delhi: Sage India.

Ciotti, Manuela. 2011. "After Subversion: Intimate Encounters, the Agency in and of Representation, and the Unfinished Project of Gender without Sexuality in India." *Cultural Dynamics* 23 (2): 107–126.

Coronil, Fernando. 1997. *The Magical State: Nature, Money, and Modernity in Venezuela.* Chicago: University of Chicago Press.

Das, Veena. 1997. "Language and Body: Transactions in the Construction of Pain." In *Social Suffering,* edited by Arthur Kleinman, Veena Das, and Margaret M. Lock, 67–92. Berkeley: University of California Press.

——. 2007. *Life and Words: Violence and the Descent into the Ordinary.* Berkeley: University of California Press.

Das, Veena, and Deborah Poole. 2004. *Anthropology in the Margins of the State*. Santa Fe, NM: SAR Press.

Desjarlais, Robert, and C. Jason Throop. 2011. "Phenomenological Approaches in Anthropology." *Annual Review of Anthropology* 40: 87–102.

De Vries, Hent. 2009. "The Niebuhr Connection: Obama's Deep Pragmatism." *The Immanent Frame: Secularism, Religion, and the Public Sphere*, June 18. https://tif.ssrc.org/2009/06/18/the-niebuhr-connection-obamas-deep-pragmatism/.

Eckert, Julia, Brian Donahoe, Zerrin Özlem Biner, and Christian Strümpell. 2012. *Law against the State: Ethnographic Forays into Law's Transformations*. Cambridge: Cambridge University Press.

Foucault, Michel. 1990. *The History of Sexuality*. Vol. 1. New York: Pantheon Books.

Fruzzetti, Lina. 1993. *The Gift of a Virgin: Women, Marriage, and Ritual in a Bengali Society*. New Delhi: Oxford India Paperbacks.

Garcia, Angela. 2010. *The Pastoral Clinic: Addiction and Dispossession along the Rio Grande*. Berkeley: University of California Press.

Geertz, Clifford. 1973. *The Interpretation of Cultures: Selected Essays*. New York: Basic Books.

———. 1983. *Local Knowledge: Further Essays in Interpretive Anthropology*. New York: Basic Books.

Geetha, V. 1998. "Periyar, Women and an Ethic of Citizenship." *Economic and Political Weekly* 33 (17): WS9–WS15.

Gramsci, Antonio, Geoffrey Nowell-Smith, and Quintin Hoare. 2001. *Selections from the Prison Notebooks of Antonio Gramsci*. London: Electric Book Co.

Halley, Janet. 2015. "The Move to Affirmative Consent." *Signs: Journal of Women in Culture and Society*, November 10. http://signsjournal.org/currents-affirmative-consent/halley/.

Han, Clara. 2012. *Life in Debt: Times of Care and Violence in Neoliberal Chile*. Berkeley: University of California Press.

Hansen, Kathryn. 1992. *Grounds for Play: The Nautanki Theatre of North India*. Berkeley: University of California Press.

Harvey, David. 1999. "Time-Space Compression and the Postmodern Condition." In *Modernity: Critical Concepts 4*, edited by Malcolm Waters, 98–118. New York: Routledge.

Hirsch, Jennifer S., Holly Wardlow, Daniel Jordan Smith, Harriet Phinney, Shanti Parikh, and Constance A. Nathanson. 2009. *The Secret: Love, Marriage, and HIV*. Nashville, TN: Vanderbilt University Press.

Holden, Livia. 2016. *Hindu Divorce: A Legal Anthropology*. London: Routledge.

Husserl, Edmund. 1970. *The Crisis of European Sciences and Transcendental Phenomenology*. Evanston, IL: Northwestern University Press.

Jaffrelot, Christophe. 2003. *India's Silent Revolution: The Rise of the Lower Castes in North India*. New Delhi: Orient Blackswan.

Jassal, Smita Tewari. 2012. *Unearthing Gender: Folksongs of North India*. Durham, NC: Duke University Press.

Jodhka, Surinder. 2014. "Emergent Ruralities: Revisiting Village Life and Agrarian Change in Haryana." *Economic and Political Weekly* 49: 5–57.

John, Mary E. 2012. "Gender and Higher Education in the Time of Reforms." *Contemporary Education Dialogue* 9 (2): 197–221.

Kapur, Ratna. 2013. *Erotic Justice: Law and the New Politics of Postcolonialism*. London: Routledge.

Kaviraj, Sudipta. 2010. *The Imaginary Institution of India: Politics and Ideas*. New York: Columbia University Press.

Kleinman, Arthur, and Joan Kleinman. 1995. "Suffering and Its Professional Transforma-
tion: Toward an Ethnography of Interpersonal Experience." In *Writing at the Margin:
Discourse between Anthropology and Medicine*, edited by Arthur Kleinman, 95–119.
Berkeley: University of California Press.

Kumar, Pradeep. 1991. "Sub-Nationalism in Indian Politics: Formation of a Haryanvi
Identity." *Indian Political Science Association* 52 (1): 109–24.

Latour, Bruno. 2004. "Scientific Objects and Legal Objectivity." In *Law, Anthropology and
the Constitution of the Social: Making Persons and Things*, edited by Alain Pottage and
Martha Mundy, 73–114. Cambridge: Cambridge University Press.

Lefebvre, Alexandre. 2008. *The Image of Law: Deleuze, Bergson, Spinoza*. Stanford, CA: Stanford University Press.

Liang, Lawrence. 2005. "Cinematic Citizenship and the Illegal City." *Inter-Asia Cultural
Studies* 6 (3): 366–385.

Loizidou, Elena. 2007. *Judith Butler: Ethics, Law, Politics*. Abingdon, UK: Routledge-Cavendish.

Lutz, Catherine 1988. *Unnatural Emotions: Everyday Sentiments on a Micronesian Atoll and
Their Challenge to Western Theory*. Chicago: University of Chicago Press.

Mahajan, Gurpreet. 2002. *The Multicultural Path: Issues of Diversity and Discrimination in
Democracy*. New Delhi: Sage.

Maunaguru, Sidhartan. 2010. "Brokering Transnational Tamil Marriages: Displacements,
Circulations, Futures." PhD diss., Johns Hopkins University.

Menon, Nivedita. 2004. *Recovering Subversion: Feminist Politics beyond the Law*. Chicago:
University of Illinois Press.

———. 2012. *Seeing Like a Feminist*. London: Penguin.

———. 2015. "Is Feminism about 'Women?'" *Economic and Political Weekly* 50 (17): 37–44.

Merry, Sally E. 1988. "Legal Pluralism." *Law & Society Review* 22 (5): 869–896.

Ministry of Human Resource Development, Department of Higher Education. *All India Survey on Higher Education (2013–2014)*. New Delhi: Government of India, 2015. http://
aishe.nic.in/aishe/viewDocument.action?documentId=196.

Ministry of Women and Child Development. *Gendering Human Development Indices: Recasting the Gender Development Index and Gender Empowerment Measure for India*. New
Delhi: Government of India, 2009. http://www.undp.org/content/dam/india/docs
/gendering_human_development_indices_summary_report.pdf.

Miyazaki, Hirokazu. 2006. "Economy of Dreams: Hope in Global Capitalism and Its Critiques." *Cultural Anthropology* 21 (2): 147–172.

Mody, Perveez. 2008. *The Intimate State: Love-Marriage and the Law in Delhi*. Delhi: Routledge India.

Murphy, Tim. 2004. In *Law, Anthropology and the Constitution of the Social: Making Persons
and Things*, edited by Alain Pottage and Martha Mundy, 115–141. Cambridge: Cambridge University Press.

Nandy, Ashis. 1983. *The Intimate Enemy: Loss and Recovery of Self under Colonialism*. New
Delhi: Oxford University Press.

Office of Registrar General and Census Commissioner of India. *Single Year Age Returns by
Residence, Sex and Literacy Status, Census Survey of India, 2011*. New Delhi: Government
of India, 2015. http://www.censusindia.gov.in/2011census/Age_level_Data/C13/DDW
-0000C-13A.xlsx.

Okin, Susan Moller. 1989. *Gender, the Public and the Private*. Toronto: University of Toronto,
Faculty of Law.

Ortner, Sherry B. 1978. *Sherpas through Their Rituals*. Cambridge: Cambridge University
Press.

Osella, Caroline, and Filippo Osella. 1998. "Friendship and Flirting: Micro-Politics in Kerala, South India." *Journal of the Royal Anthropological Institute* 4 (2): 189–206.

Pateman, Carole. 1988. *The Sexual Contract*. Stanford, CA: Stanford University Press.

Poonacha, Veena. 1996. "Redefining Gender Relationships: The Imprint of the Colonial State on the Coorg/Kodava Norms of Marriage and Sexuality." In *Social Reform, Sexuality, and the State*, edited by Patricia Uberoi. 39-64. New Delhi: Sage.

Puri, Jyoti. 2016. *Sexual States: Governance and the Struggle over the Antisodomy Law in India*. Durham, NC: Duke University Press.

Raheja, Gloria G. 1988. *The Poison in the Gift: Ritual, Prestation, and the Dominant Caste in a North Indian Village*. Chicago: University of Chicago Press.

Rajadhyaksha, Ashish. 1999. "The Judgement: Re-forming the 'Public.'" *Journal of Arts and Ideas* 32: 34–52.

Rao, Raj R. 2000. "Memories Pierce the Heart." *Journal of Homosexuality* 39: 3–4, 299–306.

Riles, Annelise. 2010. "Is the Law Hopeful?" Cornell Law Faculty Working Papers 68. http://scholarship.law.cornell.edu/clsops_papers/68.

Rouland, Norbert. 1994. *Legal Anthropology*. Stanford, CA: Stanford University Press.

Rubin, Gayle. 1984. "Thinking Sex: Notes for a Radical Theory of the Politics of Sexuality." In *Pleasure and Danger: Exploring Female Sexuality*, edited by Carole S. Vance, 267–319. Boston: Routledge and Kegan Paul.

———. 1990. "The Traffic in Women: Notes on the 'Political Economy' of Sex." In *Women, Class, and the Feminist Imagination: A Socialist-Feminist Reader*, edited by Karen V. Hansen and Illene J. Philipson, 74–113. Philadelphia: Temple University Press.

Sangwan, Nina. 1991. "Development Process in a Newly Organised State: A Case Study of Haryana." PhD diss., Panjab University.

Sarkar, Sumit. 1999. "Post-Modernism and the Writing of History." *Studies in History* 15 (2): 293–322.

Scott, James C. 1998. *Seeing Like a State: How Certain Schemes to Improve the Human Condition Have Failed*. New Haven, CT: Yale University Press.

Sinha, Chitra. 2012. *Debating Patriarchy: The Hindu Code Bill Controversy in India (1941–1956)*. New Delhi: Oxford University Press.

Strathern, Marilyn. 1991. *Partial Connections*. Savage, MD: Rowman and Littlefield.

———. 2004. "Losing (Out on) Intellectual Resources." In *Law, Anthropology and the Constitution of the Social: Making Persons and Things*, edited by Alain Pottage and Martha Mundy, 201–233. Cambridge: Cambridge University Press.

Tambe, Ashwini. 2009. "The State as Surrogate Parent: Legislating Nonmarital Sex in Colonial India, 1911–1929." *Journal of the History of Childhood and Youth* 2 (3): 393–427.

Turner, Victor W. 1986. "Dewey, Dilthey, and Drama: An Essay in the Anthropology of Experience." In *The Anthropology of Experience*, edited by Victor Turner and Edward Bruner, 33–44. Urbana: University of Illinois Press.

Uberoi, Patricia. 1993. *Family, Kinship and Marriage in India*. New Delhi: Oxford University Press.

Vanita, Ruth. 2011. "Democratizing Marriage: Consent, Custom and the Law." In *Law Like Love: A Queer Perspective of Law in India*, edited by Arvind Narrain and Alok Gupta, 338-354. New Delhi: Yoda Press.

Vatuk, Sylvia. 2008. "Islamic Feminism in India: Indian Muslim Women Activists and the Reform of Muslim Personal Law." *Modern Asian Studies* 42 (2): 489–518.

Virdi, Jyotika. 2003. *The Cinematic ImagiNation [Sic]: Indian Popular Films as Social History*. New Brunswick, NJ: Rutgers University Press.

Wardlow, Holly. 2006. *Wayward Women: Sexuality and Agency in a New Guinea Society.* Berkeley: University of California Press.

Weber, Max. 2002. *The Protestant Ethic and the Spirit of Capitalism.* London: Penguin.

Weinbaum, Alys Eve, Lynn M. Thomas, Priti Ramamurthy, Uta G. Poiger, Madeleine Yue Dong, and Tani E. Barlow. 2008. *The Modern Girl around the World: Consumption, Modernity, and Globalization.* Durham, NC: Duke University Press.

Wikan, Unni. 2014. *In Honor of Fadime: Murder and Shame.* Chicago: University of Chicago Press.

Yadav, Bhupendra. 2001. "Haryana's 'Setting Daughters.'" *Economic and Political Weekly* 36 (45): 4257–4259.

INDEX

193

ABOUT THE AUTHOR

RAMA SRINIVASAN is a writer with extensive experience in journalistic and scholarly writing. Formerly a traveler and world citizen, she is now permanently settled in Germany and is pursuing a career in intercultural competence training. She holds a PhD in anthropology from Brown University and a master's degree in gender and cultural studies from Simmons University. She pens articles on gender and sexuality, politics, cinema and popular culture, law and society, and immigration and diaspora issues. When she is not writing or conducting training workshops, she is trying to master High German and the Bavarian dialect.